THE NAZI GHOST TRAIN

MIRROR BOOKS

© Greg Lewis 2026

The rights of Greg Lewis to be identified as the authors of this book have been asserted, in accordance with the Copyright, Designs and Patents Act 1988.

All rights reserved. No part of this publication may be reproduced, stored in a retrieval system, or transmitted, in any form or by any means without the prior written permission of the publisher, nor be otherwise circulated in any form of binding or cover other than that in which it is published and without a similar condition being imposed on the subsequent purchaser.

1

Published in Great Britain and Ireland in 2026 by
Mirror Books, a Reach PLC business.

www.mirrorbooks.co.uk
@TheMirrorBooks

Print ISBN 9781917439695
eBook ISBN 9781917439701

Editing and Production: Christine Costello, Lawrence Matheson
Cover Design: Chris Collins

Photographic Acknowledgements: Alamy

Every effort has been made to trace copyright, Any oversights will be rectified in future editions.

Printed and bound in Great Britain by
CPI Group (UK) Ltd, Croydon, CR0 4YY

THE NAZI GHOST TRAIN

GREG LEWIS

MIRROR BOOKS

*For my dad, who read all the stories and 'books' I wrote when I was a child and even drew their covers.
You are remembered with love.*

CONTENTS

Author's Note — 7
Prologue — 11

1. A Bad Omen — 16
2. Promise To Resist — 28
3. Under Suspicion — 38
4. Lucky Escape — 45
5. Schräge Musik — 52
6. 'Mike, The Spirit Of LSU' — 72
7. The Carpetbaggers — 82
8. Death In The Water — 88
9. Secrets And Sabotage — 95
10. A Chateau Near Namur — 105
11. Checkpoint — 110
12. 'Here You Areat Last!' — 122
13. Working With The Resistance — 134
14. A Betrayal Revealed — 145
15. The Man With The Missing Finger — 154
16. The 'Dog House' — 165
17. No Place Of Safety — 173
18. 'Cawn't Miss' — 183
19. Dezitter's Last Airmen — 192
20. A Village In Terror — 203
21. The Dark Cells — 214
22. Agents Behind Bars — 226
23. Nacht Und Nebel — 240
24. The Train — 247

25. The Station ... 253
26. A Journey To Nowhere ... 266
27. A Battle Of Wills ... 273
28. The Last Prisoners ... 285
29. After The Train ... 296

Acknowledgements ... 309
Sources ... 310

AUTHOR'S NOTE

A SINGLE MOMENT sparked my intrigue with the 'Ghost Train'. I had travelled to Calverton, a village just outside Nottingham, England, to see John Evans, an RAF pilot who had been shot down during the Second World War and managed to evade capture for several months.

Sitting beneath a painting of his Halifax bomber in full flight, John was searching through his large box of memorabilia – items which any museum would be delighted to own: his flying logbook, the letter from his commanding officer to inform his parents he was missing, a grainy photograph taken in a walled back garden while he was on the run, and the false identity card created by the Resistance which claimed the Welsh pilot was actually a Belgian draughtsman named Albert Bastin. Then he found what he was looking for, and handed it to me.

It was a letter, creased by time and reading, from his rescuer: Florent Biernaux, the man who helped John escape after his plane was shot down. Anyone who sat with an evader like John became intensely aware of the esteem and respect in which they held these civilians who had risked everything for them. They viewed them as the *real* heroes.

The letter was written six weeks after the end of the war in Europe. 'I hope you will remember your stay in Hasselt at my home,' Florent wrote. 'I will tell you our adventure in a few words.'

After helping John and about 60 other airmen, Florent and his family had been arrested and sent to the 'big prison' of Saint-Gilles in Brussels. His wife, Olympe, teenage son, Raymond, and young daughter, Eliane, were all sent to concentration camps, but 'I alone remain to Brussels, with 1,500 other men and women to be shot'.

But, he added, 'On account of sabotage... we were liberated.'

Confused, I asked, what does Florent mean? How could 'sabotage' save what Florent claimed were 1,500 lives?

'Ah, that was *le train fantôme*,' John said. 'The ghost train.'

The ghost train! That set me off on a new trail. I finished writing John's story and began to read and research about this new one. This presented a new set of challenges. There were hundreds of people involved in this event. The vast majority were dead, but I managed to find some who were still alive. Men like Jozef Craeninckx, who was just a teenager at the time and had grown up in what would at other times seem like a rural idyll. The war changed that, and Jozef witnessed the worst of humanity. Seeing him break down a lifetime later as he described what happened to his father gave me fresh energy to complete this story.

I tracked down relatives of those on the train. Descendants of the airmen who found photographs, told me what they knew and, in some cases, even read proofs of the manuscript to ensure I was doing their loved ones justice. And relatives of the young resisters, too. One relative, Guy Jaspers, whose family had helped John Evans, gave me a real insight into what life was like under occupation and the tension between those who found themselves collaborating and those who resisted – a tension which can sometimes transcend the generations. Guy's help with translations was also invaluable.

But the research continued to present a challenge. After the events of the 'Ghost Train' everyone involved disappeared back into their lives. The airmen returned home – most often to the United States – and the Germans involved were killed or sent to prisoner of war camps. The resisters were working men and women

AUTHOR'S NOTE

who went back to their work and homes, often struggling with the trauma of having been tortured or the searing pain of loss: they did not want to relive it. The spies on the train were bound by the Official Secrets Act.

Even the train's central hero – an ordinary man who had never taken part in an act of resistance before – just walked back into work the day afterwards and got on with his job, as he had, indeed, done throughout the war.

And at the heart of this true-life drama was a story few had wanted to revisit: the life of Prosper Dezitter, a man who ranks among the Second World War's darkest villains. If he were the fictional character he sometimes seems to be, he would feel almost 'dastardly'. The story of Dezitter's treachery, British intelligence efforts to identify him, and his unparalleled 'success' as a double agent make for a riveting, at times astonishing, read. But he is not fiction. His actions and betrayals are real. People not only became prisoners because of him, but they were also tortured and executed. Hundreds, possibly thousands, of them. And what he did had nothing to do with conviction or ideology: there is no evidence that he believed in anything, only in money and achieving greater wealth for himself, while the rest of the world suffered.

Dezitter's story is buried in declassified documents from MI5, the Special Operations Executive (SOE) and the Abwehr, Germany's military intelligence organisation and, when he is revealed in the interviews given to intelligence officers by the airmen he betrayed, he is spoken of only by the aliases he used. They never knew the name of the man who tricked them.

So, the 'Ghost Train' kept me searching. I spent hours in the Belgian archives uncovering detailed information in French, Flemish and German, including unpublished interviews with the train driver and the anti-Nazi doctor who helped stop the train. I scoured the records of the UK's National Archive and the USA's

NARA (National Archives and Records Administration) for the escape and evasion reports completed by airmen on their return to England and the crews' mission reports. I found out-of-print books such as Françoise Labouverie's memoir, one of the few to devote a whole chapter to the train.

I visited the fascinating village of Meensel-Kiezegem – scene of resistance and atrocity – and the 'Dog House' where many airmen were trapped by Dezitter. I followed the route of the train to understand the geography of the story.

Over the years there have been some wonderful researchers – many of whom I have met or corresponded with. I'd like to mention one I never got to meet: Oscar Catherine.

Oscar had his own remarkable war. Wounded while defending his homeland in 1940, he had been evacuated to England, where he met and married a woman working for the Ministry of Information. Trained as a saboteur, he parachuted into Belgium in January 1942 with a wireless operator and a list of targets. After spending a year sabotaging railway lines and factories and starting an underground newspaper, he was eventually arrested and sent to Dachau concentration camp. After the war he researched and documented the Resistance and took a particular interest in the 'Ghost Train'. Finding the documents he submitted to the Belgian archive, CegeSoma, gave me a huge boost. Thank you, Oscar.

Greg Lewis, 2025

PROLOGUE

IT WAS A scene of pandemonium and terror as the heavily armed SS men corralled the prisoners into a courtyard thick with the carbon monoxide fumes of dozens of trucks.

The evacuation of the jail of Saint-Gilles had begun in the middle of the night, the Germans desperate to move the 1,400 prisoners[1] to the main railway station where a train waited to take them to Neuengamme concentration camp – and to their almost certain death.

Saint-Gilles, just outside Brussels, looked more like a mediaeval fort than a prison. With its crenellated white-stone façade, imposing towers and 20-ft high outer wall, it had housed the worst criminals in Belgium for the past 60 years.

But these prisoners were not criminals. During the German occupation, Saint-Gilles had become a *Wehrmachtgefängnis*, a German army prison packed with the enemies of the Third Reich: members of the armed Resistance who had carried out sabotage attacks and risen up against the occupier as the Allied armies had swept across northern France; young men and women of the

---

1 Estimates for the number of prisoners removed from the jail and taken to the 'Ghost Train' vary. As seen in the author's note, Florent Biernaux believed it to be 1,500. Some estimates are as high as 1,600. The author believes this figure includes the 200 'juvenile' prisoners who were released from the jail before the deportation order (see page 187). The author believes the number on the train was around 1,400 - the figure used by the international diplomats involved in trying to stop the train in 1944 and the number settled on by the magazine Le Rail's investigation in 1974.

intelligence-gathering Resistance who had sent information to London on German defences and on the V1 'Doodlebug' launch sites; SOE spies, trained in Britain to create chaos and fear; members of the evasion lines, ordinary men, women and teenagers who had risked their lives to help Allied airmen evade capture and to return them to England from where they could continue the war. To Belgians, the prison had become *l'hôtel des patriotes*.

And among the prisoners were dozens of airmen who had failed to escape. Shot down on bombing raids over Holland, Belgium and Germany, they had played a cat-and-mouse game with the Nazis as they tried to stay at liberty behind enemy lines.

Among them were men from across the United States – New York, New Jersey, Texas, California, Iowa and Alabama – along with comrades from Canada, Australia and Britain. One Canadian pilot in the prison had been condemned to death for his work as a saboteur, while the others had fallen under suspicion of being spies.

Captured in civilian clothes, all now fell foul of Hitler's *Kugel-Erlass* – the Bullet Decree – which allowed for Allied evaders to be handed over to the Gestapo. The decree had formed the basis of the secret orders to execute 50 airmen from the 'Great Escape' just a few months earlier and would be used to send others to concentration camps to be shot, starved, or worked to death.

Many of the fliers had been betrayed by one of the most heartless double agents of all – a traitor of such audacity and means of disguise that he had come to be seen as an almost mythical bogeyman. But he was all too real and, from the first weeks after Dunkirk to the closing moments of the occupation, countless soldiers, airmen and Belgian and French patriots had suffered and died because of his treachery.

In the anguish of their cells, the airmen shared the story of their betrayal, with each revealing they had been handed over to the

PROLOGUE

Germans by the mysterious man with the missing little finger on his right hand, after being lured into his trap by his dark-haired mistress and the wild Russian with the fast car who claimed to be driving them to safety.

As each airman had been captured, so had dozens of civilians who had given them shelter and clothes, provided them with fake identity cards, and shuttled them from safehouse to safehouse, knowing that they risked torture and execution.

Now all faced the same fate.

As the guards moved through the prison blocks, the inmates began to rebel, smashing the bare bed frames and hard wooden chairs against the walls, breaking light fittings, shouting through the iron-barred windows for the others to join in.

The SS men went in hard, wielding rifle butts and clubs. The prisoners had little to fight back with, and they were tired, weak and hungry. They were soon overcome.

Then the women in an adjoining block rose up. Down in the courtyard, the prisoners already gathered there shouted words of encouragement to them. But, again, the SS put down the insurrection with swift brutality. Everyone was forced into the waiting trucks.

In the distance, the thunder of shellfire: the British Army was somewhere on the outskirts of the city.

Liberation was close, but not close enough.

Friends and strangers looked anxiously at one another. Many had lived secret lives as resisters since the beginning of the occupation, more than four years earlier. Others had been on the run for months, living on their wits and praying they would one day return safely to their homes and loved ones.

But home seemed very far away and each knew they now faced the most difficult journey of all. The Nazis were on the run, being pushed out of Western Europe, but – out of spite and hatred, and perhaps believing some prisoners might become hostages – they remained determined to transport these 'enemies of the state' to a concentration camp.

As the prison convoy drove through the city, the Belgian women in one truck raised their voices and sang out their national anthem. An SS guard fired into the air to silence them.

Other prisoners frantically scribbled down messages on scraps of paper, food tin labels or even their own clothing and threw them into the streets.

'Help us!'

'Tell my family!'

Many simply wrote: 'Stop the train!'

For the patriots and their families, the spies and the airmen, all seemed lost. Was there anyone who could save them?

The lives of hundreds now depended on the courage and audacity of a small group of ordinary people who seeing the railway station fill up with men and women who had risked all for the Allied cause, pledged that the train would never reach Germany.

They had the next few hours to work a miracle.

A miracle that would go down in Resistance folklore as *le train fantôme* – the Nazi 'Ghost Train'.

PART ONE
EVASION

1

A BAD OMEN

John 'Bud' Brown and Theodore 'Ted' Kleinman

LIEUTENANT JOHN 'BUD' Brown was feeling unusually anxious as the Jeep sped across the concrete towards the rough grass where his B-17 bomber plane, nicknamed 'Dodie', stood waiting in the winter morning light.

The day had started as days of raids had done for the past few months. Before dawn a staff sergeant had come to Brown's bunk and roused him, telling him that in half an hour it would be time for breakfast and then his briefing.

Out on the field, as the cold night air still clung to the flat English countryside of East Anglia, the ground crews once again turned a flying machine into a deadly weapon of war, loading 1,000-pound bombs and packing belts of .50 calibre shells into boxes at each gunner's station.

Ground mechanics checked hydraulics, brakes and tyres, and climbed into cockpits to test the engines.

Then, as the watery sun rose, the air gunners arrived to mount and secure their guns, removing the thick coating of oil in which they had been stored since the previous raid. The sergeant gunners did not know where they were headed today; that was for the flying officers to discover over at the admin block.

Brown attended the briefing with his co-pilot Albert Fitzpatrick and navigator Theodore 'Ted' Kleinman, from the Bronx. They listened and made notes as intelligence officers gave them the mission specifics: weather, route, waypoints and, of course, the target.

The target for February 4, 1944, was Frankfurt, a city, the intelligence men explained, heavily defended by anti-aircraft guns and fighter squadrons. But every target was tough: this was the Eighth Air Force's 100th Bomb Group after all, and it was already talked about as the 'Bloody Hundredth' for the scale of its losses. The carnage had begun on June 25, 1943, the 100th's first mission from its specially-constructed base at Thorpe Abbotts, when 17 aircraft were sent to attack the submarine pens at Bremen, and three aircrafts – 30 men – did not come back. The losses started a legend which the airmen struggled to appreciate. By the time Brown and his crew arrived in November 1943 as replacements for the dead and missing, the 'Bloody Hundredth' had suffered further heavy losses over Regensburg and Münster, where the American force had been met by 350 enemy fighters. Replacements like Brown groaned when they realised which unit they were headed to.

But, in reality, the guys in the 100th faced the same odds as everyone else, and once they knew their names were down for a raid, they just wanted to get on with it. That was why for many airmen the short ride out to the aircraft was the worst part of the day, when all the fear and anxiety gathered in their gut. Before getting on the plane, some strode out onto the grass to get away from the nauseating smell of gasoline and smoke a cigarette. They looked out across the fields, the cows and horses, and little farm buildings and thought of home. Some wanted to chat; some preferred a little time with their own thoughts. The pilots, only young men themselves – Brown was just 24 – tried their best to calm them.

But the reputation of the 'Bloody Hundredth' and the bad jokes and nervous laughter of the young men around him were not the reason Brown was feeling so uneasy as he watched his crew climbing in through the rear fuselage door of the B-17. Airmen like 'Bud' were superstitious; understandably so, as anything – real or imaginary – could seem to tip the odds for or against them. No one liked a bad omen, and today Brown was faced with one: only half of Dodie's regular crew was fit to fly. The other five had gone down with food poisoning. It did not feel right.

To make matters worse, one of the replacements – ball turret gunner William Kemp – was flying his first ever mission. This only added to Brown's jitters.

Brown's fears went unspoken, but he knew Kleinman, Fitzpatrick, bombardier Lawson Clements, and gunner Gordon Keon felt it too. It was like that feeling he had sometimes before a big game: Brown had been a promising young American footballer before the war, playing halfback for the College of the Pacific team in Stockton, California, under the legendary Amos Alonzo Stagg. Different times, but Brown was still as superstitious as most sportspeople.

This was to be Brown's tenth mission. He had shared them all with 'Ted' Kleinman. Both had enlisted soon after Pearl Harbor, keen to do their bit. A talented student with a keen intellect, Brown had been chosen for pilot training. Kleinman became a navigator and found himself in Brown's crew.

It was good to know Ted Kleinman was there. But it didn't stop the last-minute change of crew members from bugging Brown. The sooner they got this mission over with, the better.

In a few hours 10 men were going into battle. Five friends, five strangers, taking the same risk.

Brown never even got to know the new guys' names.

A BAD OMEN

***

When the US Eighth Air Force had arrived in England, the war was looking bad for the Allied nations. The Japanese had occupied the Far East and Pacific empires of the British, Dutch, and French, as well as the American–occupied Philippines. Since 1940 Nazi Germany had been the master of Western Europe.

The RAF had begun its fightback by attacking industrial targets in the Rhineland and the Ruhr. At first it had flown in daylight, but high losses forced it to switch to night-time raids. As well as industrial targets, the RAF bombed cities, believing it could break the morale of the German people. When the United States entered the war, Winston Churchill and Franklin Roosevelt agreed to bring American bombers to Western Europe, with the Americans flying by day and the British by night. For the first time German air defences would need to work around the clock.

For the young men of the Eighth Air Force – flying B-17 Flying Fortresses and B-24 Liberators designed for long-range, high-altitude strikes – arrival in England meant the bulk of their training was over and they were now in a war zone. They found themselves very quickly in combat.

The earliest recruits suffered devastating losses: only one out of four who arrived in England during the summer and autumn of 1942 survived to complete a 25-mission tour of duty. There were no medics at 25,000-ft, no stretcher bearers to run to your aid. Wounded men slumped in their cramped fighting positions with perhaps only the comfort of a comrade to hold their hand.

At the station, the deaths of crews became a grim domestic ritual – anything to protect the remaining members of the squadron from breaking down. When somebody failed to return from a raid, their belongings were quickly packed into a bag by a quartermaster. Apart from the toast drank in a local bar and maybe a bawdy song in their honour, they would become a memory to be suppressed. It was the only way to cope with such regular loss.

In this young man's war, every emotion was heightened: death happened quickly, and love could too; in fact, Ted Kleinman had met the love of his life by chance, on a blind date after making an emergency landing in Eugene, Oregon. They had married within a month of meeting.

And while death was ever-present, so was adventure. They had come a long way from their homes in all corners of the US and there was much that was different: the thatched-roof cottages with crawling plants on the walls which looked like illustrations in a picture book; the strange-tasting local bitters, brown ales and stouts; and the 'blackout', the ban on all exterior lighting which left the streets in darkness. From the air, the crews would look down at the English countryside: a mosaic of fields and hedges, small villages built around the church and a pub, and the bigger towns as they reached the coast.

On nights when they were not scheduled to fly the next day, the crews would jump into a Jeep and go to the local pub, drinking heavily with villagers and singing loudly. Sometimes the lucky ones got a trip to a cinema in town with one of the girls or a couple of days drinking in bombed-out but still strangely glamorous London. Brown and his crew managed a trip to the city on their first pass, seeing the Changing of the Guard at Buckingham Palace, walking on Tower Bridge, and riding on the Underground. They stopped to talk to people who had lost their homes in the Blitz: it reminded them of the power of the bombing war but also why their attacks on the Nazi's Fortress Europe were so important.

The crews worked hard and played hard together. Bonds grew quickly. These were the people that you relied upon to help you survive, and they were also the ones you were most likely to die alongside. A short series of missions could forge a friendship which otherwise might take months to develop; it also meant that the loss of members of a regular crew through sickness or bad fortune could make colleagues uneasy.

That was how it was for Brown and Kleinman.

'Bud' Brown and 'Ted' Kleinman had trained in Idaho, Washington, and Iowa before flying their B-17 across the Atlantic in November 1943 – Kleinman leaving behind his bride of less than two months. They had navigated themselves successfully to England, unlike a friend who made an error and headed to France. He only changed course at the last moment, finding a 'big island' which he guessed was Britain. The arrival of the B-17s at Thorpe Abbotts, a massive air station created on an aristocrat's country estate, caused a sensation in the sleepy villages nearby. Sitting in the backs of Jeeps as they were transported from one part of the base to another, the airmen would look across the furrowed fields of the local tenant farmers to the high spire of Norwich Cathedral in the distance. It was a peaceful scene, as if from a John Constable painting, but one which was continually shattered by the roar of engines.

After heavy weeks of lectures and training flights, Brown and Kleinman had flown their first mission on December 22: another 100th Bomb Group raid on Münster, and it went far from as planned. The oxygen supply to the radio operator and one of the waist gunners failed, and both men almost died. The crew struggled to save their lives as Brown steered the B-17 through anti-aircraft fire – flak.

On their return they had felt that strange sense of disorientation common to most flight crew. They had flown into a world where there had been a high chance of them being blown apart, burnt or dismembered. Even as they had been concentrating on their jobs, a part of them had been tense with fear and strain. Most felt exhausted when they got back. They sat through a debrief, wolfed down sandwiches and coffee, and wandered off to their billet to hit the sack.

But now it was Frankfurt. And that target made Brown and Kleinman doubly anxious. They had been there before – or at least set out for there. Just over a week earlier they had to abandon a run on the city when flak struck a wing and left it ablaze. Brown's skill and courage had got them home. It was another bad omen.

Dawn had just broke when the green light flashed at the end of the runway. Brown opened the throttle and 60,000 pounds of aircraft and bombload lumbered forward. He marvelled at the aircraft under his control: a tube of aluminium held together by thousands of rivets and packed with bombs stacked in racks from floor to ceiling on both sides of the bomb bay. A wonderful piece of engineering – but it was a relief to clear the cottage at the end of the runway and rise into the sky. Four days earlier a B-17 laden with incendiary bombs had crashed and exploded on take-off right in front of them. Friends gone in an instant.

Navigator Kleinman and bombardier Clements were immediately busy. Kleinman scribbled and fiddled at his charts and instruments to set a course for the bomb group's rendezvous point and final target. Peering through the Astrodome above him, he felt as if he could see toward the heavens; at night from here he could read his position by the stars. Clements sat just ahead of him, with the bombsight close to his left hand and the release handle for the bomb bay doors to his right. As the aircraft climbed, Clements made his way back to the bomb bay to remove the pin from each bomb. These were a safety precaution to stop the bombs from detonating when they were being loaded.

Brown and his co-pilot, Albert Fitzpatrick, sat in the cockpit at the top of the bomber, looking out and up at the vast sky and along the curve of the far horizon. In front and around them were more than 150 switches, dials, gauges, and handles. Aside from the fact they were flying into war, there were still all the essentials of flight to worry about: airspeed, barometric pressure, wind drift, and engine revolutions.

Today there was a silence in the cockpit; that sense of unease, as they listened to unfamiliar voices in the crew. There were silent prayers that young Kemp would not jinx them. Irrational feelings, they knew, but hard to shake.

At their shoulder they felt the presence of the flight engineer, one of the new guys, as he monitored the gauges and the health of the engines. He also doubled as the top turret gunner, fitting his body into a hydraulically controlled upper turret which could turn through almost 360 degrees as his guns sought to fight off attacks.

Above the clouds, at 60 below zero, Kleinman reached up to chip frost off the Plexiglas. Only the cockpit, nose, and radio room had heating and even that was not very good. To compensate, all the crew relied on electronically-heated suits, gloves and sheepskin boots. If a gun jammed, the gunner would be forced to take off his gloves to try to fix it and bare hands would often stick to the icy metal.

Cold was one natural enemy; the other, as the crew had found out on the Münster raid, was the lack of oxygen. It was Kleinman's job to use the plane's intercom to carry out one of the regular oxygen tests, requesting each crewman to check the indicator on his equipment and reply. If the reply did not come, then the closest man had to investigate. It was possible for a guy to be completely unaware that he had a leak in a mask or hose and to fall unconscious within minutes.

Kleinman went through the crew one by one, from the pilots and flight engineer to the bombardier at his side, and to the rest of the gunners.

In a separate compartment with a small desk sat the radio operator, who also manned a topside machine gun which pointed above and to the rear.

At midships were the two waist gunners – so close in the fuselage that, when they stood to fire their guns out of the open windows, they could feel their backs almost touching – and Keon, the ball turret gunner.

Keon sat in a revolving Plexiglas bubble that hung from the underside of the fuselage, his body curved against the glass with the twin machine guns at his knees. It was a lonely, isolated, and vulnerable position in which to fight a war. To add to his misery, there was no room for his parachute, so if the aircraft were hit, he needed to crawl out of his position and find it. He would worry about that if it happened. After all, while the parachute was an essential aid, no one liked to think about it too much: in common with most air crews, none of the men had ever made a parachute jump.

In a compartment at the rear of the plane was the tail-gunner, Richard Tangradi, from Philadelphia, who sat on an oversized bicycle seat underneath the plane's tail section. He shared much of Keon's misery: few roles in war seemed as remote and exposed.

But, for now, the oxygen tests showed all was well.

Over the sea the aircraft shook as the sergeants tested their guns, and the smell of cordite filled the fuselage.

Ahead of Brown the sun was rising, but so too now was the flak wall above Frankfurt. Inside their flying suits the sweat turned cold on the men's skin. Suddenly the smoke from the explosions was so thick in the air they could smell it through their oxygen masks.

The guns on the ground had zeroed in on them, but they flew on, Brown trying to hold steady and line up for the bombing run on the target: a steelworks on the edge of the city.

Clements adjusted the bombsight, taking into account ground speed, wind drift, and the estimated time of fall of the bombs. The aircraft shook, each movement liable to upset the sensitive gyroscopes in the sight.

So much fear, so much to think about. So much in the mind of the bombardier now. Not least the essential requirement of the job: that he would not be so overcome by nerves he would forget to open the bomb bay doors.

The crew waited, wanting to just get in and get out. A wave of freezing cold air swept through the fuselage: the bomb doors were open.

Clements crouched over his bombsight, looking down through the Plexiglas nose, painfully aware of the destructive power he now wielded.

As he released the bombs, and their huge weight fell away, the aircraft lurched upwards, and Brown began to swing it around.

But fragments from the heavy flak had taken their toll.

As Brown headed back towards the Belgian border, he lost two engines; soon after, a third began to stall. They were 100 miles or so from the coast, and beyond that they still had the English Channel to cross.

Then, Tangradi in the torturously-cramped compartment under the B-17's tail noticed a speck in the cold blue sky. Although one of the newest men in this crew and aged only 19, Tangradi was flying his 23rd mission. He was wise and alert.

The speck was 1,000ft away but closing fast and he realised with horror it was a Focke-Wulf 190.

He hit the intercom to alert the rest of the crew. It was dead. He shifted, wondering if he could get back along the waist of the aircraft to shout to them.

No chance. The fighter was coming in. Any minute now it would be spraying the aircraft – *him* – with hot metal.

Six hundred feet.

Tangradi squeezed the triggers on the twin .50 calibre guns.

It was then he had the second shock. Nothing. No music.

Guessing the mechanism must be frozen, he grabbed at the charging handles and pulled like hell. But again, nothing.

He tried the intercom. Still dead.

The 190 looked big and horrible now. He was staring it down. Defenceless. Tangradi guessed the German pilot must have realised there was something wrong in the rear of the B-17, as he was 400, 300ft away and not being fired on.

At 200ft the German opened up, and all hell broke loose inside the B-17 as cannon fire raked the fuselage and hot metal peppered the crew.

Tangradi scrabbled from his position, feeling a numbness in his left arm, and grabbed his parachute.

As he reached the waist gunners, he saw both starboard engines were on fire. Gordon Keon pulled himself awkwardly out of his ball turret, his elbow a bloody mess.

Waist gunner Bill Kemp saw that Tangradi could not move his left arm and helped him put on his parachute. The other waist gunner, 'Pappy' Janderup, made his way to the cockpit and came back to say the pilots had baled out. Brown had tried to swerve and evade the attack, but the loss of engines had left him with little power and little hope. He had given the bale-out order and, unaware of the faulty intercom, had escaped through the hatch with Fitzpatrick.

As the navigator Kleinman struggled to the hatch, fragments of a 20mm shell splintered in his right forearm. He dropped 8,000ft before opening his 'chute.

In the waist of the ship, Janderup opened the door.

'See you, Tan,' he said and jumped.

As the pilotless B-17 began to dip towards the ground, Tangradi followed.

The silk 'chutes spread across the sky above Belgium. As the men fell, snowflakes fluttered around them, flying horizontally into their faces, not from the sky above. It was a strange, discomforting feeling.

But there were only nine parachutes. Tangradi had been sure that

Bill Kemp, from Florida, the young man flying his first mission, had been unhurt. But as the burning aircraft twisted in the sky, he did not escape. Remarkably, when he was found later by the Germans in the wreck, he was alive, but he died soon after of his wounds.

The rest of the crew were all taken prisoner by Germans on the ground. Except Brown and Kleinman.

The unease they had felt had been warranted. But their fate was not to be straightforward.

They had escaped death but were set to embark on a seven-month ordeal which would see one facing execution as a German agent and the other fighting for his life alongside the Resistance.

2

PROMISE TO RESIST

Françoise Labouverie

WHEN THE GERMAN army rolled into Belgium on May 10, 1940, Françoise Labouverie felt her nation's defeat as keenly as a physical pain.

A spirited and energetic teenager, soon to turn 19, she could not understand how some of her older neighbours in the rural village of Céroux-Mousty, 25 miles south-east of Brussels, accepted the occupation readily. Even her grandfather, who she loved deeply, grew surly every time she brought up the war during family get-togethers. Once he wrote in soap on the huge dining room mirror: *'On ne parle pas de politique!'* (we're not talking about politics). Françoise, however, was unrepentant and vowed that she would not continue as if their lives were unchanged. As a child she had always been slightly ashamed that none of her family had been able to fight in the First World War and she watched with growing horror as an invader once again consumed her country.

The initial humiliation had come that very first day when the Germans struck west without warning, their Stuka dive-bombers flattening towns and villages. Blitzkrieg – lightning war – had been unleashed upon Western Europe.

By May 20, a larger force further to the south had punched

through the Belgian Ardennes and Luxembourg, with rapidly moving panzer units reaching Abbeville and the Somme estuary, cutting off French and British troops in Belgium from communication with those in France. The Netherlands, also under ferocious attack, surrendered on May 15. Brussels, which had already been heavily bombed, was declared an open city so its population would not suffer further. The people stayed in their homes on May 17 when the first German troops entered the capital; those who had the stomach to look outside saw large swastika flags being raised on public buildings.

On May 27, short of ammunition, food and supplies, the Belgian army contacted the Germans to discuss conditions of surrender. The reply came from Hitler himself: Belgium's unconditional surrender was the only way to stop the onslaught. King Léopold III had little choice but to accept – although he would come under sustained criticism from Paris, London, and some of his own ministers – and at 4am on May 28 the ceasefire came into effect and the occupation began. In the short battle for their homeland, 80,000 Belgians had been wounded, killed or taken prisoner.

Life in Céroux-Mousty, which was close to the famous battlefield of Waterloo, settled back into a kind of normality. The Labouveries ran a farm with grazing land for sheep. They were not rich, but they were wealthy enough to have a small number of servants, including a cook and a teenage maid, Francine, who Françoise was very fond of. Everyone in the village knew each other and most met every Sunday at the Catholic church. Françoise had been convent educated, but she had lost her sense of religion, and she began to feel a gulf growing between herself and her home. She was growing up, but she was grieving too: her father had died of cancer shortly before the invasion.

She began to daydream about resisting the occupation, although she had no idea what form that resistance might take. After talking with her cousin, Michel, who shared her desire to act, she decided her most important role could be a humanitarian one. She turned the attic of the family's farmhouse into bedrooms for refugees from Brussels, often Jews. But the strain of looking after people who were wanted by the Germans damaged Madame Labouverie's health, so Françoise stopped providing refuge for others and moved out, finding a job in Brussels as a junior typist and renting a small attic room on her meagre wages. Once in the big city, she realised she had to be careful who she trusted and how she expressed her views. Not everyone around her was opposed to the Germans.

The occupiers exploited the cultural split between French-speaking Walloons and Dutch-speaking Flemish. Hitler's propaganda machine courted Flemish nationalists, portraying the Germans as 'brother people', which complicated the resistance. Neighbours could turn into enemies overnight. A far-right Belgian movement, Rex, became a Nazi party for Belgium, the pro-fascist groups trying to use Allied air raids to turn the population against the British and American fliers.

However, for most adults in Belgium's population of eight million, whether they were French or Flemish speakers, this was the second occupation by the Germans in their lifetime – and it hurt. The hardship and cruelty of the First World War remained a painful memory. Françoise might not have been born until after the war ended, but she was acutely aware of the dark periods of her country's history and knew that even the name of the man now in charge of Belgium and the northernmost *départements* of France was a painful reminder to everyone of 1914-1918: General Alexander von Falkenhausen's uncle had been the military governor there during the First World War.

So, controlling her anger, she kept her ears open for ways in which she might contact like-minded people in Brussels and eventually quietly confided in an old friend of the family who invited her to a meeting at a small café near the Gare du Nord. There, she found a handsome man in his early 30s, sitting in the corner, shrouded by dark glasses, a little moustache and a soft felt hat. He said his name was Etienne, although Françoise intuitively knew it was a lie.

She soon discovered Etienne was Pierre Hauman, a 32-year-old former lieutenant in the Belgian army. Fiercely intelligent, and from a liberal, middle-class family, Hauman had been forced to take off his officer's uniform upon the surrender in 1940 but had decided to continue the fight. His French wife, Paulette, worked at his side, helping to gather information about the movement of troops, assessing which factories produced the most for the German war effort, and which targets had been successfully struck during RAF raids. The Belgian security services in London knew him and his *réseaux* – his network – by the codename *Tégal*.

Hauman already had agents living near German airfields and coastal defences, but – impetuous and sometimes eccentric – he planned an information-gathering network which would stretch through Nazi-occupied northern France into the southern zone, Vichy France, which was sympathetic to the Germans. As the network expanded, he found he needed more couriers, and a young woman such as Françoise – who seemed an unlikely spy – would be perfect.

Françoise's first mission was to take a message to the town of Carcassonne in the south of France, and she accepted it with relish, crossing the demarcation line into the Vichy zone by posing as a vineyard worker. From Carcassonne, she went to Lyon and met a distant relative whom she called 'Uncle Roger', who ran a Resistance group. Although overweight and sometimes grumpy, Roger was extremely brave and prided himself on knowing how to cross not only the nearby Swiss frontier but also the border into neutral Spain. With some bravado he decided to prove his skills to Françoise and, enjoying the dangerous game, she accepted. Taking a series of trains to Cerbère, on the coast south of Perpignan, they walked through the eastern edge of the Pyrenees, bribed a customs officer with cigarettes, and wandered into the harbour village of Portbou. There they ate cream buns and drank anisette in a café before returning to France.

For a while, Françoise joined Roger's group in Voiteur, near the border with Switzerland, as his assistant. Visitors to Roger's small farm brought information on airfields and possible landing grounds, which Françoise typed up for couriers to take on to Spain. Françoise also escorted people by train to Lyon before passing them to another guide who would take them on Roger's route over the Pyrenees.

However, on one stopover in Lyon, she was eating a meal in the home of a relative when the Vichy police knocked on every door in the apartment block. As an officer entered the kitchen where she was sitting, Françoise tucked maps up inside her jumper, and they were not discovered. However, the identity papers she showed the policeman were false and, if he checked her name against the address she had given, she feared he would return to search for her.

Roger was concerned enough to send Françoise into hiding, but in November 1942, he asked her to escort a Jewish woman from Lyon to a market town close to the Swiss border. The timing was bad: as the two women travelled, the Allied armies landed in French North Africa, and Hitler responded by moving his troops into the south of France. Françoise and the woman took refuge in a small hotel while German soldiers marched along the cobbled street outside. Fearing her false papers might put them both in danger, Françoise was forced to escape, leaving the Jewish woman in the hands of the local police chief. As the woman tried to cross the border, she panicked and was caught, later dying in prison.

Learning from Roger that the Germans were indeed searching for her, Françoise paid a *passeur* – a guide – to smuggle her over a snow-covered mountain into Llivia, a Spanish enclave just inside French territory, and then persuaded the *carabineros* (frontier guard) there that she wanted to visit her Spanish fiancée for Christmas. But overnight the Spanish government closed the border to refugees and a policeman escorted her back to the French border.

Afraid to return to Roger's group, Françoise travelled back to Belgium and risked going home. In Céroux-Mousty, she listened to her mother and neighbours talking as if there was no war on. Nothing seemed to have changed in the village. There were very few Germans about, and the farms were unaffected, meaning locals were not experiencing the same lack of food that was beginning to cause suffering in the larger towns and cities. Françoise feared she was acting like an angry, frustrated youth, but she resented the fact that many of the villagers did not seem to recognise they were prisoners in their own homeland.

As soon as she could get away from the village she headed once more to Brussels, tracked down Pierre Hauman, and told him she wanted to do a lot more to help the Resistance. Hauman asked her to work full-time for him.

'I will,' she said.

She smiled at herself afterwards, joking that she had pledged herself to *Tégal* as earnestly as accepting a proposal of marriage.

Tégal was one of about 40 underground organisations in Belgium dedicated to intelligence-gathering. Many were much smaller and specialised in specific geographical areas or particular industries. One consisted of weather experts who collected meteorological data for the RAF and the United States Army Air Forces (USAAF); another included members who worked in a telephone exchange and were able to listen in to conversations[2].

---

2   It is estimated that throughout the war about 21,000 people were involved in these kinds of intelligence-gathering activities. Winston

The underground could look across to London for support from the exiled Belgian military intelligence department, the *Deuxième Section* (also known as the *Deuxième Direction*), the British Special Operations Executive (SOE) and the American Office of Strategic Services (OSS). Around 250 Belgians arrived from London to take part in resistance or espionage activities. Most dropped by parachute and carried radio sets, money and other supplies.

Taking part in any form of dissent, espionage or resistance put people in great danger. While the military governor, Falkenhausen, was a cultured man with little time for Hitler, he presided over an occupation enforced by the full apparatus of the Nazi state, including the Gestapo (the secret police); the SS (Germany's elite soldiers); and the SS police, the SD; while the Abwehr and the *Geheime Feldpolizei* (GFP) – the secret military police of the German army – created special units to carry out specific operations against the Resistance and anyone suspected of helping downed airmen. They were aided by denunciations and information provided by people terrified of reprisals against them or their families, by those sympathetic to the Nazi cause, or by traitors motivated by personal gain.

By committing to Hauman's group, Françoise Labouverie was risking torture or death in a concentration camp. However, the option of doing nothing was too bitter a pill to swallow.

Despite the dangers and difficulties, *Tégal* grew and Hauman brought in a deputy, Paul Collard, a Belgian industrialist. While Hauman could be unpredictable, Collard was the opposite: a bourgeois Catholic who preached caution and moderation. Together they developed a courier network that reached from

---

Churchill later wrote that by 1942 80 percent of information being supplied to British intelligence by Resistance groups across Europe was coming from Belgian networks.

Mons, through France and on to British agents in Spain and Portugal.

However, two waves of arrests broke the line and left the network unable to get messages to London. Hauman and Collard – who, despite the setback, still had 300 agents and helpers across Belgium and France – had to rebuild. Hauman took on Franz Manderfeld, a 35-year-old who covered for his shyness in front of Françoise by telling bad jokes, and promoted Françoise to be his personal assistant, ordering her to find a flat which could be used as a headquarters in Brussels.

That task was not as easy as it sounded. People were suspicious of a young girl seeking to rent a flat on her own and she knew any prospective landlord would ask whether she had a job and the money to pay the rent. She needed to develop a cover story which would not only persuade others but also help her to be courageous and confident while making inquiries. So, she invented the fictional figure of Madame Jourdain, a tall and elegant but reclusive older lady for whom she was a secretary, carrying out typing and domestic duties and running errands. For the pretence to be successful, Françoise even had to lie to her family.

'You are nothing more than a servant to that woman,' a relative said one day. 'You could do so much better!'

Renting a flat in the university quarter, Françoise settled into the often-lonely life of a member of the underground. As the job she used as cover did not exist, there were long periods of boredom, broken by moments of danger and the excitement of a visit from Hauman or Manderfeld, who brought information about raids or troop movements on scraps of paper which Françoise would type up as reports.

They often also brought sketches which she would tidy up and photograph, producing microfilm which would be taken through France to Spain by a courier who, for security reasons, she never met. The British also sent the group a radio operator who Françoise knew only by the codename, 'Bob'.

But the demand from London for information was such that Hauman soon briefed Françoise that she too must meet contacts to gather intelligence. One regular source was a prim and proper middle-aged blonde woman known to Françoise by the codename 'Mado' who would only agree to meet in the finest and most elegant tea rooms. There she passed Françoise folded handkerchiefs, hollow fountain pens, or matchboxes containing notes from Mado's brother, a banker who gathered information about German investments, currency exchanges, and which Belgian businesses were profiting from the war.

But danger was ever-present. The group's personnel in Antwerp and Hauman's right-hand man Collard were arrested. And, returning to the flat for an important meeting with Hauman and Manderfeld, Françoise spotted a Gestapo car in the street. Once inside the flat, the three agents burned all the documents in a small stove.

Françoise moved again, but the gathering of intelligence did not stop. Hauman learned that an architect named Gregory wanted to sell them plans of the new fortifications on Hitler's Atlantic Wall near Dunkirk. Françoise became this new informant's handler, although she did not trust him.

Gregory's information was treated with glee by London, but his demands for money put the resistance group under pressure. In September 1943, having missed two payments, the group finally celebrated a parachute drop of funds from London. Carrying 300,000 francs in a bag, Hauman told Françoise and Manderfeld he would go and see Gregory and meet them later at the Café Royal.

'If I am not there by 6.30,' he said, 'warn my family!'

Hauman shook hands with Manderfeld and kissed Françoise on both cheeks.

As he left, Franz whispered to Françoise.

'I hope we don't need to warn his family tonight.'

Their anxiety was justified. Hauman walked into a trap laid by Captain Hugo Böhme, a cunning officer of the GFP who had identified Gregory and persuaded him to give up Hauman. Gregory had also given Böhme a full description of Françoise, although he knew her only by a codename.

Françoise and Franz Manderfeld went into hiding. Francoise assumed another false identity – that of Nicole Desmanets, a 33-year-old divorcee – dyed her hair a dark red and changed her clothes to look older. She rented an attic room in the Rue de la Vanne with a view through the skylight across the rooftops of Ixelles.

Meanwhile, Böhme had been ordered to destroy the rest of the network, and he had put Françoise at the top of his wanted list. He visited her mother and took away a photograph of her.

'Your daughter has fallen in with the wrong crowd,' he said, telling her she should help him find Françoise.

3

UNDER SUSPICION

John 'Bud Brown'

JOHN 'BUD' BROWN watched his stricken B-17 hit the ground and explode. Landing safely by parachute, he suffered the moment of disorientation felt by all airmen who had to escape their aircraft in wartime over enemy lines. This was it. He was not going back to the family photos stuck to the locker in his billet or the warm beer in the local. Tonight, friends would speak his name differently, wondering about the fate of the B-17 'Dodie', and drinking to put their fears out of their minds.

From now on, everything around him represented danger. He could walk into a police station and give himself up, but he never seriously contemplated it. Perhaps he could be one of those who stayed free, just like the stories he had heard from the intelligence officers who visited the base.

He tried to remember those escape and evasion lectures now, and the first thing he recalled was, although they must be wary of everyone, airmen had to find the support of a sympathetic local if they wished to avoid immediate capture. From that first contact it was hoped they would be put in touch with the Resistance. In particular, they sought one of the evasion lines which sheltered airmen and provided them with false papers and guides to move them through France and into Spain. He also remembered being told to head towards large cities where he would be more inconspicuous and better positioned to find help.

But where was he? He knew his flight path had taken him close to where the borders of Belgium, the Netherlands and Germany meet, and although he felt sure he had crossed from Germany, he feared in the confusion of the aircraft's final moments he could be wrong.

Brussels, he was sure, was to the south-west, so using the compass and maps from his escape kit, he began to walk through the growing darkness of the February afternoon. As often as he could, he stayed close to hedges or wooded areas but, on the second day, as he was walking on a path through a field, a man on a bicycle came silently up behind him. The man passed, then stopped and stared. Just as Brown prepared to run into the undergrowth, the man spoke in broken English.

'Are you American?'

Exhausted, Brown realised the time had come to take a risk.

'Yes.'

The man nodded thoughtfully.

'Come, I take you to a house. They speak English.'

These were tense moments for Brown as he walked in silence beside the man. The stranger might be intending to betray him, either out of loyalty to the Germans, the possibility of a reward, or just because it would be safer for him to turn the American in rather than shelter him. At the house on the outskirts of the town of Olen there were two more men.

'What is your name and squadron?'

'John Brown, 349th Bomb Squadron,' he replied.

Then, a moment of dark humour, as all three of the others introduced themselves as Louis. Brown secretly wondered whether they did not want to give their names as they could not completely trust *him*[3]. After giving Brown food and finding him civilian clothing, they said they were members of the *Witte Brigade*, one of the most effective armed groups of the Belgian Resistance.

Twenty-four hours later two of the men, Louis Govers and Louis Mertens, took Brown to a café on a narrow stretch of the Chaussée de Gand in Molenbeek, a western suburb of Brussels. In an upstairs flat, Brown's new host, Phillipe Vossells, gave him instructions to try to stay alive.

'The buildings are so close together and there are so many Germans here,' he said. 'Speak only in whispers and stay away from the windows.'

Brown was not permitted to go out, but during the four weeks he was there, he was not short of visitors. Vossells had many connections within various elements of the Belgian Resistance, including Countess Limburg-Stirum, a member of an ancient aristocratic family, and a tall man who claimed to be the head of the Belgian Red Cross and told him they were trying to find the whereabouts of Brown's crew.

Brown discovered that the small flat was a 'barracks' for the *Witte Brigade*, sheltering its operatives when they needed it and providing a place of storage and exchange for black-market food. This underground trade had become a key element of life in the city where, unlike in the countryside, vegetables and meat – unless it was mostly bone – were now almost impossible to find. Food stamps – issued by the Belgian authorities on behalf of the occupier – did not provide enough bread, butter or sugar, and very few people saw luxuries like flour and chocolate.

Vossells and his comrades were even able to use their black-market connections to source coal to warm the apartment.

---

3   In fact, records show that at least two of them were indeed called Louis.

UNDER SUSPICION

***

Brown's friend and navigator Ted Kleinman had not survived quite so unscathed from the crash. Wounded in the right forearm by a 20mm shell from the Focke-Wulf aircraft which had finally brought down their B-17, he was in agony and had not opened his parachute until he was 1,000ft from the ground. He had consequently landed about 150ft from the wrecked aircraft.

He saw the red roofs of a town and decided to head in that direction. He had no idea what he would do once he got there. Knock on someone's back door?

But he had not reached the houses when he noticed a farmer standing beside a barn. He saw the man make a quick gesture to come closer. Kleinman walked quickly over, and the man, looking the airman up and down, questioned him in faltering English.

'Is the invasion coming?'

The airman gave a wry smile.

'The generals don't share that kind of information with me.'

There was an awkward moment of silence, then the man gave a nod. He knew someone who might help and, once night had fallen, took Kleinman north to the city of Turnhout and the home of Zosime Verstraeten, a 41-year-old housekeeper with a warm smile and a keen sense of humour.

Zosime disinfected and bandaged the wound to Kleinman's arm and looked after the young man for seven weeks. She told him her husband, François, had been a corporal in the Belgian army and was captured right at the start of the invasion in May 1940. For nearly four years he had been a prisoner in Germany and she had been alone. Looking after Kleinman gave Zosime a new purpose. At least a dozen more airmen and many Belgians escaping German labour camps hid with her. Neighbours became so used to seeing young men arrive at the back door of her home they vowed not to ask questions. If one did, she told them they were her nephews.

Soon after Kleinman's arrival at the house, a man who said his name was Jacques came and interrogated him about his crew. Apparently satisfied Kleinman was who he said he was, Jacques broke the news that one of his crew had died in the wreck and others had been taken prisoner. Kleinman never saw Jacques again and learned that two days after he had come to the house, he had been arrested; it was a sharp lesson in the risks people who helped him were running.

On March 27, 1944, Zosime took Kleinman by tram to Antwerp and then on to Brussels, where, in a radio repair shop, she spoke in hushed tones with other members of the Belgian underground.

She then took the airman to a café where she introduced him to a tall, grey-haired and distinguished-looking man of about 50 whom she introduced as '*le chef*'. Over the coming weeks the chief moved Kleinman between safehouses. Then, in Liège, he met Edgard Delbecq, who was happy to help Kleinman but was more interested in sabotage work.

In one of the evasion lectures which Brown and Kleinman had attended back in Thorpe Abbotts, they had been discouraged from taking part in active resistance operations, such as sabotage: it was judged that the priority for a flier had to be returning to England and getting back on operations. Becoming a saboteur put them in danger of being shot or treated as a spy.

But Kleinman grew intrigued by Delbecq's other secret life and wondered if he could help.

***

Every Belgian who helped Allied airmen evade capture risked torture, a concentration camp or execution. But, despite the danger, organisations developed to house, clothe and provide fliers with false identity papers. Operated by ordinary men and women from all walks of life, and with sabotage and attacks on German forces resulting in such severe reprisals against civilians that it proved too costly an option, the most effective service the underground could perform was to return a highly-trained airman to active duty.

Central to that service was the Comet Line, which, from August 1941, operated an evasion network of couriers and safehouses stretching from Brussels down through France and over the Pyrenees into Spain. The network was created by 24-year-old Andrée 'Dédée' De Jongh, who had trained as a nurse but was working as a commercial artist when the war began. She knew the risks the work posed to her and others.

The death penalty was always there, written on posters in cities and villages, for helping any allied airmen. To her, their own laws counted for nothing: there was only one law, the Germans' law.

By the time John Brown entered the Comet Line network, Andrée was already paying the price. Arrested in January 1943, she was sent to a concentration camp. Her father, Frédéric, who had helped her organise the line, had also been betrayed and was executed at the same time Brown was in Brussels.

Many of those who worked on the line risked not only their own lives but also those of their families. During March 1944, Brown passed through a number of Comet Line safehouses, sharing rooms with elderly people or teenagers who wanted to help him even though they could not speak each other's language. Brown was beginning to get used to living in the shadows, but moving through the streets from one safehouse to the next always put him on edge. Leaving an apartment in the Forest area of Brussels, he sat in silence in a café for seven hours while he waited for the next guide. He was eventually taken to Léon and Olga Verleysen and their 16-year-old daughter, Suzanne, who ran a fruit and vegetable shop near Phillipe Vossells in Molenbeek, where Brown had started out. He was introduced to a nondescript-looking man of average height with a studious face and horn-rimmed glasses. The man's ordinary appearance belied his extraordinary courage. His name was Henri Maca, and he ran a network of Belgian safehouses with his sister Marie, who was known to airmen by the codename 'Simone'. Showing astonishing bravery, Marie had returned to Belgium despite having previously fled to Switzerland with a price on her head.

The line had become a target for counter-espionage operations of the Abwehr, which ran English-speaking agents who could pose as Allied airmen. Maca was tasked with verifying each airman's identity, and Brown sensed immediately Maca was deeply suspicious of him. As Maca conducted an interrogation in very passable English, Brown began to understand why: when the Red Cross official in Vossells' flat had questioned him about his crew, Brown had been unable to give five of the names. To Brown this was not unusual: they were new replacements for crew members who had fallen sick – and he simply did not know them. To the Belgians this was extremely concerning.

Maca was unsure what to do. Brown's failure to name all of his crew was a strong suggestion he could be a spy for the Abwehr or SD. Failure to act now would put Maca, his family, the Verleysens and his entire network at massive risk. The safest thing to do was to shoot Brown.

Faced with this dilemma, Maca decided to make a final check to be sure, and on April 8, another American was brought to the shop on Rue des Béguines to decide whether Brown was a genuine flier or a German faking it.

The man's name was Bill Grosvenor.

4

LUCKY ESCAPE

Bill Grosvenor

BILL GROSVENOR WAS a 24-year-old P-47 Thunderbolt pilot from Colfax, Iowa, who had left college to join the air force and had been assigned to 56 Fighter Group, the first unit to take the P-47 into combat. On November 30, 1943, already a holder of the Air Medal and the Distinguished Flying Cross (DFC), he had been flying his 40th solo mission, escorting heavy bombers on a raid on Solingen, a manufacturing hub in the Rhineland.

Over Solingen the Luftwaffe attacked, and the P-47s rushed to protect the bombers. But Grosvenor felt his aircraft splutter. He was over Germany, at 23,000ft, and his engine was cutting out. He radioed his squadron commander and told him he was turning for home. He was offered an escort but said he would go alone.

With that, Grosvenor found himself in a shallow dive, and it was not until he was at 4,000ft that he got the engine restarted. He circled a thunderstorm and dropped to treetop level, coming into clear weather somewhere between Brussels and Antwerp, with the coast dead ahead.

Then, he saw puffs of smoke and movement – a train – and, following pre-existing orders to pick targets where he could, started an approach across the fields. Concentrating hard on the sights for the twin Browning machine guns in his wings, his eyes picked up the narrow vertical line of a telegraph pole far too late. He pulled back quickly on the stick but clipped the pole.

In an instant he knew the aircraft was crippled, so he launched it into a near-vertical climb to gain height fast.

Then the engine stalled.

Grosvenor slid back the canopy and unbuckled his safety belt. As he stood, his head and shoulders came up into the slipstream, and the air sucked him out.

He turned clear of the aircraft and pulled the ripcord. The 'chute had barely opened when he hit the ground.

At the same time there was a whoosh and a crash as his plane twisted in the sky and plunged into an orchard a short distance away.

Grosvenor came down at about midday. Only an hour earlier he had been taking off from Halesworth in England, knowing the worst could happen but finding it almost impossible to believe it could happen to *him*.

But now here he was. Occupied Belgium. Alone.

Throwing off his parachute and harness, he looked around. The wreck of his aircraft was a fireball. He imagined the sleepy farming village five minutes earlier – people going about their business, cows chewing grass in the fields, and in the distance the sound of an aircraft – but now Sint-Amands was alive with activity as people ran from their homes to find out what was going on. A farmer came out of a barn close by and Grosvenor, smiling to himself at the absurdity, lifted his arm and gave him a wave.

Two men arrived and said they would take him to the village. But as they began to walk, a woman pulled up on her bicycle. Looking at Grosvenor and then the two men, she gave the airman a slight shake of her head before cycling on. Grosvenor sensed she was trying to tell him the men could not be trusted or did not know how to help. So, he bid them a swift but friendly goodbye, and made off across the field in the same direction as the woman.

He reached a lane in time to see her enter a farmyard, and as he got to the farmhouse door, she was waiting, holding it open for him. Her name, she explained, was Elza Raes and she was friends with the Flemish-speaking Vermeirens family who owned the farm. The son, Vic, ushered Grosvenor into a barn and hid him among the hay bales as Vermeiren contacted another farm where he knew the daughter's fiancé, Marcel Harnie, was working for the Resistance. Harnie arrived and, in good English, began to question Grosvenor. The American was delighted to meet this handsome young man with a dark moustache and to realise that, less than an hour after crashing, he had managed to make contact with someone who could help.

Harnie said he would come back after dark with civilian clothes and take him to Brussels. But a squad of German soldiers arrived in Sint-Amands to search every house, and they were now fanning out throughout the countryside. Vic Vermeiren ushered Grosvenor into a potato pit on the farm and closed him in.

Darkness was falling that winter's afternoon when Harnie finally came back to collect Grosvenor and walked with him to the local town, Londerzeel, where they got on a streetcar to Brussels. The 40-minute journey was fraught with danger. A man sitting by Grosvenor began to chat.

'He cannot speak or hear,' Harnie told the man, hoping it would be enough.

It was, and after leaving the tram, they walked until they reached a red brick building with a religious icon set into an external wall – the rectory for the parish of Saint-Job. The church was directly opposite. Welcomed in by the Catholic priest, Camille Leclef, who Harnie trusted, as he was helping him avoid a call for forced labour from the German authorities. Leclef, a thin man with round glasses and prominent ears, told Grosvenor and Harnie he was keen to help anyone, no matter what their religion, because he was a patriot.

Over the following days Harnie went around the city hoping to make contact with Service EVA (the EVA stood for 'evasion'), a Resistance group developed during 1943 to oversee a safehouse network which could support the Comet Line. Some people belonged to both organisations. Harnie knew that finding them would be a difficult task, as EVA depended on secrecy for its security, but was eventually put in touch with Charles Hoste, who agreed to come to the rectory and meet Grosvenor.

Hoste was one of EVA's founders, and, like many of its members, he was a local government official: the perfect role for anyone in need of access to identification papers or additional food stamps. EVA's key purposes were to provide evaders with appropriate clothes, false papers and, if necessary, medical attention, before passing them on to the Comet Line for movement through France to Spain.

Hoste took Grosvenor off Harnie's hands and brought him to Prosper Spilliaert, a fishmonger in Avenue de la Reine. The business, near the Willebroek canal in the Schaerbeek area of the city, was one of the headquarters of EVA. Spilliaert took Grosvenor upstairs to where another man waited with a sheet of paper in his hands. It was a questionnaire to establish Grosvenor's identity. He noted Grosvenor's height, complexion and the colour of his eyes and hair; and asked him about his unit and his crash and about airmen slang which he would be expected to know. They were experienced and could quickly get a sense as to whether an airman was genuine, but all the information would be checked via radio with London to ensure Grosvenor was not a German plant.

Apparently satisfied that Grosvenor was who he claimed to be, Spilliaert photographed him for a set of fake identity papers, and Hoste took him to a safehouse where he was to stay with a French-speaking, grey-haired widow, Joséphine Van Der Gracht, and her daughter, Marie-Louise, who were new to EVA but eager to help.

The Van Der Grachts made a space for Grosvenor in a nook under the eaves of the roof and gave him blankets and food. Madame Van Der Gracht used her meagre rations to ensure Grosvenor ate well and gave him a special party that Christmas. She was 58 and liked to mother Grosvenor and the other airmen she helped. Neither she nor her daughter was put off by the danger; any fear was overcome by a sense of duty and a need to help those who were risking their lives for their liberation.

Early in 1944, EVA's Gaston Matthys, a 45-year-old civil servant, took Grosvenor to the Gare du Nord. There, Matthys appeared to bump into an old friend. They greeted each other as if it were a chance meeting: in fact, this was Jules Dricot, codename 'Deltour', who had become the head of the Comet Line in Brussels. Dricot took Grosvenor with him, and, as they passed into the station, the American felt a sense of elation: it seemed his journey back to England was starting.

But the pair did not board a train. Although Grosvenor did not know, Dricot was waiting to pass them to one of his most experienced couriers, but he did not appear; in fact, he had been arrested two days earlier.

Thinking on his feet, Dricot got a message to another courier, and Grosvenor was surprised to be handed over to what appeared to be a delicate teenager with a mop of dark hair. It was an easy mistake to make: most airmen who were helped by Aline Dumon – more often known by the codename 'Michou' – mistook her to be a girl of about 15. One noted she spoke with a 'soft, child's voice' and 'when she sat in a tram, her feet barely touched the floor'. In fact, she was 23 and a close associate of Henri Maca. She had been a central figure in the Comet Line since the arrests of her own family in August 1942, when the Germans had thought her simply too young and innocent to be involved in Resistance activity, but since the latest clampdown on Comet, she was one of the most wanted people in Belgium by the Gestapo. Like the airmen she helped, she now lived in various safehouses, unable to go home.

Michou took Grosvenor to Maria Buchet, a widow who ran a small printing firm with her three sons in the east of the city. Such was the shortage of safehouses since the latest wave of arrests that 70-year-old Buchet was now hiding five airmen in her home.

After a few days, guide Henri Malfait came to Buchet and took Grosvenor to Henri's father. Throughout January he was moved through several safehouses, eventually arriving with Jeanne Drieghe and her daughter Suzanne, who turned 18 on January 25 – the day of Grosvenor's own 24th birthday. Despite the strain, they all celebrated with wine and cake. After a month Grosvenor moved to the family of Jean Plas, who looked after him despite the terrible danger to their small children.

As Grosvenor was moved through Brussels, the Gestapo remained hot on his trail. Within days of helping the fighter pilot, Henri Malfait and Jules Dricot were arrested. At their Belgium headquarters in the Avenue Louise, the Gestapo gave Malfait a drug in a glass of beer and tried to make him talk. On January 22, the Germans raided the home of Maria Buchet and her son Roger. The Buchets were dragged into a waiting truck, but three of the airmen Grosvenor had seen at Maria's home managed to escape onto the roof. Roger was tortured in front of his mother, but they each looked into the other's eyes and saw a determination not to speak.

The line to Spain collapsed. At the end of 1943 Comet had been passing 16 airmen a week into Spain. Now all that stopped. The safehouses in Brussels were either blown or under tremendous pressure.

It was into this climate of fear that John Brown arrived in the city and found Henri Maca deeply suspicious of his identity.

Hearing about Grosvenor from Michou Dumon, Maca realised one American would be able to work out if another was a fake. He brought Grosvenor to meet Brown.

Grosvenor was quickly convinced that John 'Bud' Brown was who he said he was, and Maca shook the bomber pilot's hand. Grosvenor had saved Brown from a Resistance bullet to the head.

'We had to be careful,' Maca explained. 'Our escape line to Spain has been broken; you will need to stay in Brussels.'

Throughout the coming months Maca and others tried to redevelop the network, with the two airmen moving every couple of weeks. Everyone who led them through the streets of Brussels, transported them by truck or bicycle, or gave them shelter risked torture and death.

5

SCHRÄGE MUSIK

Stuart Leslie

KEY TO THE success of an Allied invasion of France would be debilitating the Germans' response to the landings and slowing down the speed at which they could move supplies and reinforcements to critical areas on the coast.

Consequently, the Allies switched the main target of their bombing campaign from Germany to the transport and communication centres of France and Belgium. And, even discounting the Americans, they had a considerable force: the RAF, by now, had swollen in scale to consist of 487 squadrons, including 100 provided by Britain's 'Dominions': Australia, New Zealand, South Africa, and Canada.

Six of the Canadian squadrons made their home at RAF Leeming in Yorkshire and among their pilots was Flying Officer Stuart Leslie, from Winnipeg, who loved to fly despite suffering terrible motion sickness.

Leslie had known some tough times as a teenager during the Depression, seeing his father's pharmacy business collapse and struggling to find work himself until he finally got a job in the instrument shop at Trans Canada Airlines. It was there he discovered a love of planes and flight, and in 1942, he lied about his age to join the Royal Canadian Air Force.

SCHRÄGE MUSIK

It was that act of courage – or, perhaps, foolishness – that had brought him here, to the controls of Halifax Mark II – 'K for King' – on May 1, 1944, as he manoeuvred it into the air and headed across the North Sea to the skies above southern Belgium.

In the darkness, as Leslie closed in on Saint-Ghislaine, near Mons, he eased the control column forward, and the aircraft's nose dropped slightly. The Canadian squinted to see through the glare of the fires which lit up the night. The leading heavy aircraft of the No 6 (Canadian) Group had marked the target, the town's railway marshalling yards, and the whole area had already taken a terrible pounding, having been hit by the USAAF earlier in the day. Leslie's aircraft was now part of a force of 137 bombers about to deliver further destruction.

'Okay, we're going in,' Leslie told his crew, sounding more confident than he had any right to in such a situation.

So many young Canadians like him had already lost their lives in the skies above Europe. The previous January, the Canadian Group had lost 48 aircraft on sorties to Berlin, Magdeburg and Stettin. In February, 18 bombers had gone down over Leipzig, and 11 crews were lost on raids on Schweinfurt and Augsburg. Leslie had no idea what the Allied leaders were planning, but the aircrew did not mind the switch to French and Belgian targets rather than the longer-range targets of Germany's heavy industry.

Not that the skies above Belgium were any safer. The Germans had recognised the change in Allied strategy. Fighters and flak batteries had been moved, and a system of defences enabled the Germans to know the aircrafts were coming. A long-range detector system, known as Freya, could identify the Allied bombers as soon as they got to height over their bases in England. As the Allied crews approached Belgium, they were picked up by the powerful Wassermann radar on the coast at Ostend, and night-fighters would be scrambled from airbases in northern France and Belgium.

Messerschmitt Bf 110s (unofficially known as Me 110) and Junkers Ju 88s were equipped with advanced on-board radar and upward-firing cannon which the pilots called *Schräge Musik* – a play on the German word for oblique and an expression for off-key music – that allowed the fighter to come at a bomber *'von unten hinten'* (from below and aft), out of sight of its guns. If the cannon fire caught the aircraft's wing fuel tanks, the bomber could explode the very instant its crew realised it was under attack.

So many odds against you. So many out there in the darkness plotting your death. In quiet moments, when he had time to be contemplative, it seemed crazy to Stuart Leslie that he was in this position, commanding an aircraft and bombing a foreign country in which he hadn't even set foot. And the very real chance of losing your life in a flash was always somewhere in his mind. Three nights before, the Canadian bomb group had lost ten of its 54 aircraft in a similar raid over Belgium.

Each flight seemed to make the likelihood of disaster even greater, and, although still only 20, he was on his tenth mission. The war waged by Bomber Command had made these young men grow up quickly.

***

For 40 minutes RAF Lancasters and Halifaxes bombarded the rail hub at Saint-Ghislaine, causing huge damage to the railway but also unintentionally destroying civilian targets too, including the market and a church. Most civilians had left the area, having experienced the onslaught from the air before – but 41 were killed that night.

Leslie's arrival at the target had been delayed due to a faulty compass, and 'K for King' prepared to go in on its bomb run alone. He brought the plane lower and held it steady. The target was easy to identify from bombing height: it was lit up by the fires and target indicators (TIs) which had been dropped by the Pathfinders.

The bomb-aimer, John Hawke, lay still in the aircraft's nose. Leslie heard his voice come through in his headphones.

'Left a bit… Good… Ease up… Fine… Steady… Bomb's gone!'

Leslie felt the aircraft surge upwards at the loss of weight, and, in a moment of relief, he turned onto a heading which would take the Halifax back across the North Sea to England. But his relief at turning for home was tempered by the knowledge the dozens of aircraft ahead of him had already followed the same path towards the coast. The Germans would be fully alert.

Every man in the crew searched the blackness of the sky for night-fighters. The air-gunners swung their turrets, their eyes following the lines of the barrels of the .303 calibre guns. The bomb-aimer remained in the nose, tracking their journey by the silver slivers of a river or a stream and the clusters of buildings of a town. Now he could see orange flames and puffs of smoke in the sky.

'Flak ahead, skipper,' he said. 'Better try some evasive action.'

As Leslie turned the aircraft to port, there was a violent crash, almost wresting the controls from his hands. The interior of the aircraft was suddenly lit by a brilliant blue flame, and something slammed into its starboard side, showering the cockpit with debris.

The crew never saw the aircraft that hit them, but it was a Messerschmitt Bf 110 night-fighter flown by *Oberleutnant* (first lieutenant) Georg-Hermann Greiner, from the deadliest of all night-fighter units, flying out of St Trond.

The bomber lurched and dropped. Leslie looked out the window; both starboard engines had cut out, and wind rushed through the holes in the fuselage as the plane went into a dive.

Leslie stayed at the controls, a cold sweat on his brow as he watched the altimeter plunge to almost 1,000ft.

The plane responded. Leslie halted the hurtling dive and pulled the nose up.

'K for King' was still going down, though. And below in the towns of Bevere and Meerspoort, people looked out to watch the flaming dark silhouette lumber across the sky. They could see the aircraft was doomed.

Leslie knew it too. There was no way he could reach the coast. Struggling hard to stop the craft from plunging downwards again, he heard the navigator Bob Webster shout.

'Don't step back, Johnny, there's a hell of a big hole here...'

But there was no reply from John Hawke. Johnny must have been caught in that shower of shrapnel, Leslie thought to himself.

There was no time to mourn his loss. Greiner attacked again, raking the bomber with cannon fire.

'Get ready to bale out,' Leslie shouted. 'I can't hold her.'

The flight engineer, George Elliot, brushed past him and disappeared out of the forward escape hatch.

'The tail's on fire, skipper,' said the voice of tail-gunner Earl 'Baldy' Baldry in his headphones.

'Everybody out!' Leslie shouted.

Holding the controls with one hand, he released his seatbelt with the other, ripped off his helmet and earphones, and donned his parachute.

As Leslie jumped into the night sky, 'K for King' fell apart, and the air around the young pilot was peppered with fiery chunks of metal. Although in shock, he fumbled at the ripcord, and his parachute opened, jerking his body with such force his flying boots were pulled from his feet.

The flames from the chunks of aircraft illuminated the ground below, and it was coming up fast.

He was hit with a tremendous bump and sprawled face down in the mud. The shock of the previous few minutes confused his brain and, as he leapt to his feet, for some reason he reached for the whistle attached to his Mae West lifejacket and blew. The shrill noise burst through the night.

A blast in the air above him sent him ducking to the ground as the aircraft's burning tail section crashed into a clump of trees nearby.

It brought him to his senses with a jolt. Unsnapping his harness, he ran towards the trees, convinced that Baldy – who was only 20 like him – was trapped inside.

But as he reached the edge of the field, he stopped. No-one could be left alive in that flaming wreck. There were lights in the distance. Headlights. A vehicle was coming, and he had been taught enough in briefings to know the only transport on the roads at night was likely to be German.

Leslie rushed back to his parachute and began to gather up the folds of silk. Frightened that the car was getting closer all the time, he realised he was wasting time. Part of the 'chute was snagged on a barbed wire fence, and he would never be able to release it and bury it in time. Instead, tired and without boots, he began to stumble across the field, heading for a dark line of trees. After running for about 50 yards, he felt the ground give way beneath his feet and plunged into a half-flooded ditch. Realising he was still wearing his Mae West, he pulled it off and pushed it down into the cold water.

Scrambling out of the ditch, he began to run again, sharp twigs and stones cutting through his socks. Crashing into the small trees at the edge of the wood, he slumped down behind a larger trunk. Panting for breath, he searched his flying suit for a cigarette. He could hear dogs barking in the distance, and for a moment fear threatened to overtake him again, but the tobacco seemed to calm his nerves, and he worked hard to get his thoughts in order.

Aircrew in his position had two choices: they could surrender to a German patrol and find themselves taken to a prison camp to see out the war, or they could try to evade capture. To be taken prisoner might mean no more missions and less danger, but how long would the war go on? Was it possible that one might be a prisoner for the next 10 years?

Evasion had to be the main priority. Like all airmen, Leslie had been briefed that it was his duty to try to escape from Nazi-held territory. If an airman got back successfully, he would be able to brief others about life on the run. If unsuccessful, he would still have diverted enemy personnel away from the war effort and into the hunt.

The first thing Leslie had to do was put as much distance as he could between himself and the burning wreckage of 'K for King'. Evasion training had stressed the importance of moving by night and hiding by day.

Stubbing out the cigarette, he struggled to his feet. A pain in his right leg made him wince, but it held his weight, and he began to run into the darkness.

He had come down in countryside about 30 miles north-east of Mons and soon saw ahead of him a church steeple and the buildings of a town. It was the Flemish town of Oudenaarde, although Leslie did not know that. All he knew was that a place of this size was likely to have a German army presence, and so he began to skirt around its edges.

He walked all night to put distance between himself and the wreck of his Halifax, eventually collapsing into a shallow trench in a field planted with daffodils. As he tried to rest, the levels of adrenaline in his body dropped, and he became aware of a pain in his head. Raising his hand to touch the wounded spot, he felt a deep gash in his right temple. His neck, collar and shoulder were soaked with blood. The discovery shocked him, but he was more worried about his right leg, which still ached badly. He rolled onto his back, suddenly feeling very cold and a little frightened.

SCHRÄGE MUSIK

The sky was vast above him. The stars twinkled, millions of miles away from the horror here on earth. He could hear a rumble thousands of feet above, the sounds of heavy bombers crossing Belgium on their way back to Britain. He imagined the crews inside, hoping they had left the worst of the flak and night-fighters behind, dreaming of the bacon and eggs awaiting them in the mess on their return. When the drone had gone, it felt as if they had deserted him. The loneliness that remained was almost as bad as any of the physical pain he felt.

Leslie slept fitfully and woke, stiff and sore, on the hard ground. Blood had congealed on his face and sealed his left eye shut. He shifted his right leg and almost cried out with pain. It was bruised from knee to hip.

He scrambled towards the nearby river and shuffled down to the water's edge. Scooping water into the small rubber bottle in his pocket, he added several water-purifying tablets from his escape kit and swallowed a few of the malted milk pills.

In the distance he could hear the voices of men working in the fields. Above, a vast armada of B-17s heading south-east left a beautiful pattern of vapour trails. He picked out the darting shapes of the fighter escort as it flanked and weaved around the bombers. The formation took two hours to pass, but Leslie was in no hurry: he had decided to use the day to restore his energy before moving on at night. Late in the afternoon the bombers returned. They were no longer in their tight combat boxes and were followed by stragglers, trailing smoke from damaged engines. Leslie imagined his fellow pilots clinging to the controls, praying their ship would get them home safely. He knew that fear of facing the coastal flak, of wanting to avoid coming down in the Channel and of the terrifying moment of landing, the fear of the aircraft bursting into flames.

As dusk began to fall, it was time to move. Realising the water was the River Scheldt, he decided to follow it.

Every step was painful. He reckoned he had covered about five miles when he felt too tired and hungry to go on. Spotting a haystack in a field, he burrowed into it. Within a few moments he was fast asleep.

On the second day of his escape, he got lucky. Approaching a farm, he was given a meal of potatoes, pea soup, and bacon, and a glass of water by the elderly couple who lived there.

His stomach full, Leslie reached into his pocket and brought out a crumpled square-shaped packet of Sweet Caporals. The farmer and Leslie puffed away on the cigarettes as they studied his escape map, and the Belgian showed him where he was: in the heart of Flanders. Leslie sat back in his chair, weighing up his options. But he was so tired he could barely think. Switzerland? Spain? Both seemed far away. Where might he get to?

'You know the Resistance? *Résistance*?' Leslie asked.

The farmer swallowed hard. He was a good man and wanted to do the right thing, the humanitarian thing. But he was not in the Resistance, and the thought of being connected to them was terrifying. The question brought home the danger of what he was doing.

Leslie understood. Waiting for darkness to fall, he thanked the couple and set off into the night. Unfortunately, the farmer was a much smaller man than the pilot, so he had no shoes which could fit Leslie. The Canadian continued to walk in his torn socks.

With the image of the map in his mind, he set off for the river and followed a towpath for an hour before a sound made him drop behind a clump of bushes. In the moonlight he could make out the shape of a barge moored to a small wharf. Shadows moved: men carrying cargo to the barge.

Leslie hesitated. To avoid the men, he would need to make a detour into the trees. In the darkness he could lose the river and his bearings. He decided to take the easier physical route and carry on down the path.

As he approached, most of the men carried on working, but one stopped and put down a heavy wooden box.

'*Bonsoir, m'sieur,*' the man said gruffly, bidding him good evening.

Terrified his voice would give him away, Leslie nodded in reply and carried on walking. The man went back to work, and Leslie breathed out.

Then, suddenly, a cigarette flared in the darkness. A German soldier stood against the trees, his rifle slung over his shoulder.

Leslie tried hard not to appear too shocked. He glanced and then quickly looked away, still feeling the German's eyes on him. Surely, he must see his uniform and notice he was barefoot. Any moment now he would shout, unsling his gun, bring it around…

But he didn't.

In the darkness Leslie's flying suit looked just enough like the overalls of the workmen for the German not to realise what he was.

He kept walking, trying to keep to the same steady speed, until he turned a corner in the towpath and could run until he was sure he was safe.

Hours later, a heavy dew was falling as dawn approached, and Leslie's wet feet became numb with the cold. Exhausted, he went into a field next to the river and burrowed into another haystack. His spirits were getting low. It was only a few hours since he had left the farmhouse, but he now felt very alone again.

Even when he woke long after dawn to find the sun high in the sky, the same hopelessness remained heavy in the pit of his stomach. He watched peasants in the fields and wondered if they could help him. Several times he tried to muster the courage to speak to them, but his low morale sapped his energy, and each time he sank back down and dozed.

It was evening when he woke with a start to the rhythmic clip-clopping of hooves. Sitting up, he saw a horse being led by a young man towards his hiding place. Leslie scanned quickly around, and seeing no-one else in sight, stood up slowly, trying not to give the man a fright.

'Pardon, m'sieur,' Leslie croaked, his throat dry as he asked for help. 'Anglais! RAF! Voudriez-vous m'aider, s'il vous plâit?'

The man held his gaze, thinking, but not apparently frightened. He gestured with his hands: *Stay here!* Then he turned his horse and hurried away.

Leslie watched, suddenly filled with fear. What if the man had gone to fetch the Germans? He had taken a gamble – with his freedom, perhaps, or his life.

Instead of sitting back in the haystack, he moved a short distance away and crouched in a hedgerow further along the path.

Eventually figures moved. But it was not a big group, and there were no army helmets. As they came closer, Leslie could see the young man had brought a woman of similar age and an older man. They turned out to be his wife and father. Leslie stepped forward, and they watched him walk towards them. They began to talk rapidly in Flemish. Leslie could see they were studying his clothes and his face, trying to work out if he might be a German agent, a spy trying to expose members of the local Resistance – someone who would mark them out for a concentration camp and death.

Finally, the old man, whose name was Maurice De Clercq, looked back down the path, saw it was clear and gestured for Leslie to follow them. The family lived in a small Flemish farmhouse in Kerkhove. In a homely kitchen De Clercq cut thick slices of coarse bread on the heavy oak table, while the woman made coffee.

They did not speak until the door opened and another young man entered. Leslie gave the man a double-take: he and the boy with the horse were identical twins. The family saw Leslie's look and began to laugh.

Fortunately, the new arrival spoke broken English. Gesturing to his uniform and stockinged feet, Leslie said he needed civilian clothes and boots.

The family nodded, but when Leslie produced a bundle of franc notes from his escape kit, they pushed the airman's hand away. The wife went into the next room and returned with blue overalls and several pairs of well-worn boots. Leslie found a pair which were only a little small and eased them onto his feet. There was enough give in the softened leather to ensure they were not too uncomfortable.

Standing, he let the family check him over. They all smiled and nodded. Leslie wondered if he should move on now: he felt the family had probably done all they could, and he was afraid of putting them in danger.

But an urgent rapping on the front door made him jump with fear. The old man gestured for Leslie to be quiet and went through to the hall. There were hurried, hushed voices.

The kitchen door swung open, and the farmer returned with two well-dressed women in their 20s. Both looked Leslie over, and then one stepped forward, placing a bottle and a first-aid kit on the table.

'How are you?' she said in excellent English, with only a trace of an accent.

She opened the bottle and handed it to Leslie. He lifted it. It was English gin.

The young woman smiled. 'We are friends,' she said.

Leslie smiled back, raised the bottle in a toast, and took a long drink of the harsh but welcome alcohol.

Leslie was quite taken with the two women, and it took some time for him to realise they were using their charm to interrogate him very subtly about his identity. Eventually, satisfied, they told him he would need to change his appearance to give him a better chance of survival.

One lifted aside the collar of the overalls and noted his RAF shirt.

He would have to take it off, she said, and his ring and his watch. Opening a valise, she pulled out a selection of dark clothing.

As Leslie got changed, the women and one of the twins conferred.

'We will leave now,' the older woman told him. 'You will follow in half an hour.'

Thirty minutes later the brother who spoke a little English led Leslie down the dark country lane. Somewhere there was the faint sound of aircraft, but it was too far away for either man to pay it any attention.

There was one other house nearby. Leslie's companion nodded in its direction and whispered.

'It is lucky for you that you did not ask those people for help. They are collaborators.'

They walked quickly, but without appearing to be in a hurry and eventually turned through a gate and set out across a field. Looming in the darkness, Leslie saw a large building behind a stone wall. It was a chateau, with high windows and ivy growing up its walls.

The brother knocked at a heavy wooden door, and the two sisters answered. The farmer shook Leslie's hands, exchanged a few words with the sisters, and left.

The older of the pair said her name was Alice van Wassenhove. Her sister was Elisabeth. Alice was in her mid-20s, was tall and dark, and she handled most of the conversation. Her sister was several years younger, perhaps not yet 20. She was blonde and blue-eyed, almost Nordic in appearance. For some reason, Leslie imagined a tall, blonde, perhaps aristocratic father and a dark, southern European mother. Alice explained the chateau was their family's country home and that they lived most of the time in Brussels.

A table had been laid, with shiny silver cutlery lying on a bright white cloth. The sisters brought steak and vegetables, with a plate of crusty white bread, and two bottles of a local wine to wash it all down. They explained they had an elderly Flemish cook who worked during the day but who must not know he was here. She would stay in the kitchen, and he would live upstairs in what was their father's room. He could move around but only in stockinged feet and he must not make a noise.

Upstairs, Leslie had a bath and found a pair of blue silk pyjamas laid out on the covers of the four-poster bed. After walking on hard ground in socks, feeling lost and tired and sleeping in haystacks, he suddenly felt as if he had entered another world. The luxuries were intoxicating. He had to remind himself that he was still in enemy territory and a very, very long way from home.

The next day he learned the sisters' mother, Madame van Wassenhove, was also a part of the escape network and was coming to arrange what to do with him. Greeting Leslie warmly, she quickly went on to discuss the reality of his situation. His presence at the chateau must be kept an absolute secret. There were many collaborators living in the area. She planned to move him, but nothing could be done until she had arranged papers for him. Work was already being done by a forger. As she talked, Leslie could see her daughters had inherited her confidence, courage, and poise.

But days became weeks, and it was May 25 before fresh word arrived from the city. He was on the move.

After tipping his workman's cloth cap at his four-poster bed, Leslie followed Alice outside, where she had two bicycles leaning against the wall.

Insects buzzed in the high crops at the side of the country lane as they cycled through. They passed old mills and crossed a canal, where bargemen waved a greeting and a lockkeeper went calmly about his work in the sunshine. But Leslie felt strangely exposed in the countryside: there were so few people about, and if a *Wehrmacht* motorcyclist rushed up behind them or a patrol suddenly appeared around the next corner, he was certain they would see him for what he was and arrest him.

The outskirts of Brussels brought a different fear. Here there were soldiers and army trucks passing on the street. Alice had warned him to be extra careful about keeping to the right-hand side of the road – cycling on the wrong side could be a giveaway to a watchful German – and about not taking too much notice of the soldiers: they had been here now for four years, and the locals paid them little attention.

Leslie kept just behind Alice so he could follow her and not appear unfamiliar with the area. But at one corner he bumped into a German soldier crossing the street. The soldier shouted at him angrily. Leslie looked humble and took the abuse – anything as long as the German did not unsling his rifle or demand to see his papers: this was not the time to try out his forged documents. Still waving his arm angrily, the German finally walked off, and Leslie caught up with Alice, who had cycled ahead.

'It is just a few blocks now,' she told him.

Eventually they arrived at a townhouse where two nurses lived. Alice came inside for only long enough to have a cup of coffee. This was a safehouse, she explained, and a new guide would come soon. She must say goodbye. At the door, she hesitated and stepped close to Leslie.

'Your crew…' she said. Leslie listened hard. He had been wondering about them, hoping their paths might cross. He had half-expected some of them to turn up at the chateau, having been passed to the evasion line.

But then he noticed the look on Alice's face. It was serious; she was struggling for words.

'They did not survive,' she said, her words hitting him like a strike to the face. 'Five or six bodies were found.'

She gripped his hand and squeezed it. It was comfort, friendship and sympathy. He tried to smile and say thanks, but the faces of his friends kept coming back to him.

Alice opened the door and was gone.

Stuart Leslie spent only one night at the house of the two nurses before being guided by a young man and his teenage sister through the streets to the tram station.

After a nervous tram journey, Leslie followed the young pair to a busy traffic junction where the man nodded to a smartly dressed old gentleman with white hair and a waxed moustache. The gent approached the airman and whispered that he was the editor of an underground news sheet, *Libre Belgique*. He then revealed with a smile that he was carrying a few copies inside his rolled-up newspaper. He liked to find places where he could leave them.

The old man's bravado rather terrified Leslie, although he could not help but find the pinched turned-up corners of the man's moustache just a little amusing.

They took another tram to the outskirts of the city where, in a quiet café, the old gentleman shook hands with the owner and whispered: *'Un parachitiste anglais!'* Leslie looked around anxiously, double-checking that there were no customers.

The woman smiled a greeting and reached out her hand.

'How are you, Mr Leslie?' she said in English. 'You just missed meeting a couple of American boys. They left for France last week.'

She felt with her hand under the bar and brought out a book and pen, showing him the names inside. The last one belonged to a lieutenant from New Jersey. She handed him the pen, and he hesitated. It seemed such a terrible security risk to keep a list of names, but as a guest he felt he could not refuse.

As he signed, a thick-set man with a large cigar in his hand came through from a room in the back. This was the owner's husband, whom she introduced by his nickname, 'Churchill'. The man puffed hard on the cigar to emphasise the similarities he imagined he had to the British prime minister. The woman explained that they both loved Britain, having escaped there as refugees during the First World War.

Churchill took Leslie upstairs to a small bedroom. He and his wife had had separate bedrooms before the war, but Churchill gave up his own for Leslie to use. There were also two young men sleeping in another room. They had the wild look of hunted men and put Leslie on edge. Churchill told him they were Resistance men – *'Armée Blanche'*, he whispered – but he could say no more.

Two nights later there was a rapping at the front door, and a breathless man with a cap pulled down over his head hurried inside the café, talking rapidly to Churchill. Leslie had to be moved. The two men hiding upstairs had been part of a trio which had attacked and killed a collaborator a few days earlier. The third man had been caught and tortured by the Gestapo, and the anxious visitor believed all the network's addresses and many of its people might have been compromised. Airmen in the evasion line were being moved to 'clean' addresses.

A young woman in a coat and beret, who introduced herself as Madeleine, led Leslie through the dark streets, hugging the walls to avoid the patrols: being caught after curfew could lead to capture for him and most likely a concentration camp or execution for her. They had moved just in time: the Germans raided the café shortly after they left, arresting Churchill and his wife.

Leslie found himself spending several difficult days in the home of an elderly couple who were terrified of being caught. Then Madeleine returned and took Leslie to a park where they could talk without being overheard. She told him their group had been completely broken and she had nowhere to take him; she had many people to talk to, and he must wait for her here.

Leslie watched her walk off and wondered if she would ever come back. He sat, alone. It was Monday morning. A few people passed on their way to work, and there were mothers with babies in prams or toddlers at their side. Leslie felt very out of place, as if everyone who saw him recognised immediately that he was an Allied airman. He even began to imagine that people were looking at him, whispering 'RAF!'

It was a long day.

Darkness was falling by the time an exhausted-looking Madeleine returned. There was no good news. All the local safehouses were either blown or under suspicion. Madeleine led him back to the home of the elderly couple. Leslie muttered to them that he was sorry, and when he lay on his bed, he could hear the couple talking anxiously on the other side of the wall. He felt awful about the fear they were going through and about the people who had already been arrested. He made up his mind to leave the following day.

The next morning, the couple made him sandwiches and packed them with a bottle of beer into a bag, and he left to wait for Madeleine in the park. Again, she appeared tired and stressed.

'I've tried everywhere,' she said with a sigh. 'But there's one chance. I know a man in the city who might help.'

They left the park and took a tram to a street dominated by large buildings which Leslie guessed belonged to the university. Across the road was a building draped with swastikas and the word *Kommandantur*. Madeleine saw Leslie's nervous glance and told him to wait on a bench under a tree. She crossed the road and entered the Nazi building. It was only then that he realised that her contact must work for the Germans. As a clerk, perhaps, a civilian worker, forced to work with the occupiers. He opened the package prepared by the couple and began to chew thoughtfully on the sandwiches.

Then his mind began to panic. Perhaps this was a trap after all. As he sat here, wringing his sweating hands, he was probably being delivered into German hands. Any minute soldiers would come out, stride across the park, and snatch him at gunpoint.

He was being irrational. He knew the risks people like Madeleine took. And she was taking one now, and all for him. He opened the beer. More than an hour passed. The taste of the beer in his mouth turned a little sour and he stretched his legs with a circuit of the small park.

Finally, Madeleine returned with a smile on her face. They walked around to pass some time and then headed to a rendezvous at the Café à la Paix. Inside, Madeleine bought a copy of *Der Signal*, the *Wehrmacht* magazine for soldiers, and led Leslie to a table in a corner.

Madeleine ordered drinks and leafed through the magazine. Her coolness made Leslie smile. He remained on edge and each time the door clicked open, he looked up and casually scanned the visitor to see if they were the worker from the *Kommandantur* who wanted to help him.

Eventually a tall, well-dressed woman came in and crossed to the table, barely acknowledging Leslie but shaking Madeleine's hand and talking as if they were old friends. Leslie noted her attractiveness had turned a few customers' heads, but they soon went back to their coffees and frothy beers.

After a few moments she turned to Leslie, touched his hand and whispered in English, 'It's time to go.'

Madeleine put some coins on her white saucer, and all three stood, the women saying goodbye to the man behind the counter. They looked like office workers heading back to work.

They walked briskly but calmly to another café where more coffee was ordered, and Leslie stayed silent as the two women chatted. Then someone brushed past Leslie and slid into the fourth seat at the table. It was a short, rather heavily-built man, who appeared rather physically sluggish but had an intelligent face.

He spoke quickly and in hushed tones with the women in French. Leslie slowly realised he was the husband of the tall woman. The man's name, he learned, was Guy Schouppe.

SCHRÄGE MUSIK

'At this particular time, Mr Leslie,' Schouppe whispered with a playful smile, 'you have become something of a liability. However, my wife, Louise, will take you and your friend to our apartment while I try and find out what can be done.'

All four headed by tram to the Ixelles area of the city and entered a smart block of flats, where the Schouppes had an apartment on the fifth floor. A large window looked out onto a hospital and church and gave a view across the city. Louise showed Leslie his bedroom and the bathroom but explained there was no hot water. Leslie bathed anyway, dressed in some of Guy's clothes, and sat in the window reading one of the couple's English language books. Later that afternoon Guy came back in with a grin and tossed the airman a packet of English pipe tobacco, and that evening they sat, ate and drank port. Once again, Leslie felt that sense of the unreal – like the clean sheets at the Wassenhove's chateau.

The meal finished, Guy smiled conspiratorially and put a record on the turntable: 'We're Going to Hang Out the Washing on the Siegfried Line!' All looked at each other and began to laugh.

But the bravado only barely covered the Resistance group's fears. The Gestapo and SD raids continued. Friends had been arrested; who knew who was being exposed by their interrogation and torture? Brussels was becoming too dangerous.

6

'MIKE, THE SPIRIT OF LSU'

Al Sanders

LIEUTENANT ALFRED SANDERS – known to his family as Al – was a university graduate with a talent for track running who would have spent 1942 to 1944 fulfilling his dream of becoming a science teacher had it not been for the attack on Pearl Harbor.

But, as a keen member of a flying club, he had only ever considered one branch of the forces. In fact, he had been in the air when the Japanese struck at the Pacific Fleet. He had landed his Piper Cub to find the local sheriff waiting at the airfield and scowling.

'What are you doing flying that airplane around? Don't you know there's a war on?'

He volunteered for the Army Air Corps but was two pounds below the minimum weight, so he had gone out and eaten six bananas in one sitting.

Air Force training had been at Blytheville, Arkansas, and Sewart Air Force Base in Smyrna, Tennessee, where he learned to fly a B-24 Liberator. He was introduced to his crew in Tucson. They were so young they made him, at 26, feel like a grandfather: only he and his top turret gunner – Sergeant William Kozulak – were old enough to vote back home in Louisiana. They flew across to Dakar in Senegal and then north to Sudbury in England.

England was another world. A world of rationing, hot beer, bombed-out streets and lonely women. To remind him of home, Al had painted the yellow tiger head emblem of Louisiana State University on the side of his B-24 Liberator, dubbed 'Mike, the Spirit of LSU'.

The most difficult thoughts of all were of his wife, Millie, back home in Kentwood, Louisiana, who was expecting to give birth any day now. Her letters, like many of those coming to airmen from back home, had grown more focussed on the dangers of the air war, as its reality was being relayed increasingly to the American public. Reporters such as Walter Cronkite, of *United Press*, had flown missions and written articles vividly describing the terror of being under attack by flak and German fighters. Bob Post, of the *New York Times*, had not returned from his assignment. Film star Clark Gable had flown five missions in a B-17 with a cameraman and sound engineer to make a documentary which had been released in 1943. William Wyler's *Memphis Belle: A Story of a Flying Fortress* had caused a sensation when it came out in April 1944. Both films allowed audiences to watch actual combat footage filmed inside a bomber. For some it was thrilling; for the many with relatives and sweethearts serving as aircrew in England it was almost unbearable to watch.

But Sanders had little time to reflect on life back home. As Stuart Leslie was arriving in Brussels at the end of May, Sanders, of 832nd Squadron, was preparing for a raid on Leipzig. He and his crew had been up since 5am, having been roused from their bunks and told to head to the mess hall as quickly as possible. There was a rush to the supply room to pick up parachutes and other bits of kit.

In the ready room, an officer had been waiting by a large curtain against the wall.

'Ready, boys?' he said, and pulled the cord to open the curtains, revealing a huge map. Sanders had scanned it and seen a plan which took them to eastern Germany. A long flight.

The crew had then been taken by truck to their ship. But then, as often happened, after the rush came a lull. Take-off was delayed by an hour. No one liked that.

In the tail, Staff Sergeant Robert Swaffield, voiced his fears about what was happening but nobody else wanted to talk about it. The rest of the crew went through their last-minute checks at their stations. Co-pilot Fred Morley; navigator Tom Zoebelein; bombardier Danny O'Connell; radio operator John Lawrence; Kozulak up top; James Sizemore in the ball turret; Lou Lujan in the waist; and Autley Smith in the nose.

As he taxied out to the runway and sat with the brakes on, Sanders felt the full weight of the aircraft in his hands. The same grim thought always passed through his mind at this point: let's make sure we get off the ground before we hit that farmer's barn at the end of the runway.

As they flew to 12,000ft, three of their counterparts were forced to return. One had a sick crewmember, another supercharger trouble and the third, engine difficulties. The main formation had assembled with bombers of 487th Bomb Group at 11.30am, but Sanders had not been able to get off the ground until noon, so he was having to catch up. As he climbed, he found his visibility becoming obscured by what he called a 'sweet cream'– fog – on the windshield. For a time, he could see nothing at all, but he kept climbing and broke through the top of the fog to find he was almost at the point where he joined the formation.

By 12.44pm the various squadrons had found each other and there were 87 Liberators flying in close formation – almost wing tip to wing tip – over the North Sea. Sanders flew near to the lead bomber, which was piloted by his friend, Lieutenant Eugene Hicks, and was identified by the special lights on its wings and tail, but he stayed a little higher so that if Hicks decided to turn they would not collide.

Sanders surveyed the sky: the feeling of cruising along at 185 miles an hour as part of such an aerial armada was awe-inspiring. They were joined by more than 80 P-38 Lightning twin-fighters before they reached the Dutch coast.

There was no communication with the other planes, the only chat being on the headphones with the rest of the crew. They called Sanders 'Sir' on the ground but in the air they followed the air force style of finding a name based on his family name: so he was 'Sandy' to them all here.

Not all the aircraft would reach the Dutch coast. Three developed mechanical problems and turned back over the sea. A fourth jettisoned its bombs and left formation; its number four engine had a runaway propeller. Another was using too much fuel and would not make it to the target. A sixth Liberator aborted the mission over the Netherlands. Two of its engines were overheating. It dropped its bombs on a barracks and headed for home.

For the pilots who flew on, seeing so many of their formation abort with mechanical problems was a blow. One, Mike Volechenisky, commented at that afternoon's debriefing:

'A large number of aborts do not keep up morale when going in.'

What had improved morale was the rendezvous with the second fighter escort of 43 P-51 Mustangs from the 339th Fighter Group. Over Lingen in Germany they took positions around the Liberators. Soon after, the Lightnings reached the limits of their range, signalled they were 'heading back to the barn' and turned for home.

One further Liberator, 'Lucille', aborted before reaching the target, but there were few other problems. The flak they encountered was light and there was no sign of enemy fighters. Shortly before 3pm 38 new Lightnings joined the formation, having taken off from Wormingford, Essex, just under two hours earlier.

Sanders' navigator informed him they were coming to the location where the formation would make its final turn for its target.

On the ground, the air-raid sirens of Leipzig blared out and people who had returned to work after lunch ran for the shelters. Anti-aircraft guns blasted into the blue sky. Sanders and the planes of the 92nd held back as the 35 Liberators from the 93rd went in first. Ahead they could see the refinery towers which were the mission's primary target. Bomb doors were opened and bombs released. It was 3pm.

Most of the bombs fell well short of the refineries. Sanders could see some were missing by as much as a mile. He understood why. The flak was extremely heavy. There was always a temptation to release bombs early and pull away. It was human nature.

Now the 92nd's wing leader called over the interphone. It would soon be Sanders' turn to try to do better.

But thick smoke from the bombing and from smoke pots lit by the German flak batteries were making it impossible to see the target, and each Liberator shook as it passed through the turbulence produced by other aircraft. A B-24 from another bomb group had lost two engines and fuel and oil was spurting from its wing tanks. Then Eugene Hicks took a direct hit on his number three engine and was forced to turn away. Sanders saw him dive and begin to circle back. It all made the stomach churn.

But Sanders went lower and held a line, even though the same flak bursts which had struck Hicks had also damaged 'Mike, the Spirit of LSU' and one of its engines was beginning to fail.

Looking around the sky, one of the crew quipped nervously.

'We're the only ones. We must be the crazy ones.'

O'Connell released the bombs on the target and Sanders turned the aircraft away, knowing they were going to struggle to keep up with the formation as they crossed back over Germany. They managed to pass over the ribbon of the Rhine, with Koblenz to their south and Cologne away to the north, but then Sanders felt his blood run cold: the indicators showed the fuel tanks were leaking gas and a second engine was losing power.

Soon after, number two engine cut out. Sanders and co-pilot Morley ran the two remaining engines on maximum power, but they began to overheat. Navigator Thomas Zoebelein checked his charts. They were passing Namur and Charleroi, but they would never make the coast.

Sanders was surprised at how calm he sounded.

'You'd better start getting out because we're going to have to leave this thing,' he advised.

Radio operator John Lawrence radioed a mayday and gave the aircraft's position. Then bombardier Daniel O'Connell opened the escape hatch in the nose of the plane and slid out into the nothingness. Zoebelein followed him.

One-by-one the crew followed. Morley and Lawrence. The two waist gunners, Autley Smith and Louis Lujan. The ball turret gunner, James Sizemore, the engineer William Kozulak, and Robert Swaffield in the tail. Some left by the nose, others by the bomb bay doors.

Only Sanders was left, wondering if he would ever see his friends again.

All he had left now was the right outboard engine. He set the autopilot to keep the ship flying as straight as possible for a few more miles, and checked the altimeter. 2,500ft.

It felt surreal as he slid out of his seat and looked around: away to the north he could see the wide spread of a large city. He knew it must be Brussels.

Down below, crowds gathered in the late afternoon sunshine to watch the struggle of the B-24. They saw the final lone figure jump, and his parachute open quickly.

By the time Sanders reached the green grass of a pasture near the town of Braine-le-Comte there were about 400 people waiting for him on the grass. Some looked blankly, unsure; others waved and smiled. A middle-aged farmer acted quickly, grabbing Sanders by the shoulder and pushing back through the crowd. Sanders tried to keep up with him as they walked quickly across the field, but the American realised he had badly hurt his ankle on landing. He stumbled along, caught his parachute harness on a fence and fell, cutting his brow and causing his nose to bleed. But the man kept him moving until they were out of sight of the others.

Then, introducing himself as Melchior Resteau, he told Sanders to hide in a hedge.

'I will be back,' he said in broken English.

Sanders watched the man disappear and wondered if he would return with help or with the Germans.

The airman spent an anxious few hours crouching in a hedge near the town of Braine-le-Comte before hearing an engine and cautiously looking out to see a 1940 Ford station wagon pull up.

With Melchior Resteau was a man who was introduced only as Roland, a young woman with red hair, and three men who stepped out to guard the road. Each carried a Thompson submachine gun.

As Roland drove, the girl handed Sanders a pile of civilian clothes then took a white handkerchief and held it to the cuts on his face. After the shock of losing the plane and having to parachute into enemy held territory it was a moment of kindness which made him realise he was still free and might even remain so.

Sanders had been told about the local resistance groups and evasion lines. It appeared he had stumbled into one. He had got lucky. All the same he was apprehensive about where they were taking him. Although he spoke a little French and asked questions, they did not want to tell him too much.

Sanders was still getting changed into the rough civilian clothes when the vehicle pulled into a garage. Once he got out, he realised the trousers were huge so, after some chat and laughter, a belt was brought and pulled tight.

Taken by bicycle to a farm south-west of Brussels, he was left with a man who said his name was Alfred. Soon after there was a knock at the door and a man entered, shaking Alfred's hand. The new man introduced himself as Bernard. He had brought with him a stock of weapons.

Alfred and Bernard then moved Sanders again, this time using a hay wagon with a false bottom. On a country lane Alfred suddenly hissed for Sanders to remain quiet: they were coming to a German checkpoint. Sanders remained still as a soldier pushed a pitchfork into the hay but, fortunately, it was a half-hearted search, and the cart moved on.

Once at another farm nearby, the two Belgians let themselves in. It was deserted. They showed Sanders to a room and, exhausted, he lay on the bed. He thought about home, family, but eventually drifted off to sleep.

Later, Sanders sat carefully at a window and watched anxiously as a man approached. He appeared to have walked from a nearby farm; and he looked around quickly before letting himself in. He was a confident fellow of about 45, handsome with a determined square jaw. His hair was greying and so were his thick sideburns. He told the American that he worked with Alfred and the airman should lay low, eat what he wanted from a bag of food, and stay away from the windows.

Sanders said he was in a lot of pain, having sprained his ankle on landing, and, the following day, the man returned with another stranger. He explained to the airman that as he did not know a doctor whom he could trust, he had brought a vet. The vet examined Sanders and said he had probably broken his ankle. He bandaged Sanders' foot and then tied the laces very tightly on his flying boot so it would act something like a cast.

Then Sanders was left alone again. His mind went to Millie. Very soon she would be hearing that he was missing in action. What would that do to her? She was heavily pregnant. Perhaps she'd even given birth by now. He tried not to think of it; exhaustion eventually overcame him, and he went to sleep.

The next day a different man arrived. Shaking Sanders' hand, he said his name was Alex. Although still a university student – studying chemistry – Alex led a local resistance organisation. Puffing out his chest, he declared he would bring some comrades to the farm very soon, shook the American's hand again and left.

Another night passed with Sanders alone in the farmhouse. The silence made him lonely but perhaps he should have savoured it because, the next day, two trucks drove up and Alex and three others jumped out of the cabs, rushed round to the rear, and opened the tailgates.

Sanders watched in horror as men in ragged German army uniforms jumped down onto the muddy farmyard. His heart missed a beat: he must have been betrayed. Alex hurried the men inside and, seeing the look on Sanders' face, laughed and explained the men were 18 Russians who had been forced into the *Wehrmacht*. Having deserted, they were seeking his organisation's help to escape.

For a few days Sanders found himself living a strange life with a large group of people who did not speak his language and who, until a few weeks ago, had been fighting for the enemy. They ate black market food and watched the road in the distance to make sure the German trucks they saw passing took no interest in the farm.

After a few days the man with the sideburns from the neighbouring farm arrived and called out to Sanders: he had brought with him a fellow American. The door opened and in walked a handsome man with close-cropped hair. They chatted, asking a few gentle questions, slowly checking each other out. Then, satisfied that both were who they said they were, they relaxed.

The new man was Lieutenant Henry Wolcott III, of Royal Oak, Michigan. He had spent the last few days hiding in a priest's room at the Catholic University in Enghien. He was a pilot the Germans would stop at nothing to find.

Wolcott was with the 406th Squadron which flew only top-secret missions for SOE and the OSS.

Henry Wolcott was a 'Carpetbagger'.

7

THE CARPETBAGGERS

Henry Wolcott's Crew

HENRY WOLCOTT III'S experience as a pilot was very different from most of his comrades in the United States Army Air Force. He did not drop bombs; he delivered packages and people. He did not fly by day in vast airborne armadas; he flew by night and alone.

His unit was one of several Special Duties Squadrons which had been created by the USAAF and the RAF to fly, hopefully undetected, without escort over enemy-held territory in order to drop supplies and agents – known to American crews as 'Joes' – to the Resistance in Occupied Europe.

Overseen by the OSS, the sense of swagger and adventure which surrounded the American squadrons was obvious from the start. While setting them up, USAAF commander General James Doolittle had suggested to OSS head 'Wild Bill' Donovan that they would go anywhere at any time, packing their bags at a moment's notice, like the notorious 'Carpetbaggers' – a nickname given to fortune-seeking government representatives in the Confederate states after the American Civil War. The nickname had stuck.

At first, Wolcott's 406th Squadron flew from the same place as their British counterparts, RAF Tempsford, a base in the countryside north of London which had been specially designed to conceal not only its purpose but its existence from the enemy. With the help of theatrical illusionist Jasper Maskelyne, the base had been made to look like a derelict airfield. Its nerve centre, an old farmhouse, featured a dilapidated roof, crumbling walls, and broken windows. But it had a second inner skin: walls built to withstand bomb damage and protect the control and briefing rooms. Outside was a pond, half-overgrown with weeds and plants, and a sprinkling of rusty tractors. The runways were painted to appear, from above, as if they were fields crisscrossed with hedges.

But, in March 1944, the 406th had moved to its own base, Harrington Airfield – Station 179 – just to the west of Kettering in Northamptonshire. There, the crews slept in newly equipped Nissen huts and had access to their own shop and post office. Security was tight. Crews were discouraged from drinking heavily in the local pubs and received regular, stern warnings that any discussion about their work would result in an immediate court martial.

The B-24 Liberator which Wolcott flew would have intrigued pilots from bomber squadrons. Inside the fuselage was a static line and handrails for parachutists, and the belly gun turret had been replaced with a cargo hatch – the 'Joe hole' – for supplies and agents to be dropped through. Any equipment related to bombing had been removed, as had the waist and nose guns. The aircraft had been painted a shiny black – a move which the experts said would reflect beams from searchlights. Everything was geared to secrecy and to flying safely below 2,000ft to avoid enemy radar detection.

As D-Day approached, General Pierre Koenig, who would lead Free French forces in Normandy, visited the crews to tell them that the agents, sabotage teams and supplies they were delivering would be essential to the invasion, so it would be a busy time for the Carpetbaggers.

Wolcott and his crew had flown 18 missions over France and Belgium during the past few weeks, delivering agents, containers and packages. Delivering agents was always more stressful. Crews knew these men and women were embarking on missions with a high chance of death. They felt responsible for them as they were the ones delivering them into danger. There were nervous smiles and jokes, an attempt to keep up everyone's morale.

On the night of May 22, the crew had flown four agents into north-western France. After struggling to find the drop zone, they had finally spotted the Resistance on the ground flashing the password K in Morse code. The drop zone had been obscured by a nearby wood. They were able to drop the agents on the second and third runs, but it was a great relief to finally turn for home.

A few days later, Wolcott's Liberator began what would be its final mission, leaving solid ground in England on May 28 – the same day as Al Sanders. Sanders had taken to the sky that morning; but it was almost midnight when Wolcott rose into the air. The mission was to drop 12 containers of arms and explosives into a drop-zone being marked by bonfires placed in a rectangle by members of the Resistance in Belgium. Having experienced the intense pressure of these low-flying missions so many times, each man trusted the other crew members.

For this mission, the Liberator 'C for Charlie' was carrying an eighth man, Lieutenant Carmen Vozzella, who was on board to gain additional navigational experience. It was the Massachusetts man's first mission. As with Brown and Kleinman, the addition of a 'rookie' made Wolcott and the others nervous. But, for Wolcott – a 25-year-old former chemistry student – learning to clear his mind of any extraneous thoughts was a fundamental part of the job: he had one of the most challenging jobs of any Second World War airman. Once airborne, Wolcott had to fly by instrument only. To help him, the artificial horizon, compass, air speed dials and radio altimeter of the modified Liberator had been grouped in front of him. There was no free time to check his progress by looking out of the windows: he was flying far too low. His eyes did not leave the dials.

His co-pilot, Lieutenant Robert Auda, had turned 24 a week earlier and had joined the air force four months before Pearl Harbor. A mechanic from Tiffin, Ohio, he enjoyed sharing stories with radio operator Sergeant Dale Loucks, who had worked on the construction of the Grand Coulee Dam but was at heart – like Auda – a car lover. They entertained the crew with their knowledge of American automobiles and how they compared to the British ones they saw in the villages around Harrington. Loucks often led the squadron in games of baseball on the base. He was a naturally calm guy with a quiet confidence about him – an ideal crewmate. He was not yet 20.

Bombardier Wallis Cozzens and navigator William Ryckman were both 22 and essential figures in Wolcott's closely-knit crew. Cozzens was a quietly-spoken, former student from El Dorado, Texas, while Ryckman was an accountant from Fresno, California – having a head for numbers was an ideal qualification for a navigator. Ryckman had access to one of only two lights in the whole aircraft. The other was placed above the 'Joe hole' and could light up red, amber or green to signal when the time had come for the agent to jump.

As well as bonfire signals from the ground, the crew had two other ways to communicate with Resistance members. The Rebecca radar system allowed Ryckman to pick up blips sent out by an Eureka transmitter and home in on them from a distance of 70 miles away. Then, once over the target, the crew could use an S-phone – a walkie-talkie type radio – to speak to *résistants* below.

Both apparatuses had worked successfully on the crews' last trip out four nights earlier.

But over the drop zone in the early hours of May 29 they received no signal of any kind from the Belgian Resistance fighters.

Three times they turned over the target, but nothing. Then as Wolcott banked to begin the homeward journey there was a burst of cannon fire as a Messerschmitt Bf-110 came in for an attack. Wolcott twisted the Liberator through a stomach-churning series of manoeuvres and seemed to shake off the night-fighter.

In the silence the crew scanned the darkness for the German. But they could see nothing. Had they lost him? Their hearts drummed in their chests.

Then the fighter came in from below and to the side, his .50 calibre shells ripping through the right wing-tanks and fuselage and blasting holes in the structure between the co-pilot's and navigator's seats, miraculously missing both Auda and Ryckman.

Flames lit up the night sky: both starboard engines were on fire. Wolcott quickly gave the order to bale out. All eight of the regular 'Carpetbagger' crew and Vozzella leapt into the dark.

Sadly, tail-gunner Dick Hawkins did not make it. The 22-year-old's parachute failed to open. Loucks, who sprained his knee on landing, limped over to find him dead, his parachute still in its pack. It would be a fortnight before Hawkins' wife, Virginia, in Ohio, received a telegram to say her husband was missing and three weeks before she would hear that he was dead. The couple had been married for seven months.

In the dark countryside the surviving crew watched a fireball rise from the fields as their blazing Liberator hurtled into the ground.

And then there was silence.

It was 2.30am and the night was pitch black. Wolcott and his crew were scattered across the countryside. Auda buried his parachute in the woods. He could see no one else so immediately tried to put some distance between himself and the downed aircraft. Wolcott also wandered into the night alone.

Cozzens bumped into his friend, Ryckman, and they discussed in whispers what to do next. Ryckman, the navigator, reckoned they were somewhere between Enghien and Aaigem, to the west of Brussels. He had hurt his knee and back on landing. They decided to stick together.

Moments earlier Wolcott and his crew had been supplying those desperate for liberation; now they could only hope that, whenever the Allied invasion forces came, they would be liberated too.

8

DEATH IN THE WATER

Gaston Masereel

WHEN HENRY WOLCOTT'S unit had left RAF Tempsford, it said goodbye to its British counterparts, the RAF's 'Moon Squadrons', including 138, the air arm of SOE.

The Moon Squadrons, like the Carpetbaggers, were busy during the nights before the invasion was to commence. On June 2, 138 flew six agents out by three Lysanders and three more by Halifax. Onboard the Halifax – a specially modified bomber, like Wolcott's Liberator – was a 36-year-old Belgian named Gaston Masereel.

Like most Belgian and French agents of SOE, Masereel's journey into the clandestine world of Britain's sabotage organisation involved resistance and escape. These were people who had already fled dangers in their occupied homeland but were so dedicated and committed that they were determined to return.

Of average height but stocky, with dark wavy hair and a moustache, Masereel had been enjoying a life of moderate wealth and gentility when the war began. The family business, which made varnishes and a range of modern plastic items for people's homes, had done well between the wars, and while his older brother Albert had gone on the road as its travelling representative, Gaston had stayed in the office as company director, watching over its 20 workers. He had a beautiful apartment in trendy Altitude 100, a community in the Forest area of Brussels which had been built during the 1930s with the striking Art Deco beauty of the church of Saint Augustin as its centrepiece. He collected art and antiques and had a particular penchant for Persian rugs. There was nothing in the first 33 years of his life which could hint at the man of action and violence he would become when war came.

Called up into a Grenadier regiment, he had been captured when Belgium was invaded, but had escaped while being transported to a German prison camp. Back in Brussels, he found the fortunes of the family firm had taken a downturn – its competitors were quicker and more willing to trade with the Germans.

Masereel loved the company of women and had few men friends, but one of them was about to change his life. Jean Crèvecoeur, an assistant commissioner in the Brussels police, was becoming an important part of a fledgling resistance group made up of police officers and municipal workers in the Forest area. He recruited Masereel and together they supported French and British soldiers by providing them with fake identity cards, civilian clothes and shelter and escorted some to the French border. They also became involved in the distribution of the clandestine newspaper, *La Voix des Belges*.

In the spring of 1943, Crèvecoeur and Masereel had their first contact with agents sent by SOE from London. Both were Belgian born: Frederic 'Freddy' Veldekens, who was dropped into a field near Enghien with the task of finding German wireless-jamming stations, and Léon Bar, who arrived a few weeks later to work as Veldekens' radio operator. Bar, a 24-year-old former regular army sergeant who was codenamed 'Dormouse', had one of the most dangerous roles in the underground. He had to carry equipment which, if checked by a German or police patrol, was hard to disguise as anything other than a clandestine radio. While transmitting his messages, he was also under constant danger of being tracked by German radio-detector teams.

Crèvecoeur and Masereel agreed to provide security for Bar. They helped him move some of his spare equipment to a safehouse near Waterloo and then set him up in an apartment near Masereel in Altitude 100. For several months, Crèvecoeur and Masereel acted as lookouts as he sent messages to London. One would stroll around the block before taking up a spot in the street from where the other, standing in the window, could see if he signalled that there was trouble. They worked hard to ensure Bar never transmitted from the same house twice.

But, knowing he was about to be recalled to London for a rest and having a series of messages to transmit for Veldekens and another SOE agent, Bar took a risk. Using his own apartment, and without notifying his security team, Bar sat down to work through his backlog of messages. SOE radio operators were trained to send a message of up to 600 letters – 120 groups of five letters – in five minutes and, if they were likely to stay on the air for much longer, to switch frequencies midway through the transmission to avoid detection. SOE trainers advised their operators never to be on air for more than 20 minutes, but – because of the volume of work – they frequently had to be. It was a nerve-wracking job. As one experienced radio operator summed it up: 'I must admit to butterflies floating in my tummy all the time. You had to have your eyes in the back of your head as well as in the front.'

On that evening of August 27, Bar stayed on air too long. His transmissions were picked up by a mobile direction-finding team which tracked him first to the area of Altitude 100 and then pinpointed his apartment. Troops surrounded the building and, noticing movement outside, Bar tried to escape out the back. Running into gunfire from troops in the building opposite, he returned fire but was wounded, pounced upon, and thrown to the ground.

DEATH IN THE WATER

Crèvecoeur and Masereel knew nothing of Bar's arrest until a report of the gun battle passed through Crèvecoeur's office. Discovering that others close to Bar, including the woman who owned his apartment, had since also been arrested, Crèvecoeur planned to go to ground. Contacting another police officer, Crèvecoeur discovered an escape route to Switzerland, which relied on the courageous work of a customs agent named Arthur Balligand. In mid-September Masereel took the route and knocked on the door of the British Consulate in Geneva. There he found that Veldekens and Crèvecoeur had arrived safely too. Veldekens vouched for Masereel and, by the end of 1943, Masereel had reached London via Perpignan, the Pyrenees, Madrid and Gibraltar. In February 1944, Masereel was recruited into SOE and began his training under the alias of 'Guy Montoisy' to protect his family back home in case of a security breach. To help him train, he borrowed some vinyl records to take a crash course in English. The records had been made in Canada so many people came to believe – from his accent – he was a French Canadian.

Months on, with D-Day approaching, and having been intensively trained as a saboteur and in techniques of silent killing, Masereel now had a major task ahead of him: he was to act as the main liaison between the Belgian government-in-exile in London and the powerful left-wing resistance group, the *Front de l'Indépendance* (FI). He sat in the 'Moon Squadron' Halifax, knowing that while his papers and clothing had been carefully sourced to ensure he would pass as an ordinary Belgian citizen, he carried with him two items which, if discovered, proved he was a spy: the hidden bottom of a specially-constructed jar of olive oil was packed with money for the FI, while the frame of his briefcase concealed microfilm which detailed plans for the 'short-term' sabotage of rail and road targets, designed to hamper German attempts to supply their troops in northern France but also to allow for easy repair when the Allies reached Belgium. The importance SOE placed on Masereel's mission was evident in his assignment of two radio operators and four sabotage instructors, two of whom were sitting with him in the adapted bomber.

The experienced pilot brought the aircraft in over southern Holland but was jumped by a night-fighter as it reached the coast. Masereel did not even hear the attack. He was immediately hit in the neck by a bullet or shrapnel and quickly received a second wound behind his right ear. But the dispatcher had already prepared him for the drop so, only semi-conscious, he stumbled towards the parachute hatch and fell through, the static line opening his parachute for him. As he tumbled through the air, the aircraft exploded, killing everyone else on board.

Coming to in shallow water off an island, Masereel realised the extent of his injuries. Feeling around his face in the darkness, he was horrified to find his nose was hanging from the side of his face. Putting his hand to his head, hair came away; it had been badly burnt. He could barely see: not only had he lost his glasses but one of his eyes had been closed by blood – and he had also lost a finger.

He spent some time struggling out of his parachute harness and then tried to bandage the wounds in his neck. He tasted the water to see if it had the saltiness of the sea or the freshness of a lake, but his mouth was too filled with blood to tell. He counted his blessings; he had landed in so little water he had not drowned. Reaching for his pistol, he fired it into the sky, hoping to summon help, but dropped it into the water and could not find it again.

As the dawn began to break, he tried to move and found himself in slightly deeper water. It was then he heard a noise: a small boat and strange voices shouting in English, 'Hello, boy! Hello, boy!'

The small boat came alongside him and Masereel asked where he was. He heard the men say in broken German, 'The man thinks he is in England'.

They hoisted him onboard.

'A British aviator is a good capture.' There were four of them. All Armenians drafted into the *Wehrmacht*. They looked at the bedraggled and disfigured man and threw him dismissively to the bottom of the boat.

Masereel had spent only five days at SOE's Special Training School in the Oxfordshire countryside, but his instructors had described him as a 'first-class man', who was 'aggressive and keen' in close combat and 'systematic and unruffled' in difficult situations. Now, at the very first opportunity, he was about to reveal just how accurate those assessments had been.

As the boat turned for shore one of the Armenians laughed and slapped Masereel. It was a cruel act and a terrible mistake; it fired up the hatred inside him and led to a burst of sudden, horrific violence.

Masereel jabbed the closest man with a flattened hand to the throat. Two others came at him. He punched one and kicked the other in the pit of the stomach. The fourth man would not shoot for fear of hitting his comrades, so rushed the bloody Masereel with a metal bludgeon and smashed him across the side of his head. Somehow he stayed on his feet and hit his attacker on the arm, forcing him to drop the weapon, before striking each of the four men on the head with the bludgeon.

His captors all dead, Masereel tied a bandage around the throttle of the boat and sent it out to sea.

After working his way ashore close to the village of Stavenisse, an exhausted Masereel collapsed in the sand, and his luck ran out again. He was found by more Armenian soldiers who – unaware of what he had done to their comrades and believing him to be an RAF airman – treated him with some kindness. Only coming around when the open truck in which he was being carried stopped in a small town, he found himself surrounded by Dutch civilians eager to greet the British 'airman' and offer him milk to drink.

Driven to the prison in Vught, he was given hospital treatment and X-rayed to assess the damage to his ribs – three were broken – and his skull. But he knew the treatment would stop if his German captors found the money or plans hidden in the olive jar or frame of the briefcase.

In a moment of privacy, two Belgian doctors whispered news to Masereel.

'The Allies have landed in Normandy.'

D-Day was underway.

9

SECRETS AND SABOTAGE

François Reeve

FOR MONTHS, PREPARATIONS for D-Day had been central to the lives of dozens of SOE agents who had gone into the field ahead of Gaston Masereel.

Knowing an invasion of north-west Europe would have to be attempted in 1944, an SOE planning group had agreed sabotage missions must take precedence over the gathering of intelligence. One of the groups from which it would take inspiration was FARMER, a network which had been built from the ground up by Michael Trotobas, a 29-year-old former regular army officer who had been born in Brighton to a French father and Irish mother.

Courageous and often reckless, Trotobas had become a legendary figure in SOE. Captured during his first mission to France, he led an escape from a Vichy internment camp in July 1942 and arrived back in London two months later. His second mission started in November 1942 when he landed blind – without anyone to meet him – and headed for Lille where, over the coming months, he created a network of hundreds of saboteurs, couriers and informers, relying heavily on those who had been members of the communist and socialist trade unions in the area. The region's railways were essential to the supply of military goods to the coastal areas of northern France and, during the early months of 1943, Trotobas carried out a series of audacious attacks on trains and the rail network.

In June 1943, working from his headquarters at the Aquarium café in the city, Trotobas planned his biggest operation yet. The SNCF locomotive construction and repair works in the city's north-eastern suburb of Fives was one of the largest of its kind in Europe, and London had long wished to see it put out of action.

Four air raids had failed – resulting in the deaths of local residents. Trotobas disguised himself as an elderly worker, surveyed the site, and reported to London that he believed a small sabotage team could seriously damage the works. SOE was delighted and, to support him, acceded to his long-standing request for an additional radio operator.

On June 23, he was introduced to Lieutenant François Reeve, who had arrived in France 10 days earlier, having been transported in a Halifax by the 'Moon Squadron', 138, the same unit which would later attempt to deliver Masereel.

Reeve was a tough-looking 24-year-old who had had a hard, rough life. Although born in England, he was fluent in French, having spent most of his life in Pas-de-Calais. He and his mother had been deserted by his English father when Reeve was 14. Leaving school, he had gone to work in a steelworks, making extra money on the side as a boxing champion. Reeve's square shoulders and hard jaw certainly gave him the look of a streetfighter. When the Germans invaded France, they arrested his British mother but Reeve escaped to England and joined SOE in February 1943.

Late on Saturday, June 26, 1943, Trotobas and Reeve, both carrying false Gestapo ID papers, German-speaking comrade Henri Vandesype, wearing the uniform of a German army colonel, and four others met a truck filled with *résistants* dressed as policemen at a side gate to the Fives works. All carried either revolvers or submachine guns. The 'policemen' and Reeve carried bags filled with explosives.

Wandering purposefully through the works, they walked into the chief security officer and then a nightwatchman. Trotobas flashed his Gestapo badge.

'We are searching for saboteurs,' he shouted. 'Help us.'

When they reached the control centre, an electrician refused to let them in until Vandesype drew his pistol and shouted angrily in German. Trotobas and Reeve went inside alone, planting a series of charges, before ordering the unwitting factory workers to take them to the transformer room. By the time they had finished, the two men had planted a total of 23 charges around the railway works. They had managed to talk themselves into such access to the site they regretted not having brought more explosives.

The first blasts went off prematurely, just as Trotobas' team was leaving, and he shouted at the nightwatchman:

'The saboteurs must still be in there. Stay under cover while I get reinforcements and the fire brigade.'

As the guard hid, Trotobas and the others escaped to celebrate their success at the Aquarium café. The fire at the factory raged well into the next day, destroying four million litres of oil, damaging 22 transformers, and disrupting German efforts to maintain good local railway networks. The attack showed what SOE-led units could do on the ground, carrying out important localised attacks without causing civilian casualties.

A GFP inspector named Lynen was ordered to put together a team to identify the 'terrorists' responsible, but, at first, he made little headway. In fact, the FARMER network's problems were developing from within. Many of Trotobas' closest associates did not get on with Reeve, finding him to be a 'show off' who thought he deserved 'prestige and respect'. Some thought he was jealous of Trotobas' reputation and standing.

To deal with the issue, Trotobas gave Reeve command of the Arras sector of the network and Reeve – known to his Resistance colleagues as 'Olivier' – went searching for suitable drop zones for deliveries of supplies from London which the network urgently needed to continue its campaign of sabotage. During August the network received two drops totalling more than six tonnes of explosives, weapons, grenades and medicines. It was a massive morale boost and suggested London held the group in high value.

Then the GFP had a stroke of luck with the arrest of group member André Martel for carrying false papers. He agreed to become a paid informer and, working on information he supplied, the Germans made a number of arrests. While searching a garage used by the group, they came across Jean Woussen, an 18-year-old apprentice mechanic and driver who had spent the last few days delivering the supplies from the parachute drops to various colleagues in the region. Woussen grabbed a revolver and shot a German police officer in the head, before jumping onto a bicycle and riding away to seek help from Reeve. In the rush, he left his false identity papers, containing his genuine photograph, at the scene.

The German administration in Brussels ordered 2,000 posters be printed featuring Woussen's photograph and that of Albéric Volckaert who, despite being 57, nearly 40 years older than Woussen, was known to drink with him. In fact, Volckaert – a butcher and horse-breeder – had been part of the team distributing supplies from the parachute drops with Woussen.

When the posters were put up in public places and reproduced in newspapers across Belgium and France, they caused understandable panic. The people sheltering the two men in their home were courageous patriots, but they had families they wanted to protect and neighbours who might denounce them anonymously and claim a 500,000 franc reward. Becoming increasingly scared, Woussen told their hosts if he was captured, many others would be arrested too. The situation grew more frightening still when Volckaert cycled into a German checkpoint on a wooded back road near Adinfer, south of Arras, and shot both soldiers dead.

There was also a third weak link in the chain. The Germans already had a description of Emmanuel Lemercier – Trotabas' longest-serving lieutenant – who had been in hiding with friends and relatives for some time. Isolated and unable to take part in any of the resistance operations, like Woussen, he had grown fearful and discontented, telling friends he was making a big sacrifice for them and they should do more to protect him. Reeve, in particular, adjudged Lemercier's words as something more than frustration: he feared Lemercier's anger could lead to betrayal and told Trotobas his lieutenant should be executed. Trotobas, though, had other plans. He wanted to send Woussen, Volckaert and Lemercier to England via an evasion line and told everyone to ignore Lemercier's remarks.

On returning to Arras, Reeve grumbled to his group that Trotobas had made a dangerous decision and, while he could do nothing about Lemercier, he believed Woussen – who had shown the same disloyalty as Lemercier – should be executed. Reeve's men said they could not execute a scared teenager, and one, Abel Guidet, volunteered to look after Woussen until he could be evacuated through the escape line. The meeting broke up, but the decisions over Lemercier and Woussen had widened the breach between Reeve and Trotobas and some of his men. Trotobas then proposed a rather unusual solution to Reeve: they should have a boxing match to settle the dispute over whose orders should be followed. While Reeve had been a boxer, Trotobas had been a boxing instructor back in the Middlesex regiment and, on wasteland in Lille, he came out on top.

Throughout this period of fear and mistrust, the FARMER network continued to carry out sabotage attacks. One man casually dropped a hand grenade down the barrel of a flak gun at Lille station before running quickly away. Railway lines were blown up near Boisleux-au-Mont and a military train was derailed on its way to Le Bourget. Freight train trucks were blown up at Douai and Orchies and over the border in Mouscron in Belgium. Trotobas himself saw his comrades blow up ammunition trucks and tanks on a train waiting at Valenciennes station. In addition, he and Reeve managed to pass 10 airmen they had been protecting on to the Comet Line.

To support this continuing campaign of mayhem, SOE arranged another parachute drop of supplies in a field near Fontaine-lès-Croisilles, south-east of Arras. On the evening of October 20, while waiting to travel out to the drop zone, Reeve and his reception team drank coffee in a farmhouse nearby. Sitting in the corner was the pilot of a Lightning aircraft which had come down north of Bapaume. He had been found by the farmer and given rough work clothes to cover his flying suit.

There was a knock at the door and two *gendarmes* walked in. They were searching for the airman.

Everyone shrugged and denied knowing anything until Reeve stepped forward, pointed at the quiet figure in the ill-fitting clothes, and announced '*he* is the American'.

Reeve pulled out his revolver and turned it on the policemen, revealing they had stumbled into a resistance group waiting for a parachute drop

'I am the British officer in charge,' he said. 'Your lives depend on the decision you make now. If you are loyal Frenchmen, we will help you; if not, you will be killed.'

The *gendarmes* said they would report nothing of what they had seen at the farm and were allowed to leave.

Reeve's men feared he had put them all at risk but, despite their concerns, they worked with him to collect the supplies and stash them in an old First World War blockhouse they used as one of their storerooms.

After losing the boxing match to Trotobas, Reeve had agreed that Woussen must live and arranged for him to be taken to Bapaume and then Paris by local members of an escape line. Then, at the end of October, it was time for Lemercier to follow. Trotobas brought him to Arras and Reeve placed him in a safehouse. But, while he waited, there was terrible news from the south: Woussen had been picked up at a railway station less than 15 miles from the Spanish border by an SD officer on the lookout for suspicious-looking strangers who may be working for the evasion lines. For Woussen, being arrested as someone hoping to escape an occupied country rather than the assassin of a GFP man must have come as a relief. But the Germans wanted him to reveal who had helped him and he was transported back to Paris for interrogation.

When news of the arrest reached Reeve on November 2, he was angry, telling his men that if he had been allowed to deal with Woussen the whole network would not be in such peril and he had 'no intention of waiting for further betrayal'. Lemercier was taken to an abandoned house on the outskirts of Arras and shot in the back of the neck. Reeve insisted Trotobas had ordered the killing, but other members of the group said it was Reeve. Whatever the truth, strains within the network were now such that Trotobas had decided to ask London to have Reeve reassigned.

The pair met on November 24 and discussed moving their stores of supplies to a safer new location. Trotobas said he was going to move as well.

'Too many people know my address in Lille,' he said, 'and the Germans are after me.'

The Germans were, indeed, closing in. After weeks in custody, young Woussen had finally broken. He had refused to give away anything about FARMER, even when hanged by his feet, whipped and burnt. He had finally given in when his mother was brought in front of him and beaten, but by then he hoped he had given his colleagues enough time to move to new addresses.

In the early hours of November 28, the GFP put Woussen in a car and drove him to Arras, where he led them to the house where Reeve was asleep upstairs. Awoken by his hosts, a baker named Henri Dewispelaere and his wife Marie, Reeve rushed to fetch his pistol, but when he looked out, he saw about 60 men and dogs and a large machine gun pointed at the house and realised there was no chance of escape.

The Germans came upstairs holding Marie in front of them. Reeve threw down his weapon, was handcuffed, shoved to the ground and beaten. GFP officer Lynen – the man tasked with destroying the network – entered the room.

'We know everything,' he said. 'We know where the ammunition dumps are and the names of the people who did the [air drop] receptions and we think we know where your *Captaine* Michel is.'

Captaine Michel was an alias used by Trotobas.

Still in his pyjamas, Reeve was dragged outside and pushed into a car where a torch was shone into his face.

'Who is this man?' Reeve heard Lynen ask someone he could not see.

'That is Lieutenant Olivier, second to *Captaine* Michel,' the voice replied.

It was Woussen.

The SOE man was taken to GFP offices, where Lynen told him he knew about parachute drops at St Leger and Fontaine-lès-Croisilles and listed names of people in the Resistance. Reeve believed he knew everything and, having been clearly identified as such, admitted he was 'Olivier'.

'*Captaine* Michel is living with a woman whose name is Denise and she has ginger hair,' Lynen said.

Reeve tried hard not to reveal on his face that what the German said was true.

'I am not on good terms with *Captaine* Michel,' he said, using elements of truth to deflect the questions. 'He does not tell me anything and wants to do all the work himself.'

Reeve was lifted onto a table and whipped. At one point he pulled free from his handcuffs but was beaten to the floor. Lynen continued to list the codenames or first names of people he knew about.

Afterwards, barely able to walk, Reeve was bundled into a car and driven to a house where the Germans arrested another member of the network. Back at the Hotel de Commerce, the beatings resumed. Lynen had been on *Captaine* Michel's tail for some time and, although his men were now making arrests across the network, he still did not have his prize: he was determined this would be the day he captured Trotobas. Having failed to get the address out of Reeve, he told him: 'You will come with us to Lille.'

Once there, Reeve was beaten again, as the Germans drove him around in search of Trotobas' address. A favoured technique of his torturers was to stamp on his bare feet. At 6.45am, Reeve led them to Boulevard de Belfort, near the address which a few days earlier Trotobas had said he planned to leave. Reeve pointed out the building where Trotobas had a flat.

Lynen ordered his men to cordon off the area and prepare to move in. Reeve remained in the vehicle, a machine gun pointed at his chest. He hung his head, hoping Trotobas had left the address as he had planned.

Then he heard shots.

He could not know it, but the first shot was a disaster for Lynen. As his men moved in, one had seen a door open in a neighbouring house and a man appear with a rifle. He shot instantly, killing the man, just as he realised it was a German soldier heading off on guard duty.

But, tragically, Trotobas had not yet moved. Alerted by the shot, he heard the GFP men run up the stairs, shouting *'Police allemande!'* As they kicked down the door to his flat, Trotobas fired a series of shots, killing the first man and seriously wounding the second.

Lynen's troops returned fire, cutting down Trotobas and wounding Denise Gilman, his courier, companion and lover, who had done so much to help build up the FARMER network. Wounded in the stomach, she was carried to the bed by the Germans and died there. Reeve was brought in to confirm Trotobas' identity for Lynen.

He realised he had killed his organiser and was led out of the building and through a street littered with glass. Behind him, the Germans fixed a swastika seal to the front door of the building where Trotobas had lived and died.

For Reeve, the fight was over, but the beatings were not. He was kept in chains at Loos Prison for four months, undergoing regular bouts of torture until, in April 1944, he was tried and condemned to death by a 'court martial' at the town hall in Arras.

All the while, in his heart, he was 'bitterly upset' about what had happened to Trotobas. Twice over the coming weeks the Germans promised him his life would be spared if he gave up everything he knew about the remaining men and women of the FARMER network. He refused.

Just over a week before D-Day, he was moved to Saint-Gilles prison in Brussels.

10

A CHATEAU NEAR NAMUR

Stuart Leslie

STUART LESLIE HAD been in hiding for almost five weeks when he heard the news of the D-Day landings while drinking morning coffee in a small cottage 20 miles outside Brussels. Louise Schouppe, his host, burst into the room, her face filled with joy.

'*Un grand débarquement!*' she cried, grabbing his arm. 'It's come.'

He shook his head, not understanding, and she began to laugh.

'The landings! The invasion!' she said. 'The Allies have landed in France!'

As she spoke, she rushed to the radio on the dark wooden sideboard and tuned it to the BBC. The slow speech patterns of King George VI burst into the room.

'Once more a supreme test has to be faced,' he stated. 'This time the challenge is not to fight to survive, but to fight to win the final victory for the good cause…'

The words dropped out in places, but both hung on the broadcast until the end when the King quoted an old hymn:

'The Lord will give strength unto His people, the Lord will give His people the blessing of peace.'

Louise slipped into a chair beside Leslie. They both stared at the radio as General Eisenhower spoke.

'The tide has turned. The free men of the world are marching together to victory.'

When the speeches finished, the pair danced a jig around the kitchen as Louise threw questions at the airman.

'Will the invasion succeed? How long will it take the Allies to get across France? When will Belgium be free?'

It was not the time to dampen spirits, but Leslie knew nothing could be taken for granted. They talked about best-case scenarios, occasionally trying to be realistic, and wondering what form liberation would take: what sort of battles might be fought out on Belgian soil? How dangerous might it be? But each time doubt set in, they reminded themselves that the Allies were on the coast of France, closer than they had been for four years.

So far, Leslie had lived a charmed life. After being taken to Brussels, he had been cared for by Louise and her husband, Guy. They were an unusual looking couple – she was tall and striking and he was short and heavily-built – but their courage and generosity had been extraordinary. Hiding him firstly in their fashionable fifth-floor apartment in Ixelles, they had recently brought him out to their small country home on the edge of a quiet village. Leslie at first felt exposed; there were so few people, but Louise told her French-speaking neighbours, whose sons were avoiding forced labour by living rough in the forest, that Leslie was a Flemish friend who was recovering after an accident. He soon grew to relax.

The weather in the countryside was warm but with June showers. Leslie spent the hours listening to the rain on the cottage roof and walking among the lush green foliage when each shower had passed or helping with chores around the cottage and its small garden. It had been a fairly idyllic week.

Late on June 6, Guy arrived from the city to say that – despite the occupation – all of Brussels appeared to be celebrating. He had met with friends from the Resistance to discuss what the invasion would mean to the men they were hiding. All had agreed that there would be massive German troop movements towards the invasion area and security would be stepped up across northern France and at the Belgian frontier. As a consequence, they believed moving airmen into France – with the hope of reaching Spain – would soon become far too dangerous.

Therefore, for security reasons, they decided to keep Leslie on the move, bringing him back to Brussels. In the city suburb of Anderlecht, the Schouppes bid farewell to Leslie and passed him to an off-duty police officer, who led him to the home of another couple. Despite the good news from France, Leslie sensed a new anxiety among his helpers. In the weeks building up to D-Day there had been more bombing missions and therefore a larger number of airmen being shot down and in need of help. More and more people were being asked to risk their lives by hiding aircrew. The invasion had brought worry as well as joy, and the news from Normandy was not all good either. Any preconceptions of a quick Allied victory were abandoned as the news broadcasts stressed the difficulties faced in breaking out of the beachhead. The Allies were not yet carving their way through France as the Belgians had hoped. Some even grumbled that people had been fools to celebrate as the liberation may never happen.

The people of the evasion lines, though, had seen harder times. They had seen friends betrayed and captured; many had risked their lives for the best part of four years in some form of resistance. They were determined to carry on and one way to protect airmen now appeared to be moving them towards the rural and wooded areas of the Ardennes.

So, on June 27, a woman Leslie had never met before came and walked him through the streets to where a small man in a grey suit sat behind the wheel of a gas-powered Ford van. The driver nodded a 'hello' but otherwise said very little. Leslie never learned his name, but it was Henri Poupier, an experienced member of the *Zéro* resistance network.

As they left the city Leslie asked where they were going. Poupier simply replied, 'Namur'. The road to the south-east of the country was crowded, with both German army vehicles and locals hitching lifts. Few Belgians now had the luxury of owning or being able to run a vehicle and the civilian train schedules had been disrupted by increased German military use and Allied bombing. Leslie thought the best option was to ignore the hitchhikers – any one of whom could work out who he was and give him away – but Poupier did the opposite: he picked up as many as he could, reasoning that a German checkpoint would see a genuine ragtag bunch and not consider any of them could be joined in any kind of conspiracy.

His theory was put quickly to the test when they turned a corner and drove straight into a makeshift checkpoint – a wooden barrier placed between two barrels, manned by a rough-looking bunch wearing dirty green and brown smocks and with machine-guns slung over their shoulders. Poupier tensed and Leslie did too, realising these were not the German military police or the *Wehrmacht* officers he had seen on patrol around Brussels. In fact, they were *Waffen-SS*, elite soldiers, battle-hardened and ruthless.

A gruff soldier yanked open Leslie's door and ordered everyone out. The fake documents the Wassenhoves had arranged for Leslie were scrutinised, but the soldiers took more time over their search of the truck, perhaps looking for weapons or something to steal.

Eventually, the barrier was removed and Poupier and his passengers were allowed to go on. In the passenger seat of the little van, Leslie felt his breathing return to normal, watching in the wing mirror as the soldiers grew further into the distance.

Soon after, Poupier's hitchhikers got out and the Ford trundled on to Namur, where the Sambre met the Meuse. Driving into the city, Poupier stopped near its fortress citadel and met with a local contact to check the next stage of the journey was clear, then headed into the countryside, pulling into the grounds of a large chateau.

The family who lived at the Chateau de Thozée were welcoming but did not wish at first to share anything about their lives with Leslie for security reasons. Eventually, he learned the chateau had been the home of a famous Belgian artist named Félicien Rops and was now in the hands of his daughter Valentine, grandchildren Élisabeth and Pierre, and their cousin Danielle. Élisabeth told him that another of her brothers, Jean, was a prisoner in Germany, while Danielle's father was with the Belgian army in England.

Élisabeth also gave him a warning: they could not be sure of the loyalties of their gardener so, during the day, Leslie would have to stay in his room. Leslie settled down to what he feared would be a lonely existence, but the following day Poupier returned in his van and delivered three more guests: two men in their 20s and a third, in his mid-30s, who were standing in the chateau's large library when Élisabeth brought Leslie downstairs.

There was an awkward silence, then Leslie – unsure what the men wanted or who they were – said hesitantly: *'Bon soir...'*

The older man laughed and said in a Yorkshire accent, 'Put a sock in it, mate!' and they all shook hands and began to share stories.

The Englishman was Flight Lieutenant Frank Shaw, a 35-year-old engineer from a Halifax bomber, who had just been collected from another safehouse by Poupier.

The two men with him were Americans – Staff Sergeant Royce McGillvary and Lieutenant John Bradley, who, at 6ft 3in, towered above them all – and they had been living a clandestine life as fugitives since before Christmas.

Bradley's evasion alone had involved dozens of helpers. He had already been on the run for eight months, having landed right on the German border.

11

CHECKPOINT

John Bradley and Royce McGillvary

ON NOVEMBER 5, 1943, 26-year-old John Bradley, of Matawan, New Jersey, had been a veteran of 24 missions – one short of completing a tour.

A clerk in civilian life, now it was his job to navigate a B-17, under Captain Booker, to its target and home again to Podington in the Bedfordshire countryside, north of London.

The target that Guy Fawkes Day for 827 Squadron, 92 Group, was Gelsenkirchen, a city with a large oil plant which had been pounded by the RAF earlier in the year as part of sustained efforts to destroy the industrial capacity of the Ruhr.

The B-17s rattled the teacups in kitchens around Podington at 10am, taking off into a grey English November day. Less than three hours later they were lining up for their bomb run. But the sky was thick with flak and Booker felt the aircraft shudder from an explosion close to the starboard wing. One of the waist gunners screamed.

'I've been hit in the leg.'

The other, while helping his friend, shouted.

'There's a fire spreading between engine three and four.'

Booker turned west and seeing German fighters come in to pick them off, dove 7,000ft to 20,000ft before levelling out. It was about 60 miles to the Dutch border and 180 miles to the coast. The way the fire was raging, they were not going to make it.

The engineer and Bradley forced open the emergency exit in the nose and Booker told them to bale out. The engineer went first, then Bradley, then the bombardier.

Bradley counted to 10 and pulled the ripcord. His 'chute opened with a jerk and oscillated wildly, making him feel sick. He ripped off his oxygen mask and gulped in the air. Looking around him, he counted seven parachutes, but he could not see the pilot or co-pilot. In fact, all had been lucky enough to escape, although only Bradley would not immediately be captured.

Bradley came down in flat land between the river Meuse and the German border, hitting the edge of a drainage ditch and sprawling forward onto his face. When he stood up, he saw a small crowd was already approaching.

'Holland?' he said.

The people nodded. One of the men gestured across the Meuse and said, '*Deutschland*.'

Bradley nodded, feeling far too close to Germany.

A young boy helped Bradley take off his flying kit and the airman left him his winter flying jacket; then he walked west and began to rely on the kindness of strangers. A farmer gave him sandwiches and some old clothes, and a young man put him in touch with the underground in the town of Bergen. There he was vetted by a local resistance leader, who took Bradley across the Meuse in a rowing boat at night and left the American for nearly a week with the family of café owner Anton Mooren. The family told him that in the cities people were almost starving, but here the farmers hid crops from the Germans. When it was time to leave, the family gave him a shaving kit as a present and the local priest brought a rosary and a medal with a blessing for safe travels.

A guide brought bikes and they cycled in several stages, staying at various safehouses – often with Dutch police officers – towards a monastery on the border with Belgium, where Bradley met Theodore Florquin, a Belgian, who knew a safe route across the frontier between Weert and Ittervoort. The pair crossed fields and a stream in the darkness and eventually Florquin turned to Bradley and whispered: 'Belgium.' He was still a long way from England but to Bradley it felt like a step forward. He began to imagine himself getting back to London.

As the moon appeared from behind the clouds, Bradley followed his guide to a farmhouse to rest and then on to the mill town of Dilsen, where Bradley was sheltered by Severin Moors. Moors, he learned, was one of those who had been inspired rather than cowed by Nazi oppression: his sister Gertrude had helped dozens of escaped airmen before her arrest by the Gestapo on June 18, 1943. Her arrest had made him determined to continue her work.

The dangers that had led to Gertrude's arrest remained, though, and, when Bradley was taken by Moors to the town of Lanklaar to stay with Martin Opdekamp, his wife and six children, he was told that there had been fresh arrests, including at the safehouse where they had hoped he would move next. Bradley became emotional when he saw the two youngest Opdekamp children crying – not out of fear for themselves but because they thought that *he* might be captured.

Opdekamp led the airman to a nearby convent. For a week the nuns looked after him, bringing food and playing cards in the evening. Opdekamp visited with cigarettes and his friend Albert Bidelot took Bradley's photograph for a false identity card, and – on November 29 – it was time to leave. Bradley set off, first by bicycle and then by 'Micheline' – a short steam train running on pneumatic tyres – to a café in Lanaken where Bidelot introduced him to Jean Schoenmaeckers, his next guide, who went ahead to the railway station to buy them tickets.

Bidelot walked the airman to the station, showed him to a seat in the waiting room, and left. Schoenmaeckers sat down, passing him the ticket.

'Get on the next train.'

Once in a quiet compartment on the train the two men had a chance to talk in whispers in English. Schoenmaeckers was an engineer whose family were all involved in the underground. His father and brother had both been taken by the Gestapo.

In the buffet at the busy railway station at Hasselt, the main town in the area, the two men were met by a handsome man in his mid-40s with dark swept-back hair. Florent Biernaux shook hands, spoke to Bradley as if they were old friends and ordered three beers. They drank them, said goodbye to Schoenmaeckers and headed off through the streets.

As they walked in silence a German soldier swung his flashlight into their eyes, but they stood aside and he passed. The encounter unnerved Bradley but Biernaux hurried him on. The 47-year-old veteran – who had received a chestful of medals for service and courage in the First World War including the *Chevalier de l'Ordre de Leopold II* and the *Croix de Guerre* – and his wife, Olympe, had already turned their home, a four-storey townhouse at 16 Boulevard Thonissen, into a hub of underground activity.

In fact, it was Olympe – a short, unassuming lady with bushy hair – who led 'Evasion', a local section of the Comet Line, having taken over control following the arrest of its initial leaders in June 1943.

Olympe and Florent Biernaux, with the help of their bespectacled son, Raymond – who was 25 but looked so youthful that Bradley took him for a teenager – and 12-year-old daughter, Eliane, not only sheltered fliers but organised false papers and clothes, and worked as guides. Olympe herself often conveyed airmen between Hasselt and Brussels or Liège.

Bradley stayed with the family for three weeks, listening to BBC broadcasts about the war – in breach of the occupier's restrictions – and cooking with meat and vegetables which Florent went out into the countryside to buy. A mother and daughter who were also part of the group, brought cakes and cookies from a café they ran in the town.

One dark December evening Bradley sat down with Florent.

'How long might it take to get me back home?' he asked.

An earlier guide had boasted he could be in London in weeks but Florent was more cautious.

'It could take three or four months. The underground are having to deal with more and more airmen. We are keeping you here so you have to spend as little time as possible in Brussels.'

Eventually, two days before Christmas, Olympe told Bradley it was time to go, and they walked to the station in the grey darkness of a December dawn. The train they took was slow and crowded, with people getting off and on at every stop. They were the only passengers to stay on all the way into Brussels.

At the station Bradley followed a few yards behind Olympe as she walked out of the main entrance and crossed the street to meet Gabrielle Baltus, a 66-year-old widow whose son was an officer serving in the Belgian army in England, and a younger woman named Marcelle Deleu. The group now split up. Olympe went back to Hasselt and Deleu went on to her family home in Rue des Fraises in Anderlecht – a Service EVA safe house run by her parents, Jean and François Deleu – to prepare for Bradley's arrival. Madame Baltus agreed to take Bradley by a different route to the Deleu home.

However, at the corner of the Rue des Fraises, they were met by Marcelle's brothers, Jean and François.

'There are soldiers up the street checking identity papers,' they warned.

Following Baltus down a side street, they took a tram and eventually came back on themselves to reach the Deleu house. Bradley was given food and introduced to the family, who smiled and welcomed him although only the father spoke English. The Deleus showed Bradley to a bedroom on the third floor, and he spent Christmas and the new year holiday in the house, learning to play chess, and even attending Mass on Christmas Day when Marcelle sang in the choir. Bradley sat separately from the family in church to keep them safe.

One day Bradley watched as Jean Deleu and his daughter prepared a stack of anti-Nazi newspapers for distribution – another extremely dangerous act of resistance which he realised could lead to their arrest and incarceration in a concentration camp.

'We hand the newspapers out in groups of under ten copies to friends to be distributed in any way they can,' Jean said.

'We collect military information too, to send to London.'

'You can use landmarks like canals and railroads,' Bradley told them as they pored over a map of the country. 'It will help bomber groups identify them from the air.'

On the evening of January 6, Charles Hoste picked up Bradley, taking him to Prosper Spilliaert's fishmonger's store, the EVA headquarters where Bill Grosvenor had been a month earlier. There, he was questioned and photographed and had what remained of his escape kit – maps, compass and French and English money – taken from him, as all could give him away as an Allied airman. In return, he was given 100 Belgian francs and 500 French francs in case he ever needed to buy himself out of trouble.

Hoste took him to his new home, an apartment above a drug store in Schaerbeek, owned by Joseph Hoebancx and Alice Van Elders. It was another centre for the production of underground newspapers and soon Bradley was happily helping Hoebancx fold and count 2,000 copies featuring stories refuting those in the Nazi-controlled press, plans for post-war Belgium, and denunciations of named collaborators. During almost a month with Hoebancx, he was introduced to a man named 'Hubert', who had been shot in the leg while escaping from a German trap. Hubert was, in fact, Jean Portzenheim, a commercial traveller who had been a key figure in EVA and was now in the beleaguered Comet Line.

Then, on February 2, Bradley was taken a few doors down the street to the home of a nurse, Yvonne Bienfait, a close associate of the EVA figures, Gaston Matthys and Henri Maca, who had also helped Grosvenor. Bienfait was an important figure in the evasion of many airmen. All knew her by her codename 'Monique', loved her smile and the comforts of her four-bedroom apartment: she was able to provide extra food from the hospital where she worked and share with them her small library of English books.

When Bradley arrived with Bienfait, he was introduced to another airman already under her care. His name was Royce McGillvary. 'Mac' was a 20-year-old waist gunner from Gary, Indiana, who had suffered engine trouble coming back from a raid just before Christmas. He had baled out over the Netherlands and made contact with sympathetic locals.

Like Bradley he had eventually been passed to the underground, crossed into Belgium and been sheltered and brought to Brussels by the Biernaux family of Hasselt. From now on EVA and the Comet Line decided to move Bradley and McGillvary together.

After only 24 hours with Yvonne Bienfait, Bradley and McGillvary were on the move again. Hoste and Portzenheim took them by tram to a hardware store in the Uccle area of Brussels and left them with a man they were to come to like very much, Jules Petryns.

Petryns ran a safehouse next to his hardware store with the help of his foreman, Henri, who was himself living on a false identity, having escaped from forced labour in Germany, and an older lady who cooked and cleaned for him and whom the airmen knew only as Isabelle. Petryns was a charismatic figure who spoke English very well and had an infectious sense of humour. He was delighted to discover that he shared a birthday with Bradley, and, on February 19, they all celebrated together.

However, one week later, as the two airmen washed the supper dishes in the kitchen of the house, the doorbell rang on the gate into the front yard and Petryns looked out to see the Gestapo. Bradley and McGillvary rushed through the scrapyard at the rear and climbed over a wall. As they stood in the sleet and cold – Bradley wearing only slippers, McGillvary in a vest – they realised they would draw the suspicion of anyone who saw them, so began to make their way through the backyards, ignoring barking dogs and hoping people would not look out their back windows.

Having put a block between them and the Germans, they knocked on a door, which was answered and then slammed in their faces by a terrified homeowner. A few houses on, they tried again, and a woman kindly gave them shoes, socks and a coat. Fully dressed, they risked walking quickly through the streets until they got to Isabelle's house where they stayed the night.

The Gestapo had not arrested Petryns, but told him he had been denounced for some indiscretion and blackmailed him into delivering a package for them. Unable to contact Portzenheim, Petryns decided it was time to get the airmen out of Brussels. He took them by train to Namur and then tram to Wépion, where his mother, Berthe Petryns-Serwy, used her rented home as an EVA safehouse. The two men stayed with Berthe for three months, sawing wood in her barn and carrying out work around the house. She told her French-speaking neighbours they were Flemish labourers.

Bradley couldn't help laughing as she began to treat them as if they were her sons, playing checkers with them in the evening, telling them off if they failed to make their beds or dropped cigarette ash, and fussing if they went out in the cold or rain without a coat. Bradley, who had been taught to play chess by the Deleus, now taught the game to McGillvary.

Only a neighbour named Arsène Colin knew the two men's true identities and, to stay active, they went to work in his vegetable garden, receiving cigarettes as payment. Then, one day a squadron of Marauders missed their target – a lock on the Meuse river – and destroyed a residential street nearby. Colin and the airmen went to see the damage. Bradley sensed the local anger against the Americans and the pair went to the funeral parlour where the bodies were laid out. It was a dreadfully sobering moment.

Colin allowed his home to be used by two Belgian agents of SOE who came to send messages to England and stayed for five days. For security reasons, neither carried their own transmitter. These were delivered by a priest and later taken away by a young woman – both of whom, the underground felt, were less likely to be searched for a clandestine radio set. The two airmen agreed to help the SOE men, taking up lookout points on the approach to the house and planning to lift their hats to signal if a German soldier or vehicle approached.

Late in May, a neighbour of Jules Petryns' hardware store in Brussels arrived at the house to warn him the Gestapo were after him again and were likely to come looking for him at his mother's. The airmen were quickly moved to a coal merchant's in Malonne. Petryns soon joined them there; he was now in hiding himself. One evening their host, a nephew of Colin's, took them to the village's tiny cemetery to show them RAF graves which were well-kept and adorned with fresh flowers.

On the evening of June 28, a guide picked up Bradley and McGillvary in a car and drove them to pick up a flight engineer from an RAF Halifax crew, Flight Lieutenant Frank Shaw, who had been in hiding for nearly seven months but almost entirely with civilians who had no formal connection to the underground – they had just wanted to help. These kind people had only recently been able to find a way to contact the evasion line.

The three men were then driven on to the Chateau de Thozée where they were met by Elisabeth Rops, her family, and the surprised Canadian, Stuart Leslie.

Over the following week, in the peaceful surroundings of the Chateau de Thozée, the four airmen played crochet and cards, would sit about chatting, and swim in a small garden pool after the gardener of uncertain loyalties had finished work and gone home. Then, on July 6, Leslie's taciturn driver, Henri Poupier, returned, this time driving a wood-burning *camion-navette* – a truck fitted with bench seats like a bus – and accompanied by a *résistant* called Paul Frapier, who told them to pack their belongings and jump in the back.

Unbeknown to the airmen, the plan was to take them to a wooden cabin which EVA had built in the south-eastern corner of Belgium, in the woods near Acremont. Only two days earlier Poupier had driven Carmen Vozzella – Wolcott's navigator/observer – to the new camp, and Gaston Matthys himself would soon be forced to flee there as the Germans closed in on him.

At Namur, the truck pulled up close to the Meuse.

'We cannot all cross the river by the bridge: there is a German checkpoint,' Poupier explained. Instead, Frapier took them to the riverbank and a rowing boat. Once across, all they could do was wait for Poupier. An hour later the *camion-navette* made it through the checkpoint and they pretended to wave it down.

As they did so, a railroad conductor and his wife – believing it was a public bus – did the same. Frapier welcomed them all, the airmen pretending not to know him.

Driving into the lightly forested countryside which marked the approach of the Ardennes, Poupier stopped to let off the two passengers and more, including a hitchhiking couple, got on. Fidgeting nervously, the airmen were eager to get off the open road, but they passed through a dozen sleepy villages without incident.

Then, as they approached the town of Spontin, about 30 miles from their destination, Poupier suddenly slammed on the brakes. Having drifted off into a light sleep, Leslie woke with a start and heard the driver hiss: 'Checkpoint!'

It was too late to turn back or let the airmen off. They were in full view of a squad of German soldiers. One of them shouted to Poupier and he cut the engine.

Waving rifles and machine guns, the soldiers ordered everyone out of the bus and two jumped inside and began to search. Another grim-faced man started to go through their pockets.

Poupier now bravely began to speak up. The airmen could not understand what he was saying, but the meaning was obvious. *What was all this about? He was just a farmer. These were labourers, hitchhikers. When could he be on his way?*

The Germans ignored him. After collecting all of the men's documents, an officer disappeared into a small guard house.

When he came back out, he seemed satisfied. The fake identity papers prepared by EVA appeared to have worked. Bradley felt himself sigh with relief.

But one of the soldiers again approached the men and started another search, roughly pulling their coats aside. Pushing his hand into the pockets of McGillvary's civilian coat, he found something unusual and pulled it out. It was Mac's USAAF dog tags.

The airmen were not going to reach the safety of the Ardennes after all.

PART TWO
CAPTURE

12

'HERE YOU ARE AT LAST!'

Françoise Labouverie

THE FIGHTING IN Normandy forced many Belgians to think about what would replace the Germans when they left. On the political right, there was concern the highly-active Communist elements of the Resistance would dominate any power struggle which might follow liberation.

Two senior members of *Tégal* – the intelligence-gathering resistance group for whom Françoise Labouverie had been working as a courier and organiser – started working for the country's most right-wing of the country's Resistance group, the monarchist armed resistance organisation, *Mouvement National Royaliste* (MNR). One was Roger Hanquinet, the landlord of the building she now had a flat in. The other was her cousin Jean Loicq. Both explained the MNR planned to create a police force which would 'keep order' in the weeks after the Germans left. Hanquinet asked Françoise for her help, but for now all they wanted her to do was sew tricolour armbands for the organisation's officers to wear on liberation.

Soon, 23-year-old Françoise grew lonely and bored. The past

year had been one of intense sadness and frantic activity. *Tégal*'s woes, which started the previous September with the capture of its leader and Françoise's friend, Pierre Hauman, had continued into 1944 with the arrests of two more of its leading figures and its radio operator. But Françoise and the intelligence-gathering operatives who brought information to her were coming under increasing pressure from London to find out about a new secret weapon it believed the Germans were developing.

The first hints of something sinister arrived with Françoise during the summer of 1943 when *Tégal* operatives on the coast began to spot 'a new kind of cement ramp'. Having no idea what these might be, Françoise typed the descriptions and information, and her reports were sent to London.

The British were very interested, as Françoise's reports chimed with information received from other intelligence-gathering groups in Belgium and France. In December 1942, Henri Roth, a citizen of Luxembourg, had been sent to Germany for compulsory labour and found himself at a top-secret research site at Peenemünde on the Baltic coast. He managed to get a message to his father, describing 'tests we have been doing since November 20, 1942, of a torpedo type machine, driven by a motor, but launched by means of a catapult'. Roth's father was in the Resistance and, on April 8, 1943, a report prepared by his network arrived in London.

For Dr RV Jones, British intelligence's scientific expert, the report was the first he received on the *Vergeltungswaffen 1* – V1 – a pilotless aircraft packed with a warhead of high explosives and propelled by a jet engine which cut out at a distance adjudged to have brought it over its target. In addition, the *Zéro* network collected information, also from forced labourers from Luxembourg, about a second weapon – *Vergeltungswaffen 2*, the V2 rocket. A report landed on Winston Churchill's desk describing the terrifying prospect of the development of rockets or new missiles by the Germans and, in August 1943, the RAF bombed the Peenemünde site.

However, by the time of the raid, the Germans had already begun to construct V1 launch sites in the Pas-de-Calais and Belgium. It was these that were described in the reports coming to Françoise in the past months. By the spring of 1944, the British made observation of these sites a priority, demanding precise information so they could be targeted by the RAF. There was even a fear that the use of the weapons might have an impact on the planned landings on the coast of France. A variety of networks were involved in collecting information and the photographs, plans and reports made by *Tégal* were routed through Françoise's flat in Brussels, where she would prepare them for the long journey to London via courier or for sending by radio. Based on this information, 96 first-generation launch sites were destroyed before D-Day, but on June 13, a week after the landings, the first V1 landed on Bethnal Green, south London, killing six and injuring 30, and a new Battle of London had begun.

On that very same day, Françoise's active resistance would end abruptly.

Roger Hanquinet told her two teenagers from the MNR needed a place to stay: his 18-year-old son, Jacques, and a friend, Georges Chantrenne. Françoise said that, as the GFP was on her trail, they would be in danger with her, but, because Hanquinet owned the flat in which she lived, and she had already been forced to move several times in recent months, she could hardly turn them away.

While waiting for them to arrive, Françoise was disturbed by shouting downstairs. Sneaking a look out of the window, she saw a young man arguing with the concierge. He saw her, pushed the woman aside and ran upstairs. Françoise felt the blood rush out of her face as he pushed open her door and looked swiftly around the room to see if there was anyone else there.

Then, he bowed arrogantly and stepped very close to her. '*M'selle* Labouverie?'

'No,' Françoise stammered, trying to sound as confident as him. 'You're mistaken.'

The man smiled. His eyes were dark and his fair hair was only just long enough to show it was beginning to curl.

'Your name is Labouverie, isn't it? Some friends of mine want a chat with you. It would be better for you if they didn't come here.'

Françoise took a deep breath.

'I don't know your friends and have no intention of following you.'

The man reached slowly into his pocket, took out a gun and pointed it at her stomach.

'Perhaps you understand this better.'

'Are you arresting me?' Françoise said, still trying to sound sure of herself.

'Not at all,' he replied with a thin smile. 'We just want to ask you a few questions. Don't talk. Come along.'

'Will you give me two minutes to pack a case?' she asked, hoping to find a way to leave a note warning Hanquinet.

The man shook his head.

'No need for that. Come along!'

Taking the door key from the table, he ushered Françoise out, locked the door and put the key in his pocket. At least there was no sign of him leaving anyone behind to arrest any visitors. Holding her close, he pushed a gun into her side – like a gangster in a Hollywood movie – so any of Françoise's friends who might see them would need to look very closely to realise she was being taken away by force.

They walked several blocks through busy streets and city parks until they eventually reached the Place Philippe de Champagne and climbed the steps to a large old house. As the man rang the doorbell

Françoise looked up at the huge Rexist flag which fluttered in the light summer breeze. Any hope she had that the man belonged to a rival resistance group quickly disappeared.

The heavy door was opened by a dark little man with a small ferret-like face. Behind him, another man came running down a wide marble staircase, saw Françoise, and punched the air with delight.

'Well done! Well done! So that's her! The *Boches* will be delighted.'

Pushing and dragging Françoise through the house, down a set of steps and along a narrow corridor lined with small black doors, they arrived at the last door. The ferret-faced man took a key from a bunch that hung from his belt and opened the lock. Strong arms thrust Françoise so roughly into the room that she almost stumbled and fell. When she turned back the three men were laughing.

'You are all pigs!' she shouted.

Their laughing stopped as they stepped into the room, threatening her with a beating. Edging back to the wall, she fell silent and as the three men left, one of them spat on the floor.

The cell was little more than a large cupboard with a plank along the back wall which was so narrow she could barely sit on it.

There was no light except the chink that came in at the top of the door. There seemed to be complete silence at first but then Françoise became aware of a shuffling and murmuring from the next room.

'A drink,' a voice said in French.

It was barely more than the low moan of someone drifting in and out of consciousness.

'A drink, please, sir. Please, please.'

Loud footsteps came and her door opened.

'Out,' the ferret-faced man ordered, pushing her along the corridor and back up the steps until they reached an office where a well-dressed man with brown hair sat behind a desk.

Without looking up, he said: 'What is your name?'

'HERE YOU ARE AT LAST!'

'Nicole Desmanets.' It was the name on her false papers.

'You're lying!' The man snapped, looking hard into her eyes.

'No,' Labouverie said, shaking her head.

The man looked back down at the notes on his desk. 'Where do you live?'

'Liège.'

The man stood up and Labouverie could see now that he was tall and broad. She felt very small as he came round the desk towards her.

'I suppose you think you are very clever.' He banged his hand on the desk. 'We'll make you speak. We'll get the truth out of you.'

Turning to the ferret-faced man, he waved his hand.

'Take her away!'

This time she was led to a larger basement with a wooden bench wide enough to lie down on. Trying to rest, she pulled her cardigan around her and began to feel emboldened. She had lived under the fear of arrest for so long that now it had happened, she felt she could deal with it. In some ways she knew she should be grateful she was not yet in the hands of the Germans, but to be arrested by fellow countrymen made her sick with anger and hatred. It felt like a personal betrayal.

It was several hours before the door opened again and a short middle-aged woman came in with coffee. It was lukewarm and ersatz but Françoise sipped it gratefully. The woman, who Françoise took to be the ferret-faced man's wife, watched as she drank. There was no pity in her eyes; she seemed completely uninterested in who the prisoners were.

'Can I have something to eat?' Françoise asked. The woman looked at her as if it was the strangest request and a few moments later returned and handed over a single dog biscuit without a word and then locked the door behind her. Françoise was already very hungry and devoured the dog biscuit in two bites.

The angry man from the room upstairs unlocked her cell door soon afterwards.

'Well, have you had time to think? Are you going to tell me your name?'

Françoise sat up and rubbed her hands up and down your arms.

'I have told you,' she said defiantly.

The man shook his head ruefully.

'What's the use of lying? If you tell me the truth, you will be released in the morning.'

Françoise held his gaze and said nothing. The man turned and left, but his words lingered: she indeed wondered whether there was any use in lying. They already knew her real name and she had been in hiding for so long she didn't know any of the recent activities of the resistance network. Was there really anything important she could give away?

She stamped her cold feet: she knew that thinking like that was the first stage to giving in, perhaps even to becoming a collaborator. Finally she slept, but only after convincing herself she would never talk.

In the morning, she was taken upstairs to the office again. Her interrogator was standing this time and the man who had arrested her sat behind the desk, ready to record what she said on a typewriter.

A chair had been placed in front of the desk and on it, a sharp-edged iron bar. Forcing Françoise to kneel on the bar, he gave her another to hold with both hands above her head. It was agony.

As the pain surged through her legs and arms, the man stepped so close to her that she could feel his breath on her face.

'You have told us lies! All lies!' he hissed.

The typewriter clicked behind as he spoke.

'You have wasted precious time. But we know *all* about you.'

He lifted a thick sheaf of papers from his desk and shook them

'HERE YOU ARE AT LAST!'

in her face. She felt her stomach churn as he read out her mother's name and address, then the names of regular visitors to her mother's home, and the names and addresses of many of her relatives.

'What have you got to say? Why have you got false identity papers? Why are you hiding?'

'You have arrested me,' Françoise said through gritted teeth, 'so you ought to know.'

The man slapped her hard across the face.

She was shocked, but when she saw the grin on the face of the man behind the desk, she was immediately defiant again.

'Why do you keep changing addresses?'

Françoise could feel a trickle of blood from her nose.

'Where were you before?'

The man leaned so close to her face that they were almost touching. 'I'll tell you!' He held up a piece of paper and showed her an address.

Françoise shook her head, and the interrogator slapped her repeatedly, calling her a liar over and over.

She could cope with the shouting and closed her mind to it. She thought about the address he'd shown her. That street, she had been to it but not stayed there. It was a time she'd thought a German was following her and she had rushed through a toy shop with a rear exit.

She told him. But he did not believe her.

As he continued, Françoise grew immune to the slaps. They hurt, but she realised these people were desperate: they did not know why she was wanted by the Germans, and they needed that information so they could negotiate with the Gestapo or Abwehr. In short, they wanted to know what they had stumbled upon. Perhaps a demand for a reward depended on it.

She thought of childhood, of games in the countryside with her friends, anything to shut out the angry face in front of her. She remembered a time when she and friends had lit a campfire in the woods. The boys had been joking and laughing and ignoring her and a friend so they had created an imaginary boyfriend called Little Victor.

Slap! Slap!

'Who were you working for?'

'Little Victor.'

The typewriter clicked away.

'Little Victor.'

The slapping stopped as Françoise described a man with a thick black beard who would meet her at cafes across the city. She even offered to take them to the Café St James to see if she could find Little Victor. Françoise imagined herself being left as a decoy in the cafe as the Rexists looked on. Perhaps she would be able to signal to a friend and show that she was under arrest; maybe she would even be able to escape.

The two men sat back and listened as she talked. They had sandwiches brought in for themselves.

'Where does Little Victor live?'

Françoise, apparently talking freely now, said he had never told her. That would have been too dangerous. They kept each other's addresses secret.

'You must know if he lives in Brussels?'

'I shouldn't think so,' she said. 'He has a lovely French accent.'

For more than three hours the conversation went on until the door swung open behind Françoise and the Rexists jumped to their feet and saluted. '*Heil Hitler!*'

It was two Germans. The senior man, a captain, ignored the two Belgian fascists and looked only to the person in the chair, her cheeks red from being struck, but her eyes defiant.

From his first words she knew exactly who he was.

'Ah, Françoise,' he said, 'there you are! We have been looking for you everywhere! I have seen your mother several times.'

It was Hugo Böhme, the officer who had been pursuing her for months. Unknown to Françoise, Böhme had kept Hauman and other members of the network he had arrested in the prison of Saint-Gilles, rather than having them executed or sent to concentration camps. He was still hoping they would help him close down the whole *Tégal* network.

Discovering the Rexists had been tipped off about her, he had come to collect one of those high on his most wanted list.

'You can come with us,' he said.

'But we haven't finished,' her Belgian interrogator protested while his colleague gestured to the paper they were typing on.

Böhme waved his hand dismissively. 'Never mind, I know all about that,' he said and, taking Françoise by the arm, he added: 'Come on!'

Outside in the June sunshine, a soldier stood by a black Opel car and opened the door for her to get into the back seat.

Böhme sat beside her, looking at her like an old friend and slapped his hand on his thigh.

'Nine months you have kept us waiting,' he said with a smile. 'But never mind, here you are at last!'

Gaston Masereel

AN SOE PHYSICAL TRAINING INSTRUCTOR had given Gaston Masereel the nickname 'Tarzan' due to his physical and mental strength. And he needed every bit of that strength now.

Having been given some basic medical attention for the wounds he received when the 'Moon Squadron' Halifax had blown up over the Dutch coast, he was moved to solitary confinement in Breda, a sub-camp of the Vught concentration camp.

Conditions were horrific. The SS commanders at Vught treated both the Jewish and Dutch and Belgian 'political prisoners' – mostly members of the resistance or left-wing organisations – with unrestrained brutality. The defenceless inmates were often set upon by the dogs or attacked by a guard wielding a club wrapped in barbed wire. Many were executed at the shooting range or gallows.

Masereel was singled out for prolonged interrogations. Barefoot, wrapped in bandages and starved of food, other than a soup which was little more than warm water sprinkled with bits of carrot, he would not wash, shave or change his bloody, torn clothes for the next two and a half months.

But he had come up with a blend of audacious lies and half-truths in a bid to keep himself alive.

His interrogators – led by a German officer who spoke French – made an early mistake when they let slip they knew he had arrived by plane because they had found the wreck 'and the six bodies inside'. Masereel then knew there was no one who could contradict anything he might say.

Deciding to admit the name and address on his papers were false (as, now he was in custody, they would have been easy to disprove), he gave the Germans his real name and the approximate date he escaped Belgium for England. He hoped the admission would help them believe the essence of the story he now began to invent, having remembered an article which he had read in a newspaper shortly before heading out on his mission.

'I came,' he said, 'to investigate a Flemish politician on behalf of the Belgian government-in-exile. He was collaborating with the Germans, and they want to know if he is acting alone or with a wider political group, and what his intentions might be if – or when – Belgium is liberated.'

Masereel maintained this fiction that he was merely an emissary for the Belgian government throughout his interrogation. To support it, he agreed he had attended a British 'training school' where he was put on a fitness course to prepare him for his parachute jump. He denied undertaking any weapons or wireless training. When asked about the location of the school, he said it was in the country, but where it was had never been shared with him. He then rambled on about conditions in England, resolving to bore his interrogators. At one point he spent 45 minutes talking in detail about what food had been available to him on the other side of the English Channel, and watched the German's eyes glaze over.

He refused to let up on his denials even when his interrogators confronted him with the money in the olive jar and microfilm in the frame of the briefcase. He told the Germans his instructions had been to hand all his belongings to a (fictitious) man named Georges, who would find him at the drop-zone. He had been used by the British, he said, as they must have planted these items on him in order to get them to Georges. They had played a 'dirty trick' on both him and the Belgian government, he grumbled indignantly.

With his story not changing and his wounds allowing him to sometimes 'faint' during questioning, Masereel realised the Germans were more preoccupied with the invasion of France than him. Eventually, his interrogator at Breda left him alone, although he remained isolated in the cell, with no clothes other than a shirt, and he never saw any person other than his guard.

The Tarzan of SOE was now left to wait.

13

WORKING WITH THE RESISTANCE

Royce McGillvary, John Bradley, Stuart Leslie, Frank Shaw

WHEN THE SOLDIERS at the roadblock on the road to the Ardennes found his dog-tags, Royce McGillvary tried to argue, but it was no use. They had already swung their rifles around on him and the others.

Shouting and pushing, they bullied the airmen, their guides – driver Henri Poupier, and his helper, Paul Frapier – and the innocent hitchhiking couple into the guardhouse and made them sit on a long wooden bench. One of the soldiers stood facing them, his MP 40 machine gun pointing directly at them. The airmen shared nervous glances; capture had completely drained them. It was July 6, 1944 – and McGillvary, Bradley and Englishman Frank Shaw had all been on the run since before the previous Christmas. Leslie had been evading for nine weeks. They each felt suddenly exhausted. The situation seemed hopeless. The hitchhiking couple held hands. The driver wiped sweat off his brow.

The next 30 minutes felt like a lifetime. No-one was allowed to speak. The MP 40 remained fixed on them.

WORKING WITH THE RESISTANCE

Then the door burst open and everyone jumped. The new arrival wore a metal gorget suspended on a silver chain around his neck. On it was an eagle and the word *Feldgendarmerie* (German military police). Revelling in the startled effect his entrance made upon the prisoners, he immediately barked: 'Stand up!'

They all did. Quickly. He searched the driver, then Leslie, taking everything out of their pockets and placing it on the table. Then he waved McGillvary and John Bradley towards him and forced them to do the same. Both carried their identity tags.

The military policeman smiled arrogantly, and shifted his gaze to Frank Shaw, who shrugged and said, 'I'm a flier too.'

'So am I,' Leslie said, and suddenly felt his body deflate. The performance was over.

The German soldiers were suddenly all talking excitedly, showing each other the men's false papers and the two Americans' tags. They had bagged four Allied airmen and maybe three members of the Resistance.

'Look at them,' Bradley sneered in his New Jersey accent. 'They act as though they'd captured Eisenhower!'

The airmen laughed weakly, but no one spoke for the next few minutes and, when the Germans gave them water and cigarettes, they drank and smoked in silence.

The news of their arrest was being passed up a chain of command. The next people to arrive were two officers; one spoke English. As he took down their names and copied the information on the identity tags, there came the sound of a truck engine being started and a vehicle being moved closer to the building. The prisoners were loaded onboard and taken to the city's prison, a square building of drab grey stone. Standing in the courtyard, the airmen were inspected by army officers who took their possessions and placed them in bags labelled with their names.

Leslie looked back at their guides, Poupier and Frapier, and the two innocent hitchhikers who were still inside the truck. Their faces were pale. They were being placed in the hands of the Gestapo, facing torture, possibly execution.

Inside the prison building the four airmen were questioned but gave only their name, rank and number. After a night together in a cell they were marched outside and loaded into a truck belonging to the Luftwaffe.

Leslie breathed a sigh of relief: it appeared that the Germans had accepted that they were airmen and not spies.

But all that would change.

Al Sanders and Henry Wolcott

IN THE COUNTRYSIDE TO THE south-west of Brussels, young Resistance leader Alex – the 20-year-old student running his own network – now had Al Sanders, 'Carpetbagger' Henry Wolcott, and 18 Russian deserters from the German army to hide.

He decided to keep them busy, fulfilling his hope of turning the farm he used as a base into a defensive stronghold, where his group could safely store arms and men, and from where they could plan and launch attacks. He put the men to work creating fortifications around the outbuildings and making homemade explosive devices.

Suddenly, Sanders looked up to see a teenage girl running across the fields towards them. The Germans had raided the neighbouring farm and killed the handsome man with the sideburns who had helped them. They were on their way there.

Alex and his men started up the two lorries and everyone jumped into the back. Careering quickly down the farm track and out onto the road, Sanders and the others sneaked a peek out of the back of the truck but could not see the Germans.

Arriving at another farm in the village of Bierghes, Alex split the group. Sanders, Wolcott, three of the Russians and one of Alex's men were to stay there; the others moved on. The farm was owned by Georges Tondeur, whose small workforce were all aware of his clandestine work with Alex. But there was now fear in the group, a paranoia that Gestapo agents were moving through it, making arrests and identifying safehouses.

In fact, the Gestapo *had* planted an agent posing as an Australian airman called Martens and he had made contact with resisters in the villages of Aaigem, Ressegem, and Burst – the area in which Wolcott's Liberator had come down. The Resistance had exposed the fake airman during his interrogation and imprisoned him in a dry water well while they decided what to do with him. But he had begged to be let out to use a toilet and had escaped over a wall. Within hours 'Martens' had returned with a force of Gestapo and soldiers with him and started the wave of arrests which was leading towards Alex's group.

***

Sunday, June 18, was a perfect sunny summer's day. All the chat in the Tondeur farm was about the fighting in Normandy and fears that the Allies might not break out. Wolcott looked out from a farmhouse window and saw German troops spreading out to surround the house.

At the same moment Tondeur rushed in with a cry of '*Les Boches!*' and hurried them all to a secret hiding place under the floorboards.

The Germans had brought a substantial force. About 150 soldiers searched the farm. Sanders listened as the soldiers shouted at Tondeur, overturned furniture and smashed and broke his belongings. Lying in the darkness, Wolcott felt some of them walk over the floorboards above him.

Then both Americans suddenly realised that the three Russians were discussing in hushed tones a plan to jump out at the Germans: they hated them so much they could not stand being so close to a German soldier and not trying to kill him. The Americans restrained the three men; Wolcott was convinced that at any moment the Germans would realise that there was empty space under the floorboards and the secret trapdoor would be opened.

But the voices were retreating; the Germans were going. Final orders were shouted, vehicles started. Suddenly it was very quiet.

In the hiding place under the floor Sanders and the others held their breath, trying to work out if the enemy had left a sentry behind.

Eventually they heard another vehicle approach. There was movement in the house and the trapdoor opened. It was Alex.

All of the Germans had gone. But, sadly, they had taken Georges Tondeur and his farmworkers. In all, 19 local people were arrested. Some – including Tondeur – were later released; others were transported to Neuengamme.

The airmen knew there was nothing they could do for Tondeur and the others, but they also realised that if they were interrogated, they could tell the Germans about them. They had to leave, and quickly. They shoved what money and food they could find into their pockets, and Alex drove them by truck to another farm near the small town of Rebecq.

Sanders, Wolcott and five of the Russian deserters hid for four days until the town's mayor warned the Germans had been tipped off and were planning a raid. The two Americans were moved immediately to a hilltop mansion – the home of a local iron manufacturer – seven miles away near the village of Clabecq. With the local Resistance concerned about the numbers of their colleagues under German questioning, they kept the airmen on the move. The airmen were eventually taken back to Rebecq and a new group of men and women who introduced themselves as members of the *Witte Brigade*. The house belonged to Jean Rowart, who fed them and told them to rest, as they would continue to be moved very quickly from safehouse to safehouse. The Rowart family had already hidden a number of Jews and airmen, and they had a young Jewish woman named Jeanette staying there at the time. Sanders passed the time talking to her and playing with the Rowarts' puppy. Jeanette took time to tell him the story of Jews in Belgium since the Germans had invaded.

In 1940, the country had been home to about 90,000 Jews. Many had headed to the south of France when the Germans had invaded but about half had later returned home. In October of that year Jewish people had been forced to register with the local authorities and have *Jude* stamped on their identity cards. In 1941, they had been barred from jobs in the press, radio, schools and universities, and in the legal profession, and Jewish doctors and dentists had been forced to close their practices. Jews had been told they were only allowed to live in four cities: Brussels, Antwerp, Charleroi, and Liège. And then, in July 1942, had come the deportation decree designed to accelerate the numbers of Jews being transported to Auschwitz. Many were helped to evade by specially created Jewish defence committees, which urged people not to assemble for deportation. These committees created false papers and financially supported people without the funds to hide. Armed members of one committee forced their way into the *Judenrat* in Brussels and burnt lists of names[4].

Jeanette's freedom, like Sanders', depended on the kindness and courage of people like the Rowart family who were willing to risk all to do the right thing.

---

4   It is estimated that 3,000 children were saved from certain death by the various Resistance groups of Belgium. However, of the 26,000 Jews who were deported to extermination camps during the occupation, it is estimated that only 1,200 survived.

These friendships with their helpers only underlined the sense of guilt the airmen felt for putting them in danger. Sanders and Wolcott had already met dozens of resisters – people they could identify to the Germans if tortured. None of the civilians had shown any resentment for the peril in which they were being put; in fact, they had often been apologetic for having only a small stash of local beer and potatoes to offer them.

Being on the run was an exhausting and uncertain life. And the frequency of the changes of location reinforced a sense that the Gestapo might be closing in. In their lowest moments it was hard to avoid the feeling that capture seemed to be inevitable.

Bill Grosvenor and John Brown

FOR A MONTH BETWEEN MAY 3 and June 3, 1944, fighter pilot Bill Grosvenor and B-17 skipper John Brown stayed with Jeanne Claes-Frix, a widow in her early 50s who lived in Evere, in the north-east of Brussels, and worked for Service EVA. The two airmen slept on the second floor of her house, stayed away from the window and made as little noise as they could. Like the other airmen, they had become very fond of their host. They sat with Claes-Frix every evening, huddled around the radio, listening to the BBC.

On May 27 they sat on the roof of her house and watched B-17s bomb Brussels. The target was a railway marshalling yard, but many bombs fell short and hit a residential area. Grosvenor and Brown could not know it, but the raid almost killed people involved in helping them. EVA courier Blanche Page was delivering messages to its headquarters at Prosper Spilliaert's fishmarket when the bombs started falling and threw herself under the building's roll-down shutter just as Spilliaert was bringing it down.

Together, they rushed to the comparative safety of the basement – just as the building took a direct hit. When they came out the street was filled with rubble and scattered with dead bodies.

That day brought more bad news when Henri Maca – originally with EVA but now a senior figure in the Comet Line – was arrested. Security was stepped up but, for some reason, the Claes-Frix house seemed isolated from the rest of the line.

All the same, the airmen could not stay too long in the same place as they were bound to draw attention from the neighbours. Over the next fortnight they were moved from safehouse to safehouse, then on June 18, with the panic after the arrests subsiding and with safehouses limited, the two men were returned to Madame Claes-Frix. Both were relieved; they had asked if they could return. It was a decision made out of necessity for the members of the line, but unknown to Brown and Grosvenor, their identities were *already* blown. The Claes-Frix house had been under observation for some time.

Claes-Frix later told Brown she feared she had been denounced for laying flowers on American graves in the cemetery. In fact, she had been caught in an elaborate and far-reaching Abwehr trap laid by the German intelligence department's office in Antwerp.

Abwehr agents were running parts of their own evasion line. Called KLM, it consisted of Abwehr agents integrating their own couriers and safehouses into a genuine network so Belgian patriots were unwittingly caught up in the deadly operation.

On January 31, 1944, a genuine Dutch resister – who was already under observation by the Abwehr – came to shelter with Claes-Frix. He left a week before Grosvenor and Brown first arrived at the widow's house in May but, by then, she was firmly in the Abwehr's files.

Towards the end of April an Abwehr agent with the codename Emile was sent through the EVA safehouses by Marcel 'Victor'

Daelemans, a former member of the Comet Line who was entirely unaware this section of the underground had been infiltrated. In fact, Emile was an agent of Martin Peeters, an Abwehr assassin, and René Van Muylem, a Belgian agent of the Abwehr. A well-travelled businessman – who had started out as a ship's steward but prospered before the war through the acquisition of a string of barber shops – Van Muylem had originally been secretly employed by the Abwehr to write pro-Nazi propaganda. But the Germans had subsequently seen his potential as a networker and informer and decided they would be better served if he was socialising in clubs and business groups, keeping his ear to the ground. In late 1943 or early 1944, while posing as an agent of the British in order to spy on suspected saboteurs, Van Muylem met Daelemans. He immediately saw an opportunity to insert his own agents and informers – including 'Emile' – into this line and expose every link in the chain.

The work of the Abwehr agent, Emile, sealed the fates of Jeanne Claes-Frix, many of her comrades in EVA, and of Brown and Grosvenor.

***

It was dawn on June 20 when Jeanne Claes-Frix ran up the stairs of her home.

'The Gestapo are in the house – get out,' she urged. Grabbing their clothes, they tried a bedroom window but it offered no escape. Instead, they opened a skylight in the attic and helped each other onto the roof. But before they had made it a few yards, a soldier poked his head out and pointed his rifle at them. They had nowhere to go.

Brown, Grosvenor, and Claes-Frix were taken to Luftwaffe headquarters. As they were led inside, Grosvenor looked up at the huge swastika flag and then at a group of elderly Belgian ladies sweeping the sidewalk across the street with their brooms. *I'd give anything just to be out there sweeping the streets with them,* he thought.

Inside, Brown and Grosvenor gave their name, rank and number but a Luftwaffe officer said, as they had been caught in civilian clothes, they would be taken to a civilian prison until they could prove their identities.

In fact, any combatant out of uniform ran a great risk after orders from Hitler to execute all commandos, saboteurs and parachutists when they landed on German-occupied territory.

Brown and Grosvenor knew, in order to prove their identities, they would be expected to reveal when they were shot down and who had been hiding them in the meantime. Grosvenor had been on the run for seven months; Brown for four: giving their helpers' names away was out of the question.

They were transported to Saint-Gilles, where the two Americans watched their friend and helper, Jeanne Claes-Frix, being dragged off to a different wing.

Brown and Grosvenor were put in a cell with deserters from the SS; three German and two Belgian.

Ted Kleinman

BROWN'S NAVIGATOR TED KLEINMAN WAS still at large, still keen to take an active part in the Belgian Resistance.

After being moved to Basècles, close to the French border, he met Achilles Batiste, the local Resistance chief. Kleinman had asked many times how he could help and Batiste was the first to take him seriously. Bordeaux took the airman to the home of Carlos Bernard, who then told him their network kept a radio for contacting London in the kiln of a nearby quarry. He asked Kleinman about his knowledge of wireless sets and whether he would be willing to work with the Resistance as one. The young man from the Bronx readily agreed.

For the next three days he left the house to meet his schedule on the radio: at 6am, noon, 6pm, and midnight. Every transmission was a risk. He was a new face in the street and he did not speak the local language. If challenged, either before or after curfew, he stood little chance. He asked if he could move the set and Batiste agreed. It was a stroke of luck: a few days later a German patrol searched the quarry and the kiln where the radio had been.

A quarry worker heard about the new American radio operator and called to see him. He said his name was Captain Fernand Barbaix, an officer in the pre-war Belgian army and the chief of a neighbouring Resistance group. Barbaix became a regular visitor to the house, seeking Kleinman's advice about what was the most valuable intelligence to send on to London. The pair focussed on sending information about a nearby night-fighter base. Kleinman became a courier, taking messages between Barbaix and Batiste; he also prepared explosives for the destruction of the local railway line between Blaton and Basècles.

But the amount of sabotage in Kleinman's area attracted a huge amount of German attention. During one search for saboteurs, Kleinman was sheltered with a family at a bakery and had to endure the terror of having to hide in the heat of a recently used oven.

Realising they had a duty to try to keep the airman safe and get him back into the air war, the underground made contact with a new group of helpers. The next stage of Kleinman's journey – a hazardous move to Brussels - was underway.

/ 14

A BETRAYAL REVEALED

Stuart Leslie

FROM HIS CELL on a Luftwaffe base, pilot Stuart Leslie lifted himself up to the window bars to watch Me-110 night-fighters scramble in the darkness. As he heard their engines take them skywards, he thought of his friends in Bomber Command and hoped the German hunters would come back without any success to report.

Leslie had been brought to the airfield near Namur after his arrest at the checkpoint, along with John Bradley, Royce McGillvary and Frank Shaw. Each was in a separate cell.

In the early hours his door was unlocked and two Luftwaffe officers stepped inside. Leslie tensed for a moment, wondering what a late-night visit could mean – revenge for a colleague shot down by the RAF, perhaps? But the visit appeared a friendly one. The two men sat and offered him a cigarette. One was silent but smiling; the other spoke in his limited English. Although relieved that he was not going to get a beating, Leslie was cautious: the intelligence bods back in England had warned about the friendly approach sometimes taken by interrogators, in which the captured man might give away more than he intended in a polite chat. The German who spoke English sensed his caution and explained they simply wanted to meet a British airman and share a smoke with him. Leslie nodded, smiled and pulled on the cigarette but said little.

At dawn on the following day, he and the other three fliers were loaded onto a truck. Perhaps eager for some morning air, the two guards with them in the back of the truck did not pull down the rear canvas flaps as the vehicle rumbled across the grass. One yawned and stretched. Both ignored the airmen. Leslie looked out at a row of cottages with red tile roofs and thought there must be a village on the edge of the airfield until he realised the roofs, picket fences, and painted verandas were simply a camouflage: these were not homes; they were the airfield's buildings. 'Mac' McGillvary, sitting next to him, made the realisation at the same time.

'Never spot that from the air in a million years,' the American whispered out of the corner of his mouth.

It was almost noon when they approached the southern suburbs of Brussels. The driver lurched through the gears in the traffic, mainly military vehicles and locals on bicycles, and the tired airmen began to feel sick in their empty stomachs. There was no space to stretch their legs and the guards would not let them stand, even for a moment.

Eventually, the driver slowed right down and steered the truck between two concrete columns and into a large parade ground. There were buildings on several sides, a barracks of some kind, but the airmen were given no time to look around. Ushered into a grey building and searched, they were pushed into small wooden cells, each separated by a partition that did not quite reach the ceiling. As soon as the corridor outside was quiet the airmen stood on their bunks and whispered over the partition to each other.

'Where are we?'

A BETRAYAL REVEALED

'Centre of Brussels.'
'Why not a prison camp?'
'Do they think we're spies?'
'This place looks like a barracks.'
'Yeah, but does the Gestapo use barracks?'

There were more questions than answers. But they were not alone. In a neighbouring cell was an RAF sergeant, who had been badly hurt when he was shot down. His broken arm was in a sling, and he had trouble talking, his jaw having been smashed when his plane was attacked. The man's morale was terribly low, and he said he was waiting to be shipped to Germany. His demeanour and words hit the others hard. Moving from friendly safehouse to safehouse had held an element of adventure, a sense of freedom even, with the promise of escape; but now they were stuck in a jail in the centre of an occupied city and facing a barbed wire hell inside the Fatherland, or perhaps something even worse. They felt very far from home.

The airmen spent the next couple of days lying on their bunks, not wishing to talk and being short with any of their number who tried to be cheerful. It was when Leslie was at his lowest that two guards came for him and brought him before a Luftwaffe officer, a sharp-faced major who made no attempt to butter up his prisoner.

'You must tell me where you were shot down,' the major said, his pencil poised over a piece of paper on his desk. 'Also, when? And who has helped you?'

His nostrils flared a little as he spoke the next words.

'Otherwise you will be treated as a spy and shot.'

Leslie, standing still in front of the man's desk, did not speak.

'You were captured in civilian clothes,' the German officer went on. 'And with forged identity papers.' He pointed at Leslie with his pencil. 'You know the rules of war.'

Leslie wearily stated his name, rank, and number. The major

slammed his fist down on the table. But it seemed more like frustration than anger, and his claim that he would treat Leslie as a spy did not show in his eyes.

'I have tried to help you,' he sighed. 'But now you will go to the Gestapo and you'll be a dead man within 48 hours…'

A guard marched Leslie across the courtyard to a different cell. It was empty and large. Leslie tried to whistle to keep up his spirits, but his mouth was dry and when he succeeded, the echo of the half-hearted tune made him feel even more alone. The major's words kept coming back to him.

Two nights later the sky was filled with aircraft and the sound of guns. Leslie listened to the crash of bombs somewhere in the distance. The walls shook and there was the heavy clatter of fragments from the flak on the roof.

Leslie's door was flung open and three guards came in, grabbing him roughly and rushing him out of the building and into a waiting truck. As the RAF pounded the city, the truck sped through the streets towards Saint-Gilles which, in the darkness, looked more like a fortress than a prison. During the First World War the nurse Edith Cavell had been held behind its high walls and grey stone Tudor-style columns. Now its cells held many of the Reich's captured enemies in occupied Belgium. The Canadian was no longer being treated as a POW but as a criminal. From his new cell Leslie could see the interior of a high outside wall. One section was heavily pockmarked with bullet holes.

One of the three men in Leslie's cell was a former Nazi named Tony who had turned against the authorities. Tony spoke English well and explained the prison contained German soldiers awaiting court-martial, Belgians suspected of resistance, and captured airmen. The airmen were quickly sent on to prison camps, Tony said, although there were rumours that some also ended up in 'special treatment camps' across the border in Germany.

As dusk fell Leslie could see that light remained burning in some of the cells. These were the rooms in which those condemned to death were kept, Tony explained. Occasionally three raps echoed along the heating pipes which extended through each cell and Tony would put his mouth close to the pipe and talk in whispers to someone next door. Female voices broke up the night as those in the neighbouring women's wing shouted news of Allied successes which they had learnt from newly-arrived inmates.

The following day a guard looked through the bars of the cell door and asked Leslie to come forward. He was about 50 and smiling. He told Leslie he had been a prisoner of the British in the First World War and that he was happy to meet a Canadian. He leaned closer to the bar and whispered that his sister lived in New Jersey.

'Her daughter, she is also married to an American pilot,' he said, and shrugged, 'Ach, this war.'

Leslie was wary but smiled and made small talk, knowing a friendly guard might be of use in the difficult times to come.

John Bradley and Royce McGillvary

ON JULY 14, JOHN BRADLEY was brought to Saint-Gilles. As the guards were checking him in, he saw Stuart Leslie's name in the register but could not see 'Mac' and wondered what had happened to his friend.

Bradley was put in a cell with three Germans: an officer who had already served six months for giving himself double rations; a deserter who had hoped to be posted to the front in France where he would surrender to the Allies; and a civilian caught stealing army supplies and selling them on the black market. He took an instant dislike to the civilian, an ardent Nazi. On July 20, when news reached the prisoners of Claus von Stauffenberg's attempt on Hitler's life, none of the others spoke to Bradley for 24 hours, instead they mumbled to themselves about Roosevelt, Churchill, Communists and Juden.

Bradley found being incarcerated with his enemies very strange. They believed London had been destroyed by V1 bombs, yet complained of Allied bombings of their cities. They said Hitler would win the war with a secret weapon but outside of their fanatic belief in Hitler, they all seemed normal.

One day when Bradley was getting the clean towel he was permitted once a week, he saw Leslie and grabbed a few words. Neither had seen 'Mac' but both had heard whistling on the wing, which they were sure was him.

As the weeks went by, both men got weaker. The food, usually a carrot mush or a thin soup, tasted foul, and they were only permitted 30 minutes of outdoor exercise every other day at the most.

But after almost three weeks there appeared to be one positive: the Gestapo seemed to have forgotten them.

But that was about to change.

***

Three weeks to the day that Leslie arrived in Saint-Gilles two guards arrived, taking him by the arms. The other prisoners in his cell looked away as he was dragged out. In the courtyard he found two familiar faces, Bradley and McGillvary. There was no sign of Frank Shaw, the Englishman they had been captured with[5].

Seeing the strain and fear on his friends' faces, Leslie realised

---

5   Shaw had, in fact, already been moved on and would spend the rest of the war in Stalag Luft 1, on Germany's Baltic coast. It never made sense to any of them why he had been treated differently.

he must look the same to them. A closed van took them through the streets to Gestapo headquarters in Avenue Louise. But, despite waiting all day with nothing to eat, there was no interrogation, and they were returned to the prison after darkness fell. Two days later the three men were again taken from the prison to the same building. As they sat in a waiting room McGillvary saw prisoners being led down a corridor. Several women, all of whom he guessed were over 50, and some much older, had been badly beaten. One grey-haired older lady had so many bruises on her legs she could barely walk. The airmen also saw a man who was bleeding from the mouth as his teeth had been pulled or knocked out and a priest whose face was swollen and his collar twisted. Nearby there were cells so small you could not sit down in them. A young boy and girl were moved in and out of them all day between interrogations.

But the guards took the airmen not to the basement cells but to a bright, furnished office, where three chairs had been placed in front of a desk. All three sat and waited until the door clicked open and two men came in. Both spoke English and wore Luftwaffe uniforms, although as the day went on the Americans began to doubt that they were Luftwaffe at all.

The lead interrogator was the officer the Saint-Gilles airmen would come to know as Charlie. He had short blond hair, was about 5ft 10in tall, and carried just a few too many pounds to be an airman.

'How do you like your prison?' Charlie asked, apparently expecting an equally friendly response.

The three airmen looked at each other and began to speak in turn, complaining about the way they were being treated.

'We're prisoners of war,' Leslie said, 'and should be treated as such.'

There was a pause and then the second German began to apologise.

'A mistake was made,' he said. 'It will all be changed.'

They would need to be questioned first, he added. But it was just a formality. Charlie asked if they would like to write letters home. It would be permitted if they told them the story of their evasion, he said.

The airmen refused.

'In that case you will be shot as spies.'

Bradley said that would be against international law. There was a new law passed since the war started, Charlie claimed, that you had to tell the story of your evasion. Bradley started laughing and Charlie looked as if he had been caught in a stupid schoolboy lie.

But Leslie sensed in the two men's confidence an arrogant superiority which suggested they knew more than the airmen and they were longing to boast.

Charlie lit a cigarette and began to tell a story which shocked them. He and his colleague, he said, had posed as members of the 'underground' and they had just 'helped' two American airmen by taking them to an address in Brussels.

'They believe they are safe,' he smiled. 'Safe in the hands of the Resistance. We will leave them there for a few days, under observation.'

Charlie said those airmen would talk freely and give away any contacts who had helped them previously and would perhaps chat about their base, their aircraft or their squadron. All information the Gestapo would be delighted to receive.

'After that, they will be transferred to a prison camp.'

The airmen could not help but exchange startled glances. They had been warned in England to be on the look-out for Gestapo or Abwehr men posing as friends, and had heard rumours the Germans were trying to infiltrate the genuine escape lines, but to have it confirmed by the Gestapo themselves and to know there was nothing they could do to warn anyone made their spirits fall.

A BETRAYAL REVEALED

Charlie smiled, knowing that by telling the story he had achieved his aim of breaking the prisoners' confidence, making them doubt even the people who had helped them and – he hoped – raising a doubt that any secrets they held were not worth the pain of withholding.

'You see,' he added dismissively, 'there's very little you could tell us we don't already know.'

What he had described to the three airmen was a major operation in Brussels which would become known as the 'Dog House' – a deception which had already cost many airmen their freedom.

Far from being a shelter, the 'Dog House' was an elaborate trap. A trap laid by one of the most despicable traitors of the war: a man named Prosper Dezitter.

15

THE MAN WITH THE MISSING FINGER

WAS EVER A man more suited to treachery and betrayal than Prosper Dezitter? Born in Passchendaele in September 1893, he was convicted of rape at the age of 19 but fled a three-year prison sentence and escaped to Canada. While living in Winnipeg he was called up for service in the RAF in the final months of the First World War and trained as an observer. Although his service ended in less than 100 days, he later exploited his knowledge of Canada and the air force as a way of putting the Second World War's Allied airmen at ease.

Short – he was about 5ft 6in tall – with a dark complexion and black hair, he was naturally duplicitous and cunning. In 1919, he married an English woman named Lillian Stanbury, signing the marriage register with a list of lies: he stated his name was 'Jack Prosper', described himself as an Anglican – he was a Catholic – and claimed to have been born in Boulogne in France.

For a few years he scraped a living as a private detective before returning to Belgium in the late 1920s, after the statute of limitations on his rape crime had passed. Settling in Antwerp, he opened a car showroom – but the business was a front. He was in fact smuggling cars across the frontier into and out of the Netherlands.

THE MAN WITH THE MISSING FINGER

At some point, while most likely working on a car engine, he was involved in an accident that resulted in the loss of a finger. Those who came across Dezitter would often contradict each other as to which finger and how much of it was missing. An SOE report of May 1944 listed eight different reported variations on the injury, but the intelligence officer who investigated most closely is clear that it was the little finger on his right hand which was missing. The injury earned Dezitter the nickname '*l'homme au doigt coupe*' – 'the man with the cut-off finger'.

His criminal activities continued throughout the 1930s. In May 1935, he was sentenced to three months in prison for forgery – most likely in relation to a fake cheque – and in February 1936 he received a short jail term in Bruges for embezzlement. The same year he was charged with the unlawful import of vehicles and, in 1938, with the use of violence.

Dezitter's wife, Lillian, was no longer on the scene and he married again, this time to Germaine Princen. The second marriage did not last long. Their divorce was finalised in September 1939. By then, Dezitter had found a new and far more dangerous love in his life. This relationship would take them both to the gallows.

He had met Florentina Giralt in 1938, and they had quickly started an affair. The wife of a Brussels-based wine and liqueur merchant, Paul Dings, she was wealthy and well-travelled, having spent time in the Belgian Congo, and used numerous addresses in Brussels. The couple had one son, Serge, who was born in 1930.

Giralt – often known as Flora or Flore – was attractive, quick-witted and as smart and two-faced as Dezitter. She also shared his 'restless disposition'. Her jet-black hair, dark complexion and dark eyes suggested a Mediterranean connection and she had in fact been born in Barcelona on June 20, 1904. Later in the war, when her distinctive appearance became a problem in Brussels, she dyed her hair platinum blonde. She spoke not only her native Spanish but also Flemish, English and some German and was described as a person who 'gains everyone's confidence'.

In early 1940 the Belgian authorities caught up with Dezitter again and he was sentenced to five years in prison for '*escroqueries au mariage*': he had been trying to con wealthy widows out of their money with proposals of marriage.

But, by this time, he had developed a second deadly relationship: with the Nazis. In 1939, he had visited Munich and returned with a job in the Brussels office of the pharmaceutical company, Bayer – which was almost certainly a cover for an intelligence-gathering position with the Abwehr. And, when the Germans established themselves in Brussels, they quickly secured his release from jail. He was – as one of their opposing intelligence agencies in London would later conclude – a 'remarkable organiser' who was 'wonderfully convincing'. He was without morals and loyalty, except to Giralt and money.

In Occupied Belgium he became the perfect agent for Rudolf Kohl, a *Sonderführer* or 'special leader' in the Abwehr, who had also used work with Bayer as a front. A tall man in his mid-30s with wavy dark blond hair and large ears, Kohl was described by one American who came across him as looking like Paul Muni, the star of the gangster film *Scarface*.

Kohl was a multi-lingual chancer, not unlike Dezitter. He was a womanising heavy drinker who could mount up huge debts. Having moved from Cologne to Brussels long before the war, he spoke English, French and Flemish and had developed a wide range of contacts, both through his energetic social life and his 'work' in pharmaceuticals. Running agents under the alias Ralph Van Der Steen, Kohl was based at the offices of Abwehr III C2, a department which specialised in tracking down Allied airmen, clandestine radio operators, and Resistance groups. He was to be Dezitter's 'handler' throughout the occupation.

THE MAN WITH THE MISSING FINGER

In July 1940, Dezitter – who spoke English fluently – arranged the arrest of a number of British soldiers who had been left behind during the Dunkirk evacuation and had been hiding in the dense woods of Flobecq in southern Belgium. He had tricked them by telling them he was a delegate of the British government trying to arrange the repatriation of soldiers. In January 1941, posing as a Canadian, he deceived more soldiers into giving themselves away to the Germans. He was helped by Giralt.

Three months later, a routine check by Belgian police in Schaerbeek caught him in possession of a British passport in the name of Herbert Call. But he was able to get a message to either Kohl or a friendly GFP officer who stepped in and Dezitter was released. He had become so important to the Germans that they decided to give him a pass which stated that 'the bearer could not be arrested or detained whatever the conditions seemed to be'.

Having kept the British passport, it now became part of a changing disguise which would elevate him to near-mythical status. As well as being 'Herbert Call', he had Canadian papers in the name of Williams from Winnipeg, a Swiss identity card, and Belgian identity cards in the names Michel Giralt and Doutrepont, which used the personal details of a dead Belgian airman. During its later investigation into his activities, SOE collected 31 aliases which he was suspected to have used during the war, only five of which it was able to discount.

As he changed his name, he also subtly changed his appearance: dyeing the white streak in his hair brown, wearing glasses of different styles, wearing gloves to hide his lost finger, and growing a black moustache.

As a man for whom betrayal was a way of life, he was deeply suspicious of others. He frequently made appointments which he did not keep, and he moved between at least five different addresses in or around Schaerbeek, a bustling middle-class suburb in the north-east of Brussels. His contacts in the black market of the motor trade ensured that he and his accomplices had a range of different cars to use, including a pre-war Graham-Paige, a chunky 1938 Chevrolet, a V-8 Ford, a Peugeot and a Citroen. To confuse his enemies further, he would spread false word that the real 'Dezitter' was in England, or had been arrested, or was even dead.

In May 1941, Dezitter found himself in Saint-Gilles prison, where many of his victims would later end up. Word spread around the cellblock that the new man had been arrested by Belgian police, but, within four days, he had disappeared. He had been sent into the prison as a stool pigeon for the Gestapo to listen to prisoners incriminate themselves or others.

Soon after, he began to pose as a Canadian captain, hoping to help English airmen and Belgian *résistants* to escape to England. In August 1941, he visited a family hiding a British airman; a short while later they were arrested and the husband shot. To add insult to injury, very often on these visits to betray patriots, Dezitter wore the lapel badge of the *Confédération des Fraternelles d'Après-Guerre* (COFAG), a Belgian veterans' organisation.

By May 1942, he had moved to Uccle in the south of Brussels and was using the name George Thomas. He told people he was a South American and, to account for any time he was seen in the company of the occupier, claimed to be working as an interpreter for the Germans.

Dezitter's team now included the pince-nez-wearing Jean-Marcel Nootens, a ginger-haired man in his mid-40s with a small moustache who used the names Marcel and Albert among others. A taxi driver before the war, he would often drive for Dezitter and would also accompany airmen as a 'guide'. Nootens recruited his friend, Charles Jenart, who pretended to be either an English officer or a French colonel, depending on who he was trying to fool. A heavy drinker with conjunctivitis, a bloated face and bloodshot eyes, Jenart had a number of mistresses and was frequently seen out in the city's bars and cafés. Nootens and Jenart also added a new element to Dezitter's operation by tricking Jews, who were fearful of the growing numbers of round-ups in Brussels, into travelling with a fake helper from the Gare du Nord to Bordeaux, where they were arrested.

During the summer of 1942, Dezitter opened a new operation in the east of the city, using a three-storey apartment building with a convenient basement garage in Woluwe-Saint-Lambert. This became a fake safehouse for supporters of the *Armée Secrète*, the MNB, *Groupe G*, and the evasion lines. Some of the victims came to the building via genuine escape organisations, most likely routed to Dezitter via Kohl whose Abwehr colleagues were running a successful counter-espionage operation in the Netherlands. He then extended this trap to include his own 'evasion line' to Paris and beyond, using Giralt and the others. It was generally easy to dupe Allied airmen who were desperate for help, could not speak the local languages, and were still disorientated at being shot down and suddenly finding themselves in occupied territory. If help was offered, they had no choice but to take it. They had no reason to doubt an Englishman or Canadian calling himself Captain Jackson.

The building was large enough to house up to a dozen evaders but, to maintain his security and cover in Brussels, Dezitter would not hand them over to the Germans until they reached Paris or Bordeaux, where a safehouse would be 'unexpectedly' raided or the airmen would be picked up by a pre-arranged street control. Genuine helpers back in Brussels would be unaware the men had been betrayed or even captured.

In fact, as a 32-year-old RAF Warrant Officer named Eric Weare witnessed, Dezitter and Giralt came up with another way to ensure genuine helpers trusted the house in Woluwe-Saint-Lambert. In July 1943, Weare was among more than a dozen airmen and several civilians sheltered by 'the Captain' and his 'secretary'. And, when Weare and six others were taken by Dezitter on a train to Paris, they were 'asked to write a note of thanks to our hosts in Brussels'. These notes would become standard practice in Dezitter's deceit, falsely assuring the genuine helpers from EVA and the Comet Line that they had passed their charges into good hands. At a small hotel near the Gare du Nord, Weare and the others were told to go to their rooms for a wash before travelling on to Bordeaux. Gestapo officers then came to their rooms and arrested them all.

But Dezitter was also in danger himself. When his agents rang or sent their coded telegrams to Brussels to give information about the numbers of airmen or underground agents to be collected from the various safehouses, the person they dealt with was an Estonian-born nurse in her late 30s called Annie Lalle.

The tall, blond Lalle had met Florentina Giralt in January 1943. They were about the same age and both knew what it was like to be foreigners in another country; they struck up a friendship. Lalle lived in a small apartment in Etterbeek, which belonged to her Swiss fiancé who was stuck in his homeland for the duration of the war, and she was taking in sewing to supplement her nursing salary. Giralt saw this as an opportunity. She suggested to Lalle that her 'Resistance friend', Dezitter, could pay Lalle to use the apartment for meetings and for her to take messages. Lalle agreed. Giralt arranged for Lalle to have a telephone.

Lalle's true loyalties are now hard to ascertain. Although she was having an affair with a junior Abwehr officer, it is unclear if she felt any commitment to the Nazi cause. Dezitter later said she was 'simply an innocent… a spectator to events'. But she had become suspicious.

In September, Lalle received a telephone call from Father Jean Derèse, a priest and patriot who was hiding a number of airmen. Derèse had grown impatient at the length of time it was taking for Dezitter's 'line' to take his group on its onward journey. Lalle warned him that Dezitter might not be what he claimed to be, and the priest and his charges escaped into a camp in the Ardennes. Frightened, she then contacted a friend in the civil service at Schaerbeek and managed to get a Swiss passport in her name, indicating she was hoping to escape.

When Dezitter discovered Lalle's treachery he sent a man to kill her. Lalle was found murdered in her flat on September 29, 1943. She had been stabbed 22 times in the chest.

For continuity with some of their contacts – and so as not to raise suspicion – Giralt now sometimes took on the alias of Annie Lalle and Dezitter's ruthlessness ensured that his own treachery continued.

***

In London, the Belgian *Sûreté*, MI5, MI6 and SOE had been receiving vague reports about a 'Belgian Quisling' (a traitor) for some time.

The first hints go back to October 1941, when the *Sûreté* was informed about a 'Canadian captain' with parts of a finger missing trying to contact as many people as he could in all social circles and then giving them away to the Germans. 'Is a very bad and dangerous man who is likely in the pay of the Germans,' it noted. That December, a former Belgian soldier reached London with stories of a 'de Zitter' who was offering to smuggle out refugees but then denouncing them to the Germans.

Then, in April or early May 1943, an underground newspaper, *Le Patriote*, described a 'Gestapo agent who, posing alternatively as a British parachutist and a British soldier, asked Belgians to assist him [but later] denounced them to the Germans.' The newspaper named the traitor as 'De Zitter' and reported he had also been using the name 'Billy Franck' and was of Canadian origin. It said he had been working in the Dinant district, south of Namur, and at Huy. *Le Patriote* added: 'Belgians, be careful, and remember that this person can easily be identified, since the third finger of his left hand [sic] is mutilated.'

The newspaper's report was picked up by *News from Belgium and the Belgian Congo* which reproduced it on May 8, and was seen by MI5, which contacted the British Security Co-ordination – a branch of MI6 in New York – and the Royal Canadian Mounted Police, which went through its records and reported that Dezitter was not Canadian but had lived there for 'some considerable time'.

On August 13, 1943, a British intelligence report suggested that SOE should liquidate Dezitter. 'It is quite certain that the death of De Zitter [sic] would be a most desirable conclusion to his career,' the officer noted drily. Consequently, it was decided that Dezitter made an ideal candidate for a proposed 'rat week' being organised by Major Hardy Amies, the former fashion designer who was now head of SOE's Belgian section.

In November, MI6 reported that Dezitter had been liquidated but MI5 stepped in to say that was incorrect. It stated that the assassination had not taken place on the advice of 'the Belgians'. The Belgian intelligence service in London consisted of two main organisations – the civilian *Sûreté* and the military *Deuxième Section* – a relationship often characterised by confusion and rivalry. They could not decide on a strategy for dealing with Dezitter and, understandably, were worried about reprisals against the civilian population – although, when the *Sûreté* confirmed that it had blocked 'rat week', it said it did so as it was 'opposed to liquidating a man without trial'. It told the British that if Dezitter was 'as bad as he is painted' then the Resistance groups would mark him as a target. Indeed, in practice, despite all the discussion in London during late 1943, only the Resistance would have had the capability to track down Dezitter: no one in London could even be sure of where he lived or any of the addresses he was currently operating from.

An attempt was made to find Dezitter. Dutch SOE agent Christiaan Lindemans – who was later turned by the Abwehr after the arrest of his pregnant wife and was to give away details of the Allies' Operation Market Garden – claimed to have been ordered by a member of the Dutch Resistance to identify and kill 'Captain Jackson/Dezitter', but nothing came of it. Dezitter's aliases, his numerous addresses, and his use of different cars helped protect him. And, as SOE itself noted, bringing him to justice was doubly hard for the Resistance, whose members were themselves living clandestine lives and 'could not openly pursue the hunt'.

However, on November 11, 1943, the resistance did act. Photographs and descriptions of Dezitter and Giralt were published in the underground newspaper *La Voix des Patriotes* under the headline, *Un Couple De Salopards* – 'A couple of bastards'.

The article, which identified the address at Avenue AJ Slegers, forced Dezitter to go to ground. He left the building in Woluwe-St-Lambert, ditched some old associates, and urged others to change their names.

Over the winter of 1943, he and his Abwehr handler, Rudolf Kohl, discussed a new plan.

They abandoned the fake evasion route to Paris and rented a house at 16 Rue Forestière – the address which would become known as the 'Dog House'.

Dezitter's treachery was only just beginning.

When Dezitter began an affair with his co-conspirator Florentine Giralt in 1939, the Spanish-born Giralt had kept a secret from both him and her then husband: she was also in a sexual relationship with Russian-born Vania Gristchenko, who was exiled from his motherland after the Revolution and had been working as a singer and musician in Brussels to pay his way through the dark economic years of the 1930s.

The affair had ended but Gristchenko – also known as Jean – remained friends with Dezitter and Giralt. Now 40 years old but always in need of money, and having undergone an operation in hospital in December 1943, Gristchenko was delighted when Dezitter offered him the chance to work for his organisation.

Acting on Dezitter's instructions and using money provided by the Germans, Gristchenko hired the large townhouse at 16 Rue Forestière in Ixelles, and Giralt and her son Serge moved in. The Russian also brought in two friends, Nicolas Fetissoff, and his wife Suzanne Bertherand, who had also fled Russia after the Revolution and were well-known in the White Russian community in Brussels. Both had already done some work for the Germans but had recently lost full-time jobs; from now on they would receive a salary from Rudolf Kohl.

German-speaking Fetissoff – dark hair, large build, aged 38 – replaced Jenart and Nootens as courier and driver. French-born Bertherand – blonde, aged 34 – would act as a courier, too, and in her role as German agent, tell genuine members of the underground that her name was 'Claire'. The couple's son, Alexis, born in 1936, also came to live at the Rue Forestière.

Number 16 also became home to a number of pets, with a large and aggressive German shepherd leading a pack of four dogs. For this reason, and with dark humour, the airmen who would be trapped there named the building the 'Dog House'.

During the summer of 1944 it would become a finely laid trap for a succession of young fliers who believed they had survived months of danger and felt the freedom promised by liberation was in their grasp.

16

THE 'DOG HOUSE'

William Ryckman and Wallis Cozzens

WILLIAM RYCKMAN AND Wallis Cozzens, navigator and bombardier from the Carpetbaggers' crew, walked by night and hid by day, with Ryckman nursing injuries to his knee and back which he had picked up on landing.

Knowing they needed help, the two men – both 23 – plucked up the courage to approach a man on the edge of the village of Grotenberge, about six miles from where they had come down while attempting to drop supplies to the Resistance. The man's name was Remi Diependaele and, although not a member of a formal evasion line, he had helped an airman before. Diependaele allowed the two men to stay with him for 22 days while friends attempted to get in touch with someone else who could help. Ryckman used 2,000 francs from his escape kit to help their hosts pay for the extra food.

A man eventually came to the house, bringing ration coupons, fake identity cards and a questionnaire which the Americans hesitated to fill in. The questionnaire was designed to get information which the Resistance could use to check the airmen were genuine. The airmen were afraid they were giving away sensitive information to strangers, but they also understood what risks the Belgian Resistance were taking and wanted to do all they could to help.

The Belgians were satisfied that the airmen were who they said they were and, on June 20, another man – who said his name was George de Vrieste – walked them a couple of miles down a country road to his farmhouse in Herzele. On the eighth day there, de Vrieste came to them in a panic – the Germans were raiding the village. Fleeing to a nearby field of grain, the two Americans could hear trucks but saw no one come to the farmhouse. The Germans had received information about the men but had gone to the wrong farm, about half mile away, where there was a family with the same surname. It was too dangerous to return to the farm in case the Germans realised their mistake, so after dark de Vrieste took them a mile down the road to Woubrechtegem and the home of Bertha Dubasters, whose husband was a prisoner of war. Bertha volunteered to help Allied airmen despite also having to bring up two children alone. Over cigarettes, she told them she had been born in Long Beach, California.

During their week with Bertha, both airmen not only fell a little in love with her, but they were also filled with admiration: she had been helping the Allies since 1940, when she hid British soldiers trapped after the evacuation from Dunkirk.

She said she knew of a contact from those days – a man in Brussels. She would try to reach him. She travelled to Brussels and the airmen waited anxiously for her return. When she came back, she said she had found him and that he would help them.

On July 4, Bertha brought bicycles for Ryckman and Cozzens and the three of them cycled the 20-minute ride to Aspelare, where Bertha's mother ran a small grocery store. Joined by a local Resistance leader called Arsene Prieels, the group spent the night at the store and before dawn broke the next day, headed to Ninove, close to where the airmen had been shot down.

From the small railway station, they caught a train and arrived in Brussels before 7am. They then walked to Prieels' sister's apartment.

THE 'DOG HOUSE'

Bertha had travelled with them because she was worried, but finding that they were safe in the apartment, she hugged the two Americans and left. Prieels told the men to make themselves at home and that the other apartments on the floor were empty.

Later that day, Arsene's sister, Elvire Willemsen, returned home carrying a basket full of food and quickly set about making them all a meal. Over the next few days they were kept well-supplied by a short man with curly red hair who introduced himself as Emile and said he ran a bar in a square nearby. He spoke English and peered at the men through thick glasses as he laid out food and liquor for them. Emile said Prieels had helped about 60 aviators before. Another visitor was Germaine Lahaye, who said she had worked with a number of liberal politicians in France before the war. Germaine and Elvire found the airmen's scruffy appearance amusing and had their hairdresser visit the apartment. When the hairdresser realised with horror he was working on two evading airmen, he threw his hands in the air. But he gave them a good cut and the men began to feel safer by the day.

Although Prieels had initially told them that they would possibly have to wait in the apartment until the Allied invasion of Belgium, one day he said that he had been told it was possible to smuggle them into Switzerland by car using someone who had worked at the Belgian consulate before the war. Prieels and Lahaye were unsure about the plan, as none of the story seemed to make any sense to them.

But the temptation of finding a way to move the two airmen on towards freedom proved too great.

They were about to hand the Americans to Dezitter.

* * *

A dark-haired woman arrived at the apartment to assess Ryckman and Cozzens and returned for a second time on July 14. She waited in silence until there was another knock at the door and a tall thin man of about 40 with a small moustache and dark silky hair came in. He told the Americans he had not been able to check security on the evasion line, but an airman named Bill Sink, of Dayton, Ohio, had travelled down it only a few days earlier. They had not received a message yet from Sink to say that he was in Switzerland, as it was too early, but they were sure he was safe.

Arsene and Elvire bought extra food and drink, and as they held a farewell party, the brother and sister gave the airmen jewellery. Then the thin man with the moustache, who had taken charge, asked for the airmen's silk maps. It was time to go.

Arsene told the men that, when they got home to Britain, they should ask the BBC to play a personal message on the radio to signal that they were safe.

'The sun will not shine tomorrow,' he suggested.

The visitor offered: 'The two babes are safe.'

The dark-haired woman walked the airmen three or four blocks through the city and on a street corner, passed them to a light-haired woman of about 30.

Told not to speak in case they were overheard talking English, the two Americans nudged and whispered to each other now: they had noticed two thickset men following them from the pavement outside the apartment.

Just then, a pre-war supercharged Graham-Paige car pulled up and the woman urged them to get in. At the wheel a grey-haired man with glasses and a thick moustache waited, drumming his fingers on the steering wheel. Ryckman noticed a finger missing from his right hand.

It was Prosper Dezitter. The Resistance had delivered the pair – and before them, Bill Sink – into his hands. Sink was, in fact, already on his way to Stalag Luft 4 in Poland.

THE 'DOG HOUSE'

The woman with them was Dezitter's accomplice, Suzanne Bertherand, who urged the two men who had been following to get into other seats.

Dezitter drove very quickly for 10 or 15 minutes before pulling up in a side street and the airmen were led through the front door of a house. To the left there were three steps going down to a living room which was below street level. Beyond, through French doors, was a kitchen which opened onto a raised patio, closed off by a large fence.

Dezitter led them up a marble staircase to two large rooms separated by a thick curtain. Ryckman wandered to the window and looked into the street. It was quiet.

As Ryckman and Cozzens waited they heard the Graham-Paige start up again and drive off. It returned and left again a number of times. The house was busy. The two Americans were introduced to a tall thin man who they dubbed 'the Russian'. He did not speak English and, although heavily bearded, could not disguise the skin disease on his cheeks. This was Betherand's husband, Nicolas Fetissoff. The 'head' of the house seemed to be the dark-haired woman who was introduced to them as 'Jacqueline Winter'. Both men found 'Jacqueline' very attractive. It was Dezitter's mistress, Florentina Giralt. There was also a servant girl who did all the cooking.

Dezitter told the airmen that he and 'Jacqueline' often went out to the countryside to arrange receptions for drops of supplies and agents. He said he had visited the United States and joked, 'I know Canada well enough to make Canadians believe I'm Canadian.'

He also claimed to work for British intelligence.

'To the British I joke that only America and Russia will come out of the war victorious,' he laughed. 'But to Americans I say it will be the British and Russians.'

As he talked, he stroked the German shepherd that sat at his side.

Late in the evening on July 17, the two airmen were told they were to be taken to France and then onto the Swiss frontier by car. Both felt excitement, trepidation, and still suspicion. At 3am the following morning, they were awoken from their light sleep by a very tall blond man who smoked Lucky Strike cigarettes.

They were driven a short distance to a garage in an alleyway, where half a dozen men in civilian clothes waited. One of the men waved Ryckman and Cozzens into a yard where there were garden chairs and tables and a glass conservatory or porch at the back of a building.

Their leader casually poured them a glass of cognac and asked them which state they were from. Another clapped Cozzens on the shoulder. 'When will the war be over?' he asked in accented English.

Cozzens shrugged. 'By Christmas.'

The first man asked Ryckman what he thought about the Russians and asked if there were many communists in America.

'Eventually,' he said, 'the Russians will be in Western Europe and America will have to go to war with them.'

One of the group pulled up a chair by Cozzens and said: 'What kind of plane do you fly?'

Forms – printed on thin tissue-like paper and headed *Front l'Indépendance* with a list of questions in French – were brought out. At first Ryckman and Cozzens filled in only their name, rank and serial number, but the leader said they had to be sure the airmen were genuine Americans, so the airmen filled in more of the form, leaving blank their unit, their base and the name of their CO.

There was chatter among the others now: one said the airmen would go on to Switzerland as planned; but another talked about taking a boat from Holland all the way to Spain. The leader said they would be taken to another address for the night and would leave the next morning.

Another car, a 1936 Dodge, pulled into the alleyway. The airmen and five of the group got in and drove through the night streets to a large building, where they climbed a wide staircase to the third floor.

A door opened and the airmen were pushed into a room where they looked up to see two large photographs: one of Adolf Hitler, the other of Hermann Goering.

Cozzens turned and grabbed one of their captors by the lapels.

The leader, who had previously drunk cognac with them, shouted: 'Sit down!'

It was Dezitter's boss, *Sonderführer* Rudolf Kohl.

Ryckman and Cozzens felt their shoulders slump, completely dejected. After everything, that nagging fear that they might be betrayed had become a cold reality.

Within moments, the door opened and the interrogator stepped into the room. They couldn't have known but it was the man so many by now called 'Charlie'. He was chatty, pally even, telling them he was from Bremen and had worked in Colombia for a number of years for the York Air Conditioning Company. He said he came back to Germany in 1939 but did not join the Luftwaffe until 1941.

No threats came, just conversational questions, asking Ryckman where he was from.

'California'.

The German smiled. 'I know the Chest Tractor Company; do you?'

The airmen said little, but Charlie kept smiling and very quickly they were marched back to the Dodge and driven to Saint-Gilles prison, where the atmosphere changed.

Stripped down to their underwear and searched, an angry German NCO asked them the date they were shot down and what had happened to them since?

They showed him their dog-tags, but he waved them away.

'If you cannot say what you've been doing then it must be espionage,' he said.

They were taken to separate cells and the doors slammed behind them.

17

NO PLACE OF SAFETY

Groupe G

AWARE THAT SOME of his countrymen had seen his photograph and description in the underground newspaper, Prosper Dezitter now largely worked behind the scenes. He sent Fetissoff to make collections while another Russian, Ludmilla Wodowosoff, used her hat shop as a letterbox for messages.

Meanwhile, despite the dangers to herself, Dezitter's mistress, Giralt, continued to use her charm to ensnare genuine patriots. When Alice Rutgeerts and Roger Dister, two members of the underground with connections to the French military intelligence agency, the *Deuxième Bureau*, heard Wodowosoff knew of an Allied escape route they asked for a meeting with the organisers. The pair had smuggled an estimated 150 escaped forced labourers out of occupied Belgium and into Switzerland. Rutgeerts, along with Micheline disappeared into the 'Dog House'. When Rutgeerts and Cyprès, and her brother Lucien Mondon, had also been helping to shelter a member of the Dutch resistance named Rudolf Van Veen.

Wodowosoff introduced Rutgeerts to 'Jacqueline', and Van Veen disappeared into the 'Dog House'. When Rutgeerts and Cyprès heard a coded personal message on the BBC that Van Veen was safe in London they were delighted and relieved: here, they believed, was a new and safe escape route to England which their friends in the resistance network, *Groupe G*, might be able to use.

But it was all a trick. The 'BBC' message had been arranged using the Abwehr's *Englandspiel*, its use of captured British radios: it was fake. Van Veen never reached England and was, in fact, in a German jail.

Rutgeerts and Dister were given false identity papers and an apartment in which to hide by Giralt, but this was just a ruse for her and Dezitter to further gain their confidence. When the 'Dog House' was in full swing, Rutgeerts and Dister were taken on a journey to a new 'place of safety' but were arrested at a roadblock pre-arranged by Giralt with Rudolf Kohl.

The faked report of Van Veen's escape – and Rutgeerts and Dister's belief that it was genuine – would have severe consequences.

Gaston Bouillon, who ran a *Groupe G* sector from his hometown of Villers-Saint-Ghislain in the southern province of Hainaut, heard of the Van Veen 'escape'.

Keen to find a means of processing the growing numbers of airmen being protected by the *Groupe G* network, Bouillon contacted Wodowosoff and was invited to a meeting in Brussels with 'Jacqueline Winter' – Giralt. The meeting took place at the offices of a gold and tin mine company, which Giralt knew from her pre-war travels in the Belgian Congo with her husband.

Bouillon demanded Jacqueline organise a message from the BBC which would vouch for her. When she stalled, he was hesitant but still took the risk of sending two airmen to her. On July 3, a P-38 Lightning pilot, Lieutenant Rexford Dettre, from California, who had been on the run for nearly three months, and Captain Richard Scott were passed to Giralt. In rooms at the 'Dog House', she followed her established procedure and asked them to write a letter of thanks to those that had helped them and to say they were safe. When Bouillon later asked Giralt for a written document to state that Dettre and Scott had made it to England, she gave him this letter. They were by then in German hands and on their way to prison camps.

The note reassured Bouillon about 'Jacqueline'. He also checked with someone at the mining company, who vouched for her.

Early in July he invited other heads of *Groupe G* to his home. Between them they covered a 50-mile stretch along the frontier with France. Bouillon told his comrades about Jacqueline's network, and they decided it could be trusted. The underground in a key section of the border had now been deceived into using a false network for the airmen they protected and, over the next four weeks, Fetissoff made a number of journeys to a spot on the road between Givry and Rouveroy, near the border with France, to collect airmen.

US pilots Lieutenants Charles Quirk and George Campbell and sergeant gunners Thomas McQueen, Donald Pierce, Charles Hillis and Donald Swanson had been part of an experienced crew of a B-24 Liberator which had been struck by flak on a raid on Munich on July 12. The aircraft made it as far as Mons before the crew was forced to bale out. While two others from the crew were protected by agents of the Comet Line, this group was helped by various members of *Groupe G* in Bouillon's area. Over the next month all were collected by Dezitter's fake line and brought to the 'Dog House', with Swanson the last to discover he had been tricked on August 12.

Giralt had Hillis and Quirk write reassuring letters to their helpers in *Groupe G*. Charles Hillis wrote his to Irma Caldow, a *Groupe G* guide.

'Just a line to let you know things have gone well. So far too good to be true, as a matter of fact. I want to say to you, thanks again for all you people have done for me. Honestly, I don't know how I'll ever be able to thank you ... Until next time. So long Irma.'

Quirk wrote: 'Everything is going well. I should be on the final leg soon. I can never find words to thank you ...'

A week after Quirk's Liberator was shot down, a Lancaster with a mixed crew of New Zealanders, Canadians and British came down in the same area after being jumped by a night-fighter. Bomb aimer William Cunningham, a 22-year-old accountant from Toronto; wireless operator Joseph Murphy, a 21-year-old farmer from North Island, New Zealand; and 19-year-old tailor's apprentice Bill Mason, from Yorkshire, all independently managed to find help.

Cunningham and Murphy were both sheltered by local *Groupe G* resisters who remained convinced of the safety of the line run by Giralt. They were picked up on different days on the roadside near Givry by Fetissoff and found themselves reunited at the 'Dog House'. They were well-treated, and Cunningham did not mind when asked to write to tell his helper, also Irma, to say he was safe.

However, they became suspicious when they were asked to fill in a form asking for military details such as squadron and targets. It was then their helpers revealed themselves as Luftwaffe police and they were sent to Saint-Gilles.

Their tail-gunner Bill Mason found himself in the hands of a different branch of the underground, the *Armée Secrète* at Mons. For the time being, he was safe from Dezitter and Giralt.

Meanwhile, Fetissoff remained busy, working with a 32-year-old Belgium-born Abwehr spy named Robert Boen who was now posing as a Resistance worker in Diest, north-east of Brussels. He had befriended a local network of people who were assisting airmen in the city and suggested they use his friend 'Jacqueline'. They were grateful, as they had five airmen whom they did not know what to do with.

On June 22, Fetissoff arrived in Diest to meet Ottawa-born Flying Officer William Elliott and Sergeant Maurice Muir, from Beeston, England, the co-pilot and flight engineer on a Halifax from 424 Squadron which had been shot down by a night-fighter over Leopoldsburg just over three weeks earlier. The pair were taken on bicycles by a genuine helper to a rendezvous point on the roadside and collected by Fetissoff and taken to the 'Dog House'. It was not until July 3 they were told they were being smuggled into France. They were driven to the building with the glass conservatory and offered cognac. Their photographs were taken, and they were asked to show their forged Belgian papers and to answer questions about their squadron and crew. Then the four men at the house drew revolvers, marched them to another car and took them to Gestapo headquarters in the Avenue Louise.

Lieutenant William Baer arrived at the 'Dog House' a few days later, followed by two men from a Liberator crew who had been helped by the same civilians who had helped him. Staff Sergeant Cecil Spence, a factory worker from Michigan, and Technical Sergeant Ken Holcomb, an office worker from Illinois who had been a top turret gunner and radio operator – had come down in northern Belgium on July 20 when their Liberator encountered engine trouble. Fetissoff collected them on August 14 and brought them to the 'Dog House', where they stayed for three days before they were delivered to Kohl and they realised they had been tricked.

Baer was transported out of Belgium and sent to Stalag Luft 3, while the others awaited their fate in Saint-Gilles prison.

Sadly, British intelligence was completely in the dark about Dezitter's new operation at the 'Dog House'.

For almost three years London had been receiving such confusing and conflicting reports from occupied Belgium that it had come to view Dezitter as a near mythical figure. At one point, SOE had briefed Special Branch to investigate whether Dezitter was running agents in London and, at least twice, MI6 investigated whether Dezitter had actually come to Britain as a spy. The wild stories which Dezitter himself passed around the underground in Belgium added to the confusion. At least one agent in Belgium began to believe Dezitter was 'a fiction of German counter-espionage'. Members of his group, which had been betrayed by Dezitter, told ever-wilder stories, for instance, that Dezitter slept in a coffin and he never undressed. The agent found the 'rumour' of Dezitter's missing finger a little too much like the 'sinister villain' of John Buchan's *The Thirty-Nine Steps* to be true. The only reliable information that London had on Dezitter remained the article in *La Voix des Patriotes* in November 1943, which had printed his name, description and photograph, and so, several months on from the proposed 'rat week' in which Dezitter was to be assassinated, SOE knew very little more about the man with the missing finger.

In fact, the damage Dezitter had inflicted on both the Resistance and London's operations over the past year and a half was huge. Posing as a British officer he spent months gaining the confidence of members of the resistance group, *Corps Franc Belge*, which resulted in mass arrests. Among those captured in April 1943 was Charles Claser, codename 'Bull', a regular Belgian army officer charged with organising the Resistance to attack German observation posts near the Belgian coast as well as telephone and wireless systems. Claser had been arrested previously, then released to be observed by the Abwehr and the undercover Dezitter. After giving himself and the information away he was rearrested.

Dezitter's work on Claser also helped ensnare Colonel Jules Bastin, Claser's boss and the head of all underground military personnel in Belgium. Senior members of the Belgian Resistance organised a meeting in Liège, unaware that the 'British officer' working with them was Dezitter. Bastin – who, during World War One, had become something of a legend after making nine attempts to escape from a POW camp and succeeding on the tenth – was uneasy and hesitated to attend. He arrived late and alone and was barely in the door when the Gestapo burst in, firing submachine guns indiscriminately. Wounded, Bastin almost managed to talk himself out of incarceration by persuading the Germans he was there to discuss how to stop the Communists seizing power. He had been so unsure about the meeting he had typed up a fake agenda and had the document in his pocket. William Ugeux, of the Belgian *Sûreté*, held Dezitter responsible for Bastin's arrest.

Dezitter's web also ensnared British agents. SOE liaison agent Edmund Marechal, codename 'Labrador', and his wireless operator JP Janssens, 'Calf', had been in Belgium since January 1943. While working to organise a Resistance network, they met some genuine Canadian airmen and promised to get them help. They made the mistake of not only delivering the airmen to the Dezitter 'line' but doing so personally. Both SOE men were arrested, as were other members of their network.

Frederic Wampach was a Belgian soldier who had escaped to England when Belgium surrendered in 1940 and volunteered for SOE. Trained as a wireless operator and given the codename 'Vermilion', he had been dropped into France, where he was arrested in March 1942. But, after a year in a French jail, he had escaped with the help of fellow Gaullist inmates and a sympathetic warder. It was by then May 1943 and Wampach had not seen his wife in Belgium for three years. He could not resist travelling home for a brief reunion.

Having seen her, he needed to get back to England and sought help from an escape line: unfortunately, it was Dezitter's. Giralt persuaded him to stay at the building in Woluwe-St-Lambert with a party of fellow escapers waiting to be taken to Spain. In September 1943, all were arrested. Wampach was shot on December 10, 1943, at the Tir National – the former Belgian Army shooting range in Schaerbeek which was used by the Germans for executions.

In the end, detailed intelligence on Dezitter was to come from another of his victims. During 1942 the success and expansion of the leading genuine evasion network for Allied airmen, the Comet Line – named because of the speed with which it guided airmen to

Spain – made it vulnerable to infiltration by the Germans and their network of informers. Prime among these was Jacques Desoubrie, a loyal Nazi, who gained genuine helpers' trust very quickly because he appeared to have found a way to smuggle large numbers of people across the Belgium-France frontier. He infiltrated the line twice, first using the name 'Jean Masson' and then 'Pierre Boulain'. Both times he organised mass arrests and brought the organisation to its knees. He even gained the trust of Frédéric de Jongh, whose daughter Andrée had founded the Comet Line, and helped deliver him to the Germans.

Born in 1922, Desoubrie was less than half the age of Dezitter and was motivated by ideology rather than money. He nonetheless knew Dezitter and was described by one source as an 'intimate friend'. The pair had shared information and intelligence about the Comet Line, and Dezitter's team targeted it in Brussels.

On May 6, 1942, 40-year-old Henri 'Miche' Michelli, who ran a network of safehouses for Comet, held a secret meeting at his home in Rue Stévin to decide the next stage in the evasion of six airmen and two Belgian wireless operators, Edouard Van Hooff and Marcel Thonus. The group had been brought to the house by Charles Morelle, a former French soldier who had supported Andrée de Jongh in the months she worked to develop the line. Morelle planned to guide the evaders into France.

Also in Michelli's house was Gérard 'Brichamart' Waucquez, who had recently returned from London by parachute, Anne-Marie Roberts – Michelli's helper – and a new face, a recent volunteer who had been brought along by Madame Roberts. It was Florentina Giralt.

Everyone at the meeting was arrested soon afterwards by the GFP.

Firefighter Eugène Mayne was identified by the Gestapo as a member of the underground in August 1942 but managed to evade capture in Brussels for almost a year until, with many of his Comet friends compromised or arrested, he sought the help of another escape line. It was the one run by 'Captain Jackson'. Mayne was arrested and deported to Buchenwald and Belsen, where he died shortly after the camp was liberated.

But Michou Dumon, the 23-year-old Comet Line courier who had survived the arrest of her parents and sister, had become a key figure in rebuilding the organisation after a swathe of arrests. And she was on the trail of a traitor.

In March 1944 she talked her way out of a French police cell after being arrested in Paris and, on returning to Brussels, was told that the man who had betrayed her had been identified as 'Pierre Boulain'. Dumon had met Boulain back in February at a Comet Line meeting in Paris. He had told her he was a medical student from a farm near Charleroi and that he had already helped about 30 airmen to safety. But there had been something familiar about him and, after investigation, she realised they had met before and that at that time he had called himself 'Jean Masson'.

On May 8, Michou was back in Paris to arrange the passing of six airmen between couriers. At a meeting at Gare St Lazare the other courier, Mr Gilbert, arrived with another man: she recognised him immediately as Boulain/Masson.

A shocked Michou acted as if nothing was wrong, but, as soon as she was away, she had the exchange of airmen called off.

The next day Michou had one of her agents follow Gilbert and she saw him meet at St Lazare station with two other men. One was the man she knew as Boulain/Masson – in reality, Jacques Desoubrie.

The other was Prosper Dezitter. Michou knew Dezitter. Her father, Eugène, had been suspicious of Dezitter since late in 1940 when, under the name Call, he appeared to have betrayed a number of British soldiers. Later the Dumons realised Dezitter was using two Englishmen as agents provocateurs to ensnare their friends in the underground.

The Resistance in Paris arranged to kill 'Masson' – although tragically they were to kill the wrong person – but Dezitter disappeared back to Brussels.

Compromised – and having lived by her wits and on luck for so long – Michou used her own escape line to get to Spain.

By the end of June 1944, she was at MI5 in London telling them all about 'the most dangerous traitor at large' – Prosper Dezitter.

18

'CAWN'T MISS'

JH Singleton, James Levey, William Muse, Harry Blair

IN BELGIUM WORD of the new evasion line continued to spread and put more resisters and airmen in danger.

In Tournai, doctor's wife Gilberte Watteau-Picard needed support for the airmen she was housing with the help of her local commander, Simone Ghisdal, and priest Father Georges Dropsy, a veteran of the First World War and a former member of another evasion network, the Pat Line.

Watteau-Picard was a well-dressed blonde woman who always smelt heavily of her perfume and spoke excellent English. A key member of the local *Armée Secrète*, she knew Micheline Cyprès. Cyprès's friends Alice Rutgeerts and Roger Dister, had been tricked by Giralt. Cyprès still thought the Dezitter 'line' was genuine and told Watteau-Picard about it.

Watteau-Picard was suspicious at first but Dropsy, who was himself in hiding from the Germans, told her they desperately needed support. They decided they must trust the line.

That decision exposed the *Armée Secrète* in Tournai, which although set up as a sabotage and armed resistance group, had become a lifeline for Allied airmen during the summer of 1944. John Singleton was one such airman.

A 23-year-old who had grown up in poverty in rural Florida, his family worked as fruit-pickers. They had no money and did not know anybody with any. They had been through the Depression and still felt they were living in it. The war had not changed their circumstances much. Life was hard and, although Singleton had found work as a car mechanic, he had to supplement his work by picking strawberries too: leaving him with a lifelong hatred of the fruit.

Thoughts of home were now particularly painful: he knew his parents had been hit hard by the death of his younger brother, Virlan, who died when he had fallen off a fruit truck on Christmas Day 1943. The family had been out picking oranges – some for their own dinner and a few boxes which they could sell for three dollars each.

Singleton was named after his dad, John Henry Singleton, but he was known to everyone as JH. His mom, Janie, was the daughter of Baptist preacher, Reverend Charley Chafin, who, as a teenager, had fought in the Civil War and was buried in the cemetery at Cypress Creek. He told JH he had been discharged by General Sherman himself.

JH had escaped into the air force to continue to learn his trade as a mechanic. When war came, he had been sent to train as aircrew. He found himself with 614 Squadron, 401 Group, which arrived in England from Great Falls, Montana, in November 1943 and set up home at Deenethorpe, a base purpose-built for American bombers on farmland near the town of Kettering in Northamptonshire. The longer of its two runways stretched for 2,000 yards but early on, a Flying Fortress had failed to lift off and had careered through a cottage. The crew had escaped from the aircraft and shouted to the locals to run just before the aircraft's bombload exploded.

Singleton's crew was like hundreds of others: guys from all across the States who did not really know why the war had started yet were determined to play their part. Young men like Sergeant Harry Blair, a student from Pittsburgh who was only 19 and 23-year-old Bill Muse, from Laurinburg, North Carolina, in the top turret gun. Only James Levey DFC, the navigator, had any real experience. He was flying his 25th mission – the completion of a tour.

The crew had chosen a name for their Flying Fortress and painted it confidently on the fuselage: 'Cawn't Miss'. They had flown two missions together when, at 7.15am on April 29, 1944, 'Cawn't Miss' cleared the runway at Deenethorpe and headed for Berlin as part of a huge bomber formation. The primary target was the German capital's marshalling yards, but the crews had been told they could drop their deadly cargo on Brandenburg or Magdeburg if the 'opportunity' arose.

Their troubles started somewhere over western Germany when 'Cawn't Miss' developed engine trouble and Singleton had to drop out of the formation and turn for home. It was then attacked by three fighters but, through some incredible flying, Singleton shook them off, then flew on, jettisoning his bombs over Cologne.

They were down to just over 5,000ft and, over Lille, they took flak hits to the wing which took out two engines.

'Cawn't Miss' lumbered on but there was to be no miracle. Six Focke-Wulf 190s came out of the blue sky and fell on the easy prey. A burst of 20mm cannon fire took out Singleton's controls and the ship was suddenly completely ablaze. He gave the order to bale out, but half the crew was already dead.

He, Levey, Muse, Blair, and co-pilot Clarence Barsuk tumbled out into the bright afternoon sky as the B-17 twisted into a dive, its fuselage now a fireball.

Barsuk, a student from Philadelphia, who had only escaped when the B-17 was already in a spin, made an amazing solo evasion.

Dodging a German patrol, he jumped onto a slow-moving train, then walked and cycled for four weeks – at one point stealing a bicycle a German soldier had left outside a café – until he reached Baupaume in France. He survived mainly on raw vegetables taken from fields on which a generation earlier the Battle of the Somme had been fought. As the Allies approached Paris, he made his way to the city and was there to greet them.

The last time 23-year-old Barsuk saw his four comrades they were white parachutes in the blue skies above him. Their story after being shot down would be very different from his.

Singleton, Levey, Muse and Blair came down in fields close to the border between Belgium and France. A member of the *Witte Brigade* called Albert reached Singleton first. He gave the young pilot some civilian clothes and shelter at his home before taking him to a church in Néchin, a Belgian border village. He was interrogated by a doctor and a young priest[6]. They looked through his escape kit and took away the Horlicks tablets, chocolate bar, Benzedrine tablets, water purifying tablets, matches, tape, chewing gum and water bottle. Seemingly satisfied the items were the real thing, the men were joined by the local chief of police. He and Singleton then rode three miles south to the village of Templeuve and stopped in the house belonging to another policeman, Angel Van Leuerck.

Sitting in the policeman's front room was Singleton's top turret gunner, William Muse, an office clerk who had joined up after Pearl Harbor. He revealed his own tale – the same priest had found him hiding in a ditch and taken him to the police chief who brought him here. One of Muse's hands was bandaged up, having been struck by fragments of metal during the attack by the Focke Wulfs.

The two airmen were moved to nearby Blandain on the edge of Tournai and spent three weeks at the home of Edmond de Wolf. On

---

6   Néchin is less than ten miles from Tournai so it is probable that the priest was Father Dropsy.

'CAWN'T MISS'

May 10 Singleton and Muse watched bombers completely destroy the railway station at Tournai, noting that for the next three weeks the Germans struggled to restore any service to the line.

After keeping the airmen for a further five days at a house in the town belonging to Monsieur Daniel, the *Witte Brigade* moved them again, this time to Edgard Guilbert-Merchez's Templeuve home, a redbrick corner house with heavy shutters and a bedroom in the attic. They were brought fake identity cards and enjoyed food and wine from local farms.

Singleton and Muse spent two long months there, spending each day carefully looking out of the attic window and watching the traffic on the road right outside. It was mostly German army vehicles. But, despite the seemingly constant closeness of the enemy, they felt surprisingly safe.

Towards the end of July, they were told plans were being made to take them to Switzerland and somebody would soon arrive for them. The Resistance gave Singleton a message with information about German troop movements which they hoped he would be able to pass to British intelligence.

On August 1, a car pulled up with a blond woman – Gilberte Watteau-Picard, of the local *Armée Secrète* – in the passenger seat. She knocked on the door and gave the password: '*La cerise est une drogue*.' (Cherries are addictive.)

Once inside, she asked to take the identity discs from the two airmen who argued about it and ended up giving her only one of their two dog-tags.

Watteau-Picard's driver had a black moustache and a goatee beard which covered a skin rash. The two airmen quickly dubbed him 'the mad Russian'. It was Fetissoff who Gilberte believed was a genuine member of the underground.

All four got in the car and sped off. They were going to pick up their comrades, Watteau-Picard told them.

Elsewhere, the most experienced member of the 'Cawn't Miss' crew, 25-year-old navigator James Levey, had come down close to a town and was greeted on the ground by a large group of people. Spotting German trucks some distance away, Levey – an athletic director in civilian life – ran and hid in a ditch. He was nursing a wound to his hand, when he heard somebody approaching. A face cautiously looked down at him and then jumped into the ditch beside him. It was a young man who called himself 'Jean'. Despite his fear Levey could not help smiling because on the lapel of his jacket, Jean had a tin badge on which were written the words 'Deputy Sheriff, Texas'. Levey's mind immediately went back to his boyhood games of 'cowboys and Indians', and he realised with a laugh that he was in one heck of a high-stakes game now.

Jean led Levey into the woods and met up with a man who gave the airman his coat to cover his flying suit. They then hurried through the trees to a quiet road where another two men waited with bicycles. They rode through the lanes, one of the men always cycling a little way ahead to watch out for German patrols and checkpoints. At one point two Germans saw them, and they had to ride quickly away.

Eventually, they entered a small and secluded village, and the men left Levey with an elderly spinster who was already hiding four members of a Liberator crew. Levey and the other men waited there a week while Jean went to Liège to try to contact an evasion line. On his return another underground group argued with Jean about what should be done with the men. It was decided that Jean would look after the four men from the Liberator while Levey was taken to Templeuve. Levey was now in the hands of the same network that was helping Singleton.

He was taken to the house of Angel Van Leuerck, where his two friends had been earlier and then to another house on the Rue de Tournai owned by Monsieur Denille. Singleton and Muse were a short distance away and were able to visit each other. Levey was also able to write a note to his tail-gunner, Harry Blair, who was in a safehouse in Roubaix, about 10 miles to the north-east, over the border in France.

A few days into Levey's stay, Sergeant Roy Brown, a 20-year-old Canadian from 425 Squadron, was brought to the house. Brown had parachuted from his Halifax and landed 10 miles to the north of Tournai where local farmers had supplied him with food and clothes. Brown, who had previously been given a Belgian identity card, was now given papers which stated he was Turkish, to help account for his inability to speak French or Flemish.

Levey and Brown were joined by another Canadian, Leon Panzer, a navigator on a Halifax bomber who had been shot down by night-fighters on May 9 while returning from a raid on Haine-Saint-Pierre in Belgium. With a damaged parachute, he only just survived the jump and was lucky to get away with bruises and sprains.

Alone in the darkness, the 28-year-old chartered accountant from Goderich, Toronto – who had graduated only weeks before joining up – felt very far from home. But despite his injuries, he made a break for freedom. Removing all insignia from his uniform and sleeping by the day in haystacks and walking by night, he headed into France. But he found north-western France bristling with German troops and he was advised by a member of the French Resistance to head back to Belgium and find help there. Returning across the border, he had taken refuge in a monastery. The monks had put him in touch with Father Georges Dropsy.

***

On August 1, the car driven by Fetissoff which had just picked up Singleton and Muse arrived to collect Levey, Brown and Panzer.

Gilberte Watteau-Picard left the group there, shaking each man's hand and wishing them luck; she believed they were safe.

Levey, Brown and Panzer got in the car, and it sped off on a two-hour drive to Brussels. At 16 Rue Forestière, they were first introduced to a very attractive woman with dark eyes who said her name was Jacqueline. She, in turn, introduced them to a middle-aged man, 'Georges the chief', who claimed to be Jacqueline's husband. The airmen were told they would eventually be going back to England. Both Giralt and Dezitter were greatly enjoying the deception, but there were signs something wasn't quite right. Singleton noticed Jacqueline's teenage son, Serge, was terribly afraid of 'Georges' and stole from everyone; he was considered by the airmen to be a holy terror.

The next day two other airmen from the Liberator crew were brought to the house by the Russian. Lieutenant George Campbell and Sergeant Donald Pierce – who would later end up in POW camps – were asked, along with the other men to fill in the questionnaire. All refused.

That night 'Jacqueline' suggested writing a letter to all the people who had helped them, to tell them they were well. Taking the paper and pencils, the airmen went to their room to talk. They all wanted to say thanks and let people know they were okay, but they knew that such a letter was a terrible security risk, and they had begun to have suspicions about this house. Each wrote a vague note, mentioning no names and not addressing it to anybody. Their letters would later be received by Gilberte Watteau-Picard who would share them with Edgard Guilbert-Merchez, believing the men were safe.

On August 3, a slim man with thinning blond hair, who told them he was an English colonel – a favourite lie of Dezitter's accomplice Charles Jenart – drove Singleton, Levey, Muse, Brown, and Panzer in two trips to the same alleyway used in the betrayal of Ryckman and Cozzens, and into a garage at the back of the house, where Rudolph Kohl waited. The German intelligence man introduced himself as a professor of languages at Cologne University.

The 'English colonel' said his goodbyes and the five men went inside, where two other men offered them cognac. Everything seemed friendly until the airmen refused to fill in forms giving information about their service, homes, target and evasion, and a violent argument broke out. Kohl – still pretending to be a member of the underground – said if they could not prove who they were he would have to turn them in to the Gestapo. Confused and completely unsure what to do, the airmen gave in and filled out the forms.

Satisfied, Kohl picked up the forms and the airmen were taken to the front of the house where a lorry was waiting, its engine running. As soon as the airmen jumped into the back, they heard the clatter of boots and two German soldiers with machine guns climbed in behind them.

Singleton felt sick with despair and then remembered the written message for British intelligence that he had been given when leaving the home of Edgard Guilbert-Merchez. The note could not only lead to the arrest of members of the Resistance, but it could also give the Germans cause to shoot him as a spy.

Passing his hand across his mouth, he popped the small piece of paper inside and began to chew. By the time they reached their destination, he had swallowed it.

19

DEZITTER'S LAST AIRMEN

Al Sanders, Henry Wolcott, Ted Kleinman

THROUGHOUT 1944 THE Abwehr had grown increasingly at odds with the Nazi hierarchy. Viewed as both a failure and a hotbed of Hitler's opponents, it was completely disbanded after the July 20 assassination attempt on the Führer.

By that time the degradation of Abwehr power in Belgium and the Netherlands had been underway for some months. Its counter-espionage operations were gradually shifting into the control of the intelligence apparatus of the Nazi Party, mainly the office of the *Frontaufklärungskommando* – Front Reconnaissance Command – (FAK) 307, which had been led by Hermann Giskes, an expert in penetrating Allied intelligence operations, since January 1944.

By early August, with the Allies still fighting in Normandy, Dezitter saw no reason to stop his work as long as the Germans kept paying. The fact Dezitter's handler Kohl now reported directly to the Party was a good reason to work even harder for him…

A week after the round-up of the five airmen from Tournai, the time finally came for the two Liberator pilots, Al Sanders, who flew bombing raids, and Henry Wolcott, the 'Carpetbagger' who dropped agents and supplies, to begin their escape to Switzerland.

On August 10, Melchior Resteau, who had been risking his life for the past two months to help them, arrived at their hiding place in the village of Trop, about 15 miles south of Brussels, to say they should start preparing to leave.

Resteau went to a local cemetery for a rendezvous with a short, thin woman in her late 20s, who was looking out across a field and he gave her the code phrase.

'There are not many rabbits this season.'

Introducing herself as 'Anita', she explained that, if he told her where the airmen were, she would collect them the following day. Taking her to the safehouse, he told the airmen she would help get them out of the country and they all shook hands.

The woman was Suzanne Bertherand.

The next day Bertherand and Fetissoff collected the two Americans and headed for Brussels. Fetissoff drove very fast: too fast, they felt, for someone hoping not to be noticed but they assumed he knew what he was doing.

As they came to a roadblock, they held their breath as a German soldier inspected the driver's papers and sent the car to a large building draped in a huge Swastika. Fetissoff went inside, and the Americans waited for an excruciating 45 minutes for his return. Any German soldier wandering past the car, they thought, only had to look inside to guess they were imposters – but none did.

Eventually Fetissoff returned and they drove on, to the 'Dog House' and Dezitter.

Sanders had been given a list of seven evaders Resteau had helped. Dezitter said he wanted the list 'to check against his books', and Sanders saw no reason not to give it to him.

Sensing there was something different about Wolcott, Dezitter asked him who he was, what his mission had been, and who helped him. Wolcott avoided the questions and would only fill out his name, rank and serial number on the questionnaire he was given.

Dezitter lost his patience and, uncharacteristically, his temper, shouting at Wolcott. Wolcott feared they were truly suspicious of him – and without them he was completely helpless. They might even shoot him. He agreed to write out the names of his crew.

Dezitter looked at the form and added: 'What's the name of your base?'

'England,' Wolcott replied.

The 'Dog House' was intensely busy now. Airmen were coming and going every few days. Over the two nights that Sanders and Wolcott stayed there, six more American fliers and two escaped Russian prisoners of war arrived. One of the Americans, 26-year-old Lieutenant Thomas Smith, was a Thunderbolt pilot from Connecticut who had been sheltered by the underground in Hainaut until collected by Bertherand on August 4. The people who had risked their lives to protect him for almost four months thought they were sending him to freedom.

On the third day Sanders, Wolcott and Smith were told it was their turn to go to Switzerland. A short, blonde man arrived and asked them to hand over their identification tags. This was a frightening request, as it could well mean they would be treated as spies and not airmen if they were captured. They did as they were told, having to put their trust in the people helping them. The blond man told them to follow him in silence.

They were led through the streets of Brussels and down an alleyway into a courtyard where the blond man handed the airmen over to a small group of men who were waiting. Their 'guide' turned and left, and the Americans were led inside the glass conservatory – by Kohl.

He gave the airmen forms to fill in and studied their identity cards. These were now no good, he told them in heavily-accented English. They would be given new ones. He had their forms and their fake cards, so he was satisfied. He led them through the building to where a lorry was waiting. There were no uniformed soldiers this time; they still did not know they were in German hands.

The truck hurried through the cobbled streets, lurching with each crunching gear change, before stopping outside a large building. Kohl led them inside, telling them that they would need passports to get to Switzerland. It was an administrative building. Their boots echoed on the floors. What was going on?

He opened a wooden door and all four went inside to see a man sat at a desk. He was wearing a German officer's uniform.

Kohl was now holding a Luger pistol, which he laid calmly on the desk. He smiled.

'I suppose you now know that you are prisoners of the German intelligence,' he said.

The revelation came like a blow to the stomach, but Sanders remained unruffled.

'Perhaps you would like to come with us to Switzerland,' he quipped.

Becoming angry, Kohl shouted at them. Sanders sighed. His bravado was hiding a feeling of devastation. After more than 10 weeks of freedom, his evasion was over.

The airmen were told to strip. Sanders refused and Kohl, smirking, called him a 'wise guy' before he was pushed into the next room at gunpoint and forced to take off his clothes.

All the men's clothes and bags were searched, and everything was taken from them. Questions were fired at them:

'Who are you working for?'

'What are your orders?'

Kohl noted with a wry smile that they had no dog-tags. It was a dark joke, considering the traitors or the Germans themselves had taken them from them. As they had no identity disks, they were told, they could be executed as spies.

Outside, the 'Dog House' kept gathering its victims.

***

JH Singleton's tail-gunner, Harry Blair, was still on the run and taking refuge in a safehouse just over the border in the French city of Roubaix, close to Lille. He had been slowly getting over the injuries he had received when 'Cawnt Miss' had been attacked.

In hiding since the end of April, Blair had been helped by two friends, Gaston Ponzeeles and Ludovic Anceau, who had found a series of apartments in which to hide him. They helped him even though many of their comrades had been arrested and the pair could have been given away at any time. One day Anceau was stopped on the street by a Gestapo agent, and although he was allowed to go on his way, he became certain he was being watched. They moved Blair a few blocks from Anceau's apartment to Ponzeeles'. Dr Delannay, who also helped Singleton, Levey and Brown in their safehouse nearby, visited regularly to make sure Blair was holding up okay – both mentally and physically. Desperate to move the airman on, Ponzeeles made inquiries with his contacts in Tournai.

During his stay, Blair was able to exchange messages with Levey and Singleton, who were then just over the border in Belgium. On August 8, a note arrived at the apartment.

'Your friends have already left,' it read in English. 'You too must set out before August 9.'

It was signed 'your French friend'.

Anceau called the next day and took Blair to the police station in Templeuve. The policeman there – almost certainly Angel Van Leuerck – then took him to the house of Edgard Guilbert-Merchez where his photograph was taken for a new identity card. That night another airman, Sergeant James Wagner, was brought in. Wagner, a 20-year-old tail-gunner from Arlington, Massachusetts, was a veteran of 23 missions and had been evading for almost a month. Unusually among the evaders, he would not qualify for the 'Caterpillar Club', an informal association of people who had had to use a parachute to escape a stricken aircraft. Wagner's pilot, Jack Webber, had managed to put their Liberator – stricken by engine faults and struck by flak on the way back from Munich – down in a field. All of the crew were quickly captured, except Wagner, who found shelter in a convent near Tournai and was helped by a young *résistant* who had recently returned from Normandy where he had been carrying out sabotage attacks.

Blair and Wagner were told there was a plan to take them to Brussels and onto England by plane. On August 15, a car arrived. Of course, it was Fetissoff behind the wheel. This time, there was a strange and terrifying moment on the journey: on the outskirts of Tournai two Germans stepped into the road to stop the car. They opened the door and got inside. Hearing their Russian driver speak to them in German, the airmen had no idea what was going on but the Russian seemed calm.

In Mons the Germans signaled for the car to pull over and they got out. The Russian drove on a little further and then picked up an RAF Lancaster tail-gunner called Bill Mason, from Castleford in Yorkshire, England. Mason had been in the same crew as Cunningham and Murphy, both now already in Saint-Gilles. While *they* had both fallen foul of Dezitter's infiltration of the Resistance network known as *Groupe G*, Mason had been helped by a separate group. But, Dezitter had now infiltrated that group, the *Armée Secrète* of Tournai and Mons, as well.

Once in Brussels, they were driven straight to Rue Forestière. Blair and Wagner stayed in the 'Dog House' for eight days before the 'English colonel' drove them to the house with the glass conservatory. They were offered the traditional cognac before being taken outside to a waiting German military car. They were interrogated and driven to Saint-Gilles, where Blair was reunited with his crewmates Singleton, Levey, and Muse.

Mason spent four days in the 'Dog House', still believing he was being helped, before being taken to the other house. As well as being given the usual questionnaire, he was also asked about the 'effects of the V1' flying bombs on England.

A couple of hours later Mason was in a cell at Saint-Gilles.

***

The five airmen remaining under the protection of the *Armée Secrète* at Tournai, among them John Brown's navigator Ted Kleinman, who had been working with a sabotage unit of the Resistance for months, still believed they were safe.

But Dezitter was about to pick them all up.

So busy was his network now he had to draft in his old driver from the days of his fake Paris line, Jean-Marcel Nootens, to collect them. On August 24, Nootens picked up two airmen who had both been shot down exactly a month earlier when taking part in a day of action involving 1,500 bombers targeting 33 locations in France and Belgium. Sergeant Hugh Bomar – a 20-year-old top turret gunner on a Liberator – and ball-turret gunner Staff Sergeant Ray Smith were waiting for him at a safehouse in Isières, to the east of Tournai. Smith had turned 26 the previous day but there was to be no late birthday present.

He and Bomar began to have their suspicions in the car. Stopping at a garage to repair a flat tyre, an SS officer and two soldiers approached. The airmen watched as they spoke to Nootens out of earshot but did not ask for their papers. Setting off again, Nootens drove so fast people turned to stare. Again, it seemed strange behaviour for someone trying to be inconspicuous.

At the Rue Forestière they were given magazines and Penguin paperbacks – westerns and detective fiction – and told they would be sent to Switzerland by diplomatic car.

The next day, despite rumours that elements of the Free French armies were about to enter Paris, Dezitter's fake line did not let up, scooping up three more airmen. After five months Kleinman's time on the run – including his work as a wireless operator and sabotage support to the Resistance – had come to an end. Fetissoff and Micheline Cyprès, who believed she was helping the airman begin his journey to Switzerland, arrived in the Dodge and they set off for the Belgian capital.

Along the way they collected Halifax bomb aimer Sergeant Nigel Beamish and wireless operator Flight Sergeant Lancelot Bodey, from Mount Gambier, South Australia, who had only escaped a burning Halifax two weeks earlier by the skin of their teeth. In a steep dive they frantically unjammed an escape hatch with seconds to spare. They survived only thanks to the courage of their 21-year-old pilot, Flying Officer Owen MacPhillamy, of the Royal Australian Air Force, who held the aircraft steady enough for them to escape, losing his life in the process[7].

At the 'Dog House', Dezitter came forward, shaking Kleinman's hand. He was 'the chief', he said, but something made Kleinman uncomfortable. Perhaps it was the way some of their hosts spoke to each other in whispers, out of his earshot. He told the chief one of the people he had met – in fact it was Mme Bordeaux – had warned him about an escape organisation which helped some airmen escape, to prove its worth, but then turned others over to the Germans.

---

7   After the war, Beamish and Bodey would support a campaign for him to be Mentioned in Despatches.

Dezitter, confident and conceited behind his moustache and glasses, said he found the tale to be an unlikely one.

***

Hugh Bomar, from El Paso, and Ray Smith, from Denver, left the 'Dog House' for Saint-Gilles on August 26. Four days later, Kleinman, Lancelot Bodey and Nigel Beamish were driven to the building with the conservatory. As the driver turned the car into an alley at the back of the house, two men in crumpled suits jumped onto the running board. One was the tall, blonde interrogator who had already become known to the previous victims of the 'Dog House' as Charlie.

Charlie told the airmen to run quickly inside the house where they sat in the glass room with the door open into the garden. The sun shone as Charlie gave them the usual questionnaires. When Charlie saw that Kleinman had written down John Brown's name in his crew list, he remarked good humouredly that the American 'was here in June'.

Asked if they had photographs for fake identity cards, Bodey revealed he had used his, and Charlie told him to come with him. Kleinman and Beamish insisted on going too. They all got into a Ford V-8 and sped off down the road, Charlie riding outside on the running board. The two airmen glanced at each other with concern: this was hardly the way someone looking to avoid attention should have behaved.

But it was not far[8]. Even before they got to Gestapo headquarters, Kleinman knew in his heart his evasion was over. Sitting in a

---

8   Kleinman was the only airman to try to identify where the house with the conservatory had been. He said it was 'opposite a park' in the Avenue Louise about 'a ride of three to five minutes' from the Gestapo headquarters where the prisoners were always taken next.

waiting room on the top floor, he watched a civilian in his late 30s stumble past. He had obviously been tortured. The American could not know but this was Marcel Van Buekenhout who had helped his pilot John Brown. He later saw Van Buekenhout again. This time he was being half-dragged, half-carried and was barely conscious.

As Kleinman sat there, he heard the Belgian prisoners around him whispering to each other and realised many had helped Brown and another airman they called Grosvenor. Sitting apart from them was another man, who he had seen upstairs talking with the Germans; he suspected he was a stool pigeon. Kleinman tried to explain to the Belgians they should be careful what they said as the Germans might be listening.

A number of other airmen also came through the waiting room, among them Singleton, Levey and Leon Panzer, all being brought back in for further interrogation from their prison cells at Saint-Gilles.

Charlie worked his usual routine on Kleinman: that he was a spy and a saboteur rather than a downed airman. He demanded to know the names of the people who had helped him, but Kleinman said only that he had passed through major cities such as Brussels and Liège.

Then the New Yorker, who had turned 25 during his evasion, was taken to Saint-Gilles where he was given nothing to eat for over 24 hours. In the prison he saw one of those who had helped him, Max Varley.

Outside the prison walls, time was running out for the Nazi occupiers of Brussels. Charles de Gaulle, head of the Free French, had already made a triumphal parade down the Champs-Elysees and the Allies were racing towards the Belgian border at speed. US Army General Omar Bradley later described the British and American forces' dash across France from the Seine river to the Belgian border as 'the headiest and most optimistic advance of the European war'.

Consequently, the Germans never got a chance to interrogate Kleinman again. This was doubly fortuitous. Kleinman had risked his status as an evading airman by taking part in active Resistance operations in a way most airmen had not.

And, unlike many Jewish airmen who were shot down, he had also refused to get rid of his dog-tags, both out of fear of being shot as a spy and to ensure he got an appropriate funeral in the event of his death.

Had any of the Nazi interrogators or guards inspected them, they would have seen they were clearly marked with an 'H' for Hebrew.

20

A VILLAGE IN TERROR

Teddy Blenkinsop and the People of Meensel-Kiezegem

THROUGHOUT THE WAR the Flemish-speaking community of Meensel-Kiezegem became a microcosm of an occupied country: some people resisted, most got on with their lives, and others actively collaborated.

The local right-wing MNR resistance group developed around local notary Victor Mertens and the chief of the local tram station, Oscar Beddegenoodts. Oscar's daughter, Jeanne, became its courier, carrying messages to other groups in the Leuven area. The local left-wing *Front de l'Indépendance* flourished under Constant Wittemans and his sons, Joost and Jules. About 20 to 30 of the town's 900 inhabitants were loyal to these groups. They sabotaged railway lines and derailed an ammunition train. They helped escaped Polish and Russian prisoners of war, many of whom had fled from forced labour in coal mines. Residents brought food to their hiding places in the surrounding woods, while others offered them shelter in their barns or attics. The groups also set fire to at least one town hall in the area so that civil records would be lost to help cover up the creation of false identities for members of the

Resistance, those avoiding forced labour in Germany, and for some Jewish people in hiding.

Josef Craeninckx, who lived on his family farm with his twin brother Frans and father Vital, sheltered a Jewish woman and her two children, as well as three airmen. Like many, he never considered himself a formal 'member' of the Resistance. Although on the left himself, he was great friends with Mertens and had joined his MNR group.

Since May, they had an unusual ally in their work, a Canadian airman named Squadron Leader Teddy Blenkinsop, from Victoria, British Columbia. In civilian life he had been a trainee accountant, but war turned him into an exceptional pilot. During 1943, he flew 30 missions in a Wellington bomber from his base in north Africa, almost succumbing to an attack by a fighter over Naples. He had started his second tour of operations, this time with a Pathfinder squadron flying Lancasters, early in 1944. He had been awarded the DFC for 'high skill, fortitude and devotion to duty'.

However, on the night of April 27, returning from a raid on Montzen in Belgium, his aircraft was attacked '*von unten hinten*' by a night-fighter and its wing fuel tanks exploded. As the aircraft broke up, its target indicators – coloured marker flares – lit up the sky. All the crew died, either instantly or soon afterwards of wounds – except Blenkinsop.

Since then, the 23-year-old had been evading capture with the help of the residents of Meensel-Kiezegem, in a remarkable hiding place on the Pypen family farm: they had built a room *inside* a haystack, where Blenkinsop and young people escaping forced labour could hide. To ensure their young children did not ask too many questions about Blenkinsop, the Pypens told them he was the boyfriend of the oldest daughter, Paula. A French-speaker, Blenkinsop could communicate with some of the villagers, and he joined in a variety of underground activities. He had recently accompanied the local resistors on an attack on a collaborator, during which they shot up the house with rifles and pistols.

But there were others in the community who supported the Nazis, either facing up to the reality of the occupation as they saw it or because of a Flemish-nationalist kinship with the Germans. The Merckx were one such family; they were convinced that the Germans would win the war and support a right-wing nationalist government which would unite Flanders with the Netherlands. Clementine Merckx-Swinnen regularly hosted her black-shirted friends at the family farm and all her sons were connected to right-wing groups: Maurice, Marcel, and Albert were members of the Flemish fascist group, VNV; Gaston belonged to the Flemish Guard, a military organisation which collaborated with the Nazis; and the youngest boy, Ernest, was a member of a Flemish Nazi youth organisation.

Despite this, they lived in a fragile peace with their neighbours. They all knew each other well and had been tolerant of their political differences. It was understood the Merckx family were sympathetic with the occupiers for ideological reasons and because they could trade with them, but that they would not denounce their fellow villagers. Everyone in the village knew who was *zwart*, 'black', a collaborator, and who was *wit*, 'white', on the side of the Resistance.

Those in the community loyal to the Resistance had refused to take action against the Merckx family, partly out of local loyalty but also to avoid bringing trouble to the town. Perhaps for the same reasons the Merckx had not reported their neighbours to the Nazis.

However, in the summer of 1944, with the promise of liberation on the horizon, that changed.

Sunday, July 30, was planned to be a special day in the area, with the busy fair at Attenrode acting as a reminder of the pre-war days; a traditional celebration of country life with beer to drink in the sunshine and young girls from neighbouring villages to chase. A few days earlier a member of the Resistance overheard 24-year-old Gaston Merckx talking in the village café about his plans to attend. Word was passed to the armed wing of the *Front de l'Indépendance*, the *Partisans armés* (PA), and three young resisters – two men and a woman – decided they should be the ones to act. On the day of the fair, they cycled to Meensel and wandered out to a crossroads between the Merckx farm and Attenrode, a spot known locally as Boekhout, and lay in wait.

It was just after 2pm and the sun was high in the sky. The three ambushers found their mouths were suddenly dry and the palms of their hands, gripping pistols in their pockets, were damp with sweat.

Then they heard voices. It was Merckx and three workers from his farm, laughing and joking, teasing each other about different local girls. They looked up when the three stepped out onto the road but were not unduly alarmed until Gaston Merckx looked again at the hard faces and one spoke.

'Gestapo. Show us your papers!'

Merckx refused and, realising it was a trap, pulled out his pistol and raised it. But the gun jammed. His three assailants fired, hitting his foot.

As Merckx's companions ran, the three *résistants* made a grab for him, but he pushed them away and ran through a gate into a field. He could hear his pursuers close behind and as he rushed behind a haystack he stumbled and fell, trying desperately to hide.

The three people were suddenly standing right in front of him. One of the young men raised a revolver and shot repeatedly. Then all three ran to the edge of the field, got on their bicycles and cycled hurriedly away.

When word of the attack reached the family farm, Clementine Merckx-Swinnen rushed to the scene and cradled Gaston's head in her lap.

A VILLAGE IN TERROR

As workers from her farm loaded the body onto a cart, she said the Germans must take 100 hostages in exchange for the death of her son.

Word now spread around Meensel-Kiezegem about the killing and all sense of this being a carefree summer's day quickly disappeared.

In fact, in the skies above the town there was a sudden crack of thunder and heavy raindrops began to fall.

That night a grief-stricken Clementine presided over an angry meeting at a café owned by Julien Stroobants, another collaborator. As she talked her sons plotted revenge, writing a list of all the people in the area who they knew or suspected to be in the Resistance. Some of her friends tried to persuade her that, with the war almost over, it made no sense to bring violence down on her neighbours, but her grief and anger were too strong.

The family spent the day after Gaston's death in discussion with the SS and Gestapo both in Leuven and Antwerp. The Gestapo had a file on Meensel-Kiezegem, logging its suspicions about acts of sabotage and evasion of forced labour. The killing of a member of the Flemish Guard represented an act of outright resistance and had to be crushed. To organise a raid the SS brought in *Sturmbannführer* (Major) Frans Packet who had already revealed himself to be a ruthless hunter of the Resistance in Antwerp. The raid would be conducted by Packet's SS men and members of the Flemish Guard who were eager to avenge their comrade.

At daybreak on Tuesday, August 1, the community woke to angry shouts and gunshots. One SS officer pulled a man through the streets, ordering him to point out houses where members of the Resistance lived. Villagers recognised him as a *résistant* who had been hidden in the area but had recently been arrested and tortured. The SS had made him give up some of those who had helped him.

One of the first buildings they went to was a cafe owned by Pauline Bollen, the wife of Resistance leader Oscar Beddegenoodts. Oscar was beaten as they demanded to know where the local Resistance kept its supplies and ammunition. Two other soldiers held Pauline at gunpoint, demanding to know where their daughter Jeanne was. Both refused to speak, even when their 12-year-old son Maurice was threatened. Jeanne could hear as her parents were abused: she had managed to crawl into an attic space which she had prepared as a hideout and the Germans did not find her.

After smashing up the family home, the SS dragged Oscar, Pauline, and Maurice to the home of the town doctor, 66-year-old Hendrik Goyens, a man deeply respected by and known to all. Packet turned the driveway and garden of the doctor's home into a collection centre for all those he planned to take away. One man jumped a wall and escaped, bullets flashing through the air all around him.

Meanwhile, a squad of SS went to the home of the Craeninckx family. Kicking down the door, they dragged out 24-year-old August, pushing and shoving him into the farmyard. Ducks and geese flew off in all directions as the Germans shouted and struck the young man with rifle butts, demanding to know where he was sheltering other Resistance members. His wife, Germaine, tried to go outside to help him but a soldier pushed her back.

At the window she watched as two soldiers took August across the lane outside their house and onto the path to the local church where they made him kneel and shot him in cold blood. Dr Goyens and another man were made to carry August's body into the doctor's house.

Other townsfolk were being gathered at a house a few hundred yards away. Under blows and threats, they were asked to reveal which of them was in the Resistance. In another house, 47-year-old Maria Boesman watched as Packet threw her husband, Jozef, to the floor and began to whip him. Elsewhere, Maria and other women from neighbouring houses were stripped naked and beaten.

On a lane outside the town an SS officer and a masked man stepped into the road to stop farmer Petrus Van der Meeren as he cycled home from one of his fields. Van der Meeren was a member of the *Front de l'Indépendance* and was disliked by the Merckx family. He and Oscar Beddegenoodts were taken by a small group of German soldiers or Flemish SS into a nearby wood and told they would be forced to reveal where the Resistance kept its supplies. They were only a few yards inside the wood when the soldiers lifted their guns and killed both. Several men from the town were marched into the wood to carry the two bodies back and lay them out alongside August Craeninckx.

Packet then gathered 15 villagers, loaded them onto a lorry, and transported them to the SD headquarters in Leuven, where one – a teenage girl – was released. The rest, including Pauline Bollen, were interrogated and then sent to the state prison. Pauline was still unaware that her husband, Oscar, had been executed.

Throughout the raid Vancouver airman Teddy Blenkinsop and others hid in the hollowed-out haystack.

The next day the Germans arrested Dr Goyens and took him to Leuven where he received the same treatment as the others: kept awake, repeatedly interrogated, and flogged. Gaston Merckx's three older brothers were often present for the interrogations, advising the SS with their local knowledge.

On August 5 most of the group already in custody at the SD headquarters were transferred to Saint-Gilles. By then, the Germans had built up a picture of the Resistance presence in Meensel-Kiezegem. They arrested and tortured Adolf Hendrickx, a senior member of the local MNR, and obtained further information from local collaborators.

But the hunger for revenge for Gaston Merckx which burnt in

the bellies of the German and Flemish SS had not been satisfied. Worse was yet to come.

***

The three resistance men of Meensel-Kiezegem executed on August 1 were buried quietly and without fuss. Locals were afraid to attend the funerals as tension remained high. By contrast, Gaston Merckx was buried with military honours, a volley of shots fired over his grave and a line of Flemish Guard giving the Hitler salute.

Following the funeral Clementine Merckx-Swinnen met with two Flemish members of the SD and asked if the interrogations had given up the names of her son's killers. The answer was no, so she travelled to Brussels to meet *Obersturmbannführer* Robert Verbelen, of the Flemish SS. Merckx knew Leuven-born Verbelen had made a name for himself as a Belgian who was at least as brutal with the Resistance as any member of the German SS. She offered him money to ensure there was a second raid on Meensel-Kiezegem, to keep the operation going until the killers were identified.

Pocketing the money and keen to enjoy the success of arresting a large group of Resistance suspects, Verbelen spent August 7 getting the security clearance for an even larger second raid on the town. In all, he managed to put together a force of 350 men, mainly from the Flemish SS. He brought in one of his key accomplices in anti-Resistance work, *Untersturmführer* Tony Van Dijck, of the Waffen SS, who had taken part in brutal anti-partisan activity during the invasion of the Soviet Union, to ensure the operation would be carried out with the extreme violence that could satisfy the Merckx family.

Before dawn on Friday, August 11, trucks dropped his troops at three different locations outside the town. As the men moved in, they began to fire shots and batter on the doors. This time it was clear the SS were not only targeting those suspected of being in the Resistance: everyone was being dragged out of their homes. Most were in their pyjamas. It was 4.30am.

Adult men were taken to a church and the local boys' school for identification. As names were collected it became apparent that many of those who had been named as Resistance members during the interrogations in Leuven had fled the area since the first raid. A search at the farm owned by Constant and Germaine Wittemans failed to find their sons, Joost and Jules, who had been identified as members of the *Front de l'Indépendance*, so both parents and their daughter were taken away.

Intelligence supplied to Verbelen also brought him to a small-holding owned by 36-year-old Jules Schotsmans, who had hidden Blenkinsop in the early weeks of his evasion and had treated him like a brother. Schotsmans refused to come out of his house and the soldiers threw in hand grenades which set his home ablaze. He burnt to death in the fire.

In a field outside the town Teddy Blenkinsop and three other men decided their hideout in the haystack was unsafe and ran towards the woods but as they neared the trees two members of the Flemish SS stepped out and lifted their rifles.

Blenkinsop was taken to the girls' school in Meensel where a couple of hundred people were now gathered at gunpoint in the yard. At the entrance gates stood two masked men, whose disguise could not conceal their identities from people who had known them all their lives: Marcel and Albert Merckx. As people were brought in through the school gate the two brothers pointed out Nazi sympathisers who were allowed home. Everyone else was taken into a classroom where their names were recorded. Verbelen checked them against a list the Merckx family had written at their kitchen table. Those on the list were considered dangerous, people who helped the Resistance or escaped forced labourers, and were taken to one classroom with the doors closed. They were hit and abused on the way so the corridor soon became spattered in blood.

Those not on the list were corralled into another classroom and made to squat on the floor. In this awkward position they could only listen to the cries and shouts from the other room. All were terrified. The sound of sobbing filled the room and the guards shouted without mercy for them to shut up. The SS then began to filter this group through a door and into the school yard where they were made to stand in a line.

Adolf Hendrickx and another local *résistant*, Prosper Natens, were brought to stand in front of them. They wore handcuffs and appeared to be in a desperate state, having been subjected to torture and mock executions. Both men stood with their heads bowed but the SS shouted at them to raise their heads. The people in the school yard were slowly brought forward one by one and the two men were told to nod if they recognised someone who had helped the Resistance. Marcel and Albert Merckx stood to one side and sometimes when Hendrickx and Natens shook their heads to save a friend the brothers saw through the lie and dragged the unfortunate person to the side. All through this awful scene, people were threatened, kicked and struck with rifle butts.

Those chosen as enemies of the state were made to kneel facing a wall; the others allowed to go home.

A badly beaten Teddy Blenkinsop was dragged into the yard. Under interrogation he gave only his name, rank, and number, but the Germans had been told he had taken part in Resistance activity, and he was shoved to his knees against the wall. Kneeling with him were the Wittemans family and relatives of August Craeninckx, who had been shot in the first raid. All had brought food to Blenkinsop and resisters hiding in the surrounding fields and woods.

The horror at the school went on for several hours until, at noon, trucks were brought and Verbelen told his NCOs: 'Take everyone away!'

A total of 76 people from the community were driven to Gestapo headquarters in Leuven where their photographs were taken before they were beaten and abused. Many were also interrogated in the basement of the Gestapo headquarters on the Avenue Louise. Soon after, most were transferred to Saint-Gilles.

On arrival at the prison, farmer and *résistant* Vital Craeninckx put his arms around his 16-year-old twin sons, Frans and Jozef, as the prisoners were selected for different cell blocks.

'We'll keep together,' he said.

But a Flemish SS man approached and, seeing Vital clinging to his loved ones, punched the 51-year-old full in the face.

As the SS dragged the boys away, Jozef looked back, his eyes filling with tears at the sight of his father bleeding on the floor.

Jozef and his brother would never see him again.

21

THE DARK CELLS

THERE WERE AROUND 2,000 prisoners behind the high walls of Saint-Gilles prison. Some were criminals, some German military deserters, but most were 'political prisoners' whose opinions or past put them at odds with the occupier, or members of the Resistance, underground newspaper networks, and evasion lines. It had become *l'hôtel des patriotes*. There were also dozens of people who had been arrested simply because they were related to *résistants* or had been taken hostage to force people to give themselves up. There were agents and wireless operators and dozens of Allied airmen – victims of Dezitter, Abwehr deception or misfortune.

The cell blocks radiated outwards from a central building. One held only women prisoners, mainly members of the underground. One was designated as a military section and brought together the captured Allied airmen and German soldiers who had been tried for desertion or other violations of the military code.

On arrival prisoners were stripped and searched, and most of their possessions were confiscated. For civilians, often personal items such as photographs, watches and jewellery. For airmen it was usually the compasses, hacksaw files and bank notes they had held onto from their escape kits. They were only allowed to keep handkerchiefs and combs.

Each prisoner was led to cells where typed cards in slots on each cell door identified who was to be kept inside. Each cell contained old straw mattresses laid out on the floor. Although prisoners were not allowed to lie down during the day, most did not want to as the straw was dirty and infested. Quickly their clothes were crawling with lice. As the days wore on, though, prisoners grew hungry and lethargic: their diet consisted of weak ersatz coffee, small portions of carrots and potatoes, a sour-tasting bread, and – occasionally – thin tasteless soup. They were unable to brush their teeth and were allowed only a five-minute shower with unheated water once a week. 'Carpetbagger' bombardier Wallis Cozzens tried to stay in the water a little longer one day and was slapped in the face by one of the guards. Sometimes instructions would be shouted into cells with the prisoners' surname. The order to walk – 'Promenade!' – was the only one to be welcomed. The others were: 'Tribunal!' (Trial) and 'Transport!' (Deportation).

In many cells prisoners did not speak each other's language so the days were long, but the airmen sometimes got lucky and shared a cell with other fliers. After a few days Cozzens' fellow 'Carpetbagger' William Ryckman was taken to a cell with two other victims of the 'Dog House', Halifax co-pilot Flying Officer William Elliott and Sergeant Maurice Muir. But he found the two men were hungry, tired, and suspicious, so there was very little conversation: they had lost any sense of trust and suspected any newcomer could be a spy.

However, as time went on the airmen managed to develop some friendships. James Dykes, a 23-year-old from Clayton, Alabama, had been a radio operator on a Liberator which was shot down near Waterloo in January 1944. Although small in stature, Dykes was a courageous young man with a big heart. He had endeared himself to the evasion line members who had helped him and had twice escaped German raids – once by running out of the back of the mill where he was hiding and the second time by jumping from a window. The second escape ended as he tried to run across a field and stumbled into a German patrol. Dykes befriended a lieutenant named Ford Babcock, from Glendale, California, who had been shot down over the Netherlands and had been on the run for as long as Dykes. He had also been captured in June. Dykes' warm personality eventually also won over the wary Canadian, Bill Elliott, and they began to talk.

Stuart Leslie spent some time with John Bradley, so at least each had company. Muse, Murphy and Panzer shared a cell, and also befriended P-47 pilot Jack Terzian, a Long Islander born in Turkey to Armenian parents and a veteran of 65 missions. Terzian had been bombing a bridge and flak tower when ground fire had struck his oil line and engine, and he belly-landed in a field. He had spent seven weeks on the run before being arrested in a raid on the house in which he had been sheltering. He never got over the pain of seeing the family that had helped him being taken into Gestapo custody.

And the airmen's interrogations continued. Having been captured in civilian clothes and carrying false identity papers, they were still being treated as suspected spies and in danger of being shot – particularly men like Kleinman and Blenkinsop who had taken part in Resistance activity. In addition, with the Allied armies a short distance away in France and Germany being bombed by *terrorfliegers*, there was always an uncertainty as to how ruthless their captors could become.

Those in Saint-Gilles during July and the first three weeks of August faced regular interrogation from both Luftwaffe intelligence and the Gestapo in Avenue Louise. Some were beaten, sent back to the prison and solitary confinement, and then brought back to be beaten again. Often airmen did not know from which branch of the Nazi state their interrogator came, although most were subjected to questioning by the man they knew only as 'Charlie'.

During their interrogations Ryckman and Cozzens decided to

ignore Charlie's questions and just chat about any general aspect of the war, from the Russian front to Normandy, throwing questions back at the interrogator about the V1s and his pre-war journeys to the United States. Most of Charlie's questions concentrated on who had helped them throughout their evasion. They refused point blank to say anything about that.

For much of his two-week incarceration, Ryckman found himself in a similar situation to John Bradley: sharing a cell with criminals and deserters. One of his cellmates was a Belgian volunteer who had spent two years on the Russian front with the Walloon SS before going on the run while on leave.

Other members of Wolcott and Ryckman's Carpetbagger crew members were elsewhere in the prison. Co-pilot Robert Auda, from Tiffin, Ohio, had been helped by Francois Hennebert and his friend Diserai, two people whose kindness and courage the airman would never forget. But he had fallen foul of the Dezitter gang's deception of agents of the French intelligence service, the BCRA, and had been rounded up by Suzanne Bertherand.

Wolcott's radio operator Dale Loucks had been helped by men who housed him in his quaint terraced town house in Avenue d'Itterbeek in Anderlecht. Loucks was arrested there during a Gestapo raid on the building.

Often many of the airmen's helpers were in custody too and the interrogators tried to play them off against each other. John 'Bud' Brown, whose bad feeling about his sick crew had been proven right, was intensively interrogated in July when the Germans still thought they had time to dismantle the evasion lines. When he refused to name the people who helped him, he was slapped repeatedly across the face by his interrogator.

The interrogator switched his attention to Brown's shoes. Where had he got them from? An innocuous sounding question but disguised to provide clues as to who had provided him with his civilian disguise. And one positive answer to a question could lead to another – although Brown gave nothing away.

Five days later his interrogator came to Saint-Gilles to question him again. This time the German claimed the person who had been so kind to Brown and Grosvenor, Madame Claes-Frix, had 'talked'.

But as the interrogation continued Brown realised Claes-Frix had only mentioned that one day the airman had been taken by tram to Anderlecht. She had certainly not given the name of her comrade in the Resistance, Marguerite Quintard-Legrain, who Brown had been taken to see. Brown refused to say anything.

On taking over the evasion line investigation from the Abwehr, the SD and Gestapo brought in every *résistant* they had under observation. When Brown was interrogated four weeks later – towards the end of August – he was shown custody photographs of many of those who had helped him. The Van Den Eedes, Marguerite Quintard-Legrain, Marcel Leborgne, and Marcel Van Buekenhout. All had been arrested and were locked up in the prison.

It was emotionally devastating for Brown to see the custody photographs of people who had risked their lives for him, and to think they were now facing torture – had perhaps already been tortured – and would almost certainly be executed or sent to a concentration camp.

Sadly, many of those arrested from Service EVA and the Comet Line during July and August believed they had been betrayed by John Brown; they were unaware of the infiltration by the Abwehr.

In fact, Brown had not only said nothing, he had also worked hard to keep any hint that he recognised the people in the custody photographs off his face.

And he maintained his silence, despite having to spend weeks in the loneliness and torture of Saint-Gilles chambers of special punishment – the 'dark cells'.

The 'dark cells' – the *Dunkle Zellen* – were each no bigger than a broom cupboard, far too small to lie down in and the only time an inmate saw any daylight was when a guard opened the door and threw in a bowl of food. The prisoner shared this tiny space with a *kübel* – a slop bucket – for their own waste.

Many of the airmen had a spell in one of these cells, but one suffered more than most. Bill Grosvenor crouched in a dark cell next to his iron bucket for 31 days while his interrogators played in 'whisper recordings' to try to break him. As the recordings repeated questions over and over, Grosvenor tried everything not to think of the names of those who had helped him in case he spoke them out loud. Later his tormentors played messages which endlessly suggested his guilt. When the airmen saw him again, he was in an extremely bad mental condition and wanted to commit suicide.

Grosvenor said his prayers to help him through and sometimes fixated on the three holes drilled in the top of the iron door. He moved the slop bucket to one side, stood on it and looked through cell block, just to get a glimpse of somewhere beyond his tiny torture chamber. But that did not always bring much comfort.

'I heard a man beaten up after a failed suicide attempt,' he said.

Each time their interrogators lost patience with the airmen they were sent to the dark cells. Wolcott, Auda and Cozzens arrived in these windowless hells on August 25. For the next five nights they slept curled up in a ball on the concrete floor. The toilet bucket in the corner of the room was not emptied and they were given no drinking water.

Wolcott got through by reciting a version of an old poem he had learned when he was a child, leading him to dream that the sun would shine on him again in his own country. He prayed his young wife, Rosemary, was well at home and that her strong Catholic faith was giving her comfort. He knew she would be saying the rosary every day that he was missing.

Cold, tired, hungry, and in pain the men were dragged out one by one after five days and interrogated again. This time the questions were about their duties on the aircraft. The men mumbled and avoided giving away any more than they could help.

P-47 pilot Jack Terzian was given a printed 'confession' which stated he was a spy. He refused to sign it and was locked in a dark cell.

The punishment of the dark cells was sometimes used in an attempt to turn prisoners against each other.

Stuart Leslie, John Bradley and Royce McGillvary had been captured together. Leslie and Bradley were brought to the dark cells where a guard kept reminding them that McGillvary was in his own, regular cell. The fact that they were being treated differently stung for a moment, but Leslie understood it was a deliberate ploy to divide and conquer; to make the pair think McGillvary had talked and was getting special treatment and if they talked too, it would work out for them. It was certainly a game, as a few days later McGillvary found himself in their place.

The prisoners experienced the occasional moment of humanity from their guards. One day, while still in the dark cell, Leslie was half asleep and sweating almost feverishly in the heat when the door opened and light flooded in.

'Come,' said the voice.

But it was not an angry shout and, as Leslie's eyes adjusted to the light, he saw the guard who had befriended him in his regular cell and told him about his sister in New Jersey.

Leslie struggled to his feet and found the guard had unlocked Bradley's cell too. He took them upstairs to the washrooms and told them to hurry. When they were finished, he led them back to their tiny punishment cells, gave them cigarettes and a blanket each to lie on, urging them not to say where they got them.

Back in his regular cell, Bradley spent two days painstakingly going through his clothes to kill the lice. Examining his body, he found it was a mass of welts from untreated bites. But, he thought, it was heaven to sleep on a straw mattress and eat food in the light again.

Helpers And Couriers

WITHIN THE WALLS OF SAINT-GILLES, the cells swelled with members of the evasion lines.

Although neither Brown nor Grosvenor had given anything away, the infiltration of the line meant the civilian wings of Saint-Gilles continued to fill up with people who had helped them. Jean Plas and Jules Dricot, a father of four, were quickly sent to concentration camps, from which they would not return. Blanche Page – who had escaped death when Prosper Spilliaert's fishmarket was bombed – Catholic priest Camille Leclef, the Eliot family, the Leysens, and Jeanne Drieghe and her 18-year-old daughter Suzanne were awaiting deportation with the airmen. So, too, was Henri Maca, who had helped so many by organising safehouses for EVA and Comet, and 41-year-old Charles Servais, who ran his own safehouse for airmen.

The very active Biernaux group in Hasselt had also been broken. On August 5, the Flemish SD had raided the Biernaux home and arrested the whole family: Olympe, the leader of their evasion group, her husband, Florent, their son Raymond, and their daughter Eliane. The family had sheltered more than 50 airmen in all, including John Bradley and Royce McGillvary. They had also helped Bram Van der Stok, one of the three prisoners who succeeded in getting home from the Great Escape. Florent and Raymond were now in Saint-Gilles, while Olympe and 12-year-old Eliane were in Ravensbrück.

Others who had aided airmen in the area were also picked up, including Jules Jaspers – who was in Saint-Gilles – and his 18-year-old son René, who was taken to Breendonk. One couple – a young man and his pregnant wife – had only taken in an airman for a couple of days but were caught up in the arrests. The woman gave birth to her baby in Ravensbrück concentration camp where it was taken away and she never saw it again.

Sometime in that last week of August, 58-year-old Josephine Van Der Gracht-Broeckx, who Grosvenor had spent Christmas with, was arrested and brought to Saint-Gilles. Punched in the face by her torturer she looked at him defiantly.

'Don't you have a mother?' she asked.

They hit her all over her body with a length of pipe.

'Each airman sheltered is the equivalent of a battalion of Germans shot down,' her interrogator told her.

He had unintentionally given her even greater heart.

By good fortune, 'Carpetbagger' radio operator Dale Loucks was never taken to the dark cells. His cell was right next to the women's section of the prison. Once a week, the women got to go outside and walk around the courtyard, and Loucks and the others would stand on a table and watch what they referred to as 'the biggest event of the week.'

With Loucks was Flying Officer Jacob Thurmeier, a Morse code expert from Saskatchewan, Canada, who loved to tap out messages to other prisoners via the heating pipes going through each of the cells.

They shared with Spitfire pilot, Flight Sergeant Brian Harris. A handsome man with dark swept back hair, wide eyes and a square jaw, Harris had been studying medicine at Nottingham University when the heroism of 'The Few', the already-legendary fighter pilots of the Battle of Britain, had inspired him to ditch his studies and join the RAF. He had been fascinated by flying ever since his father had paid 10 shillings for his young son to take a flight with a travelling 'flying circus'. After training in Canada and the United States, he was posted to the legendary 74 Squadron, home to some of the deadliest aces of the Great War, including Mick Mannock, Ira 'Taffy' Jones and Sydney Carlin.

In the run-up to D-Day, the squadron had been making low-flying strafing runs and, on May 22, as Harris dived down to machine-gun a German convoy on a road outside Meslin-l'Évêque in Belgium, he clipped the top of a poplar tree, buckling the propeller and ripping off the aircraft's overload tank. He pulled up, receiving fire from the convoy, but the aircraft had no power at all. Banking away, he spotted a stretch of fields which might just be flat enough to put down.

It was then, he realised in horror, his route took him through a line of high-tension cables. Unable to climb above them, he dipped the Spitfire and flew between two pylons and beneath the cables. It was a near-impossible manoeuvre. He hit the ground and crashed through a series of hedges before coming to a stop. By holding the aircraft straight, he managed to remain largely unhurt.

His Spitfire starting to burn, he jumped out and ran to the protection of a hedge, where he hid his Mae West and revolver in the undergrowth. The aircraft being well alight, he had no need to stop and set it on fire, so he headed quickly away. The shock of the crash had left Harris – who was a week shy of his 24th birthday – with an almost insatiable thirst. His heart pounded in his chest: either from the exhilaration of having survived a brush with death or the sudden realisation that he remained in extreme danger.

He knocked on the door of a cottage, and a woman gave him bread and coffee, and pointed him to a nearby wood. After getting further help from local farmers, he arrived in Meslin-l'Évêque where he was put in contact with Jean Delcourt – sometimes known as Oscar – who worked for the underground *Groupe G*, and he was given shelter by Charles Lepoivre and Sylvie Fourmanoir in Gondregnies, a 25-minute cycle ride away. During this period other members of *Groupe G* visited to interrogate him as to whether he was really an RAF airman or was in fact a German spy. Harris was not sure he had convinced them until they took him to another farmhouse where his cuts and bruises were examined by a doctor.

From June 5 until August 10 Harris stayed at another safehouse in the village belonging to Léon Degand and his daughter Yvette. But due to the use of fake agents in the KLM line, the GFP had become aware of the safehouses being used in the area and were closing them down. Two German agents posing as resisters visited the farm in Gondregnies and asked Lepoivre to take in two airmen. Smelling a rat, he refused. The Germans revealed who they were and beat and tortured the farmer before confronting him with another member of the underground who was already under arrest. They said they already knew about Brian Harris and had arrested another airman they had helped the day before. His name was Robert Piarote and he was a 20-year-old B-17 radio operator from Lebanon, Pennsylvania. Piarote had been arrested with his helpers, Jules Versavel and his daughter, Georgette.

Faced with interrogators who knew so much, Lepoivre confessed to having helped Harris and Piarote, but made no mention of the 10 others he had sheltered.

As Lepoivre was taken away, the GFP headed to Meslin-l'Évêque. Harris heard shouts in the street as cars screeched to a halt. One of the GFP men stood behind a car and shouted in almost perfect English.

'RAF airman, come out or we will shoot you.'

Harris opened the door and stepped into the street.

As he stood under arrest, Harris was horrified to see the Degands and their daughter Yvette also being taken away. Madame Degand fingered the crucifix around her neck and saw his concern

'Don't worry,' she said. 'We will all meet again in Paradise.'

THE DARK CELLS

Harris felt sick as the Germans loaded him into a car and it sped off through the countryside and into Brussels. Despite the uncertainty of his own future, he could not help but be overwhelmed by fear and concern for all the people who had helped him and were now in terrible danger.

For each airman there had been dozens of helpers. Many – such as Versavels, the Degands and the Lepoivre family – were now, like Harris himself, among the civilian prisoners in Saint-Gilles, wondering what the upcoming battle for Brussels would bring.

22

AGENTS BEHIND BARS

Robert Beckers, Frans Flour, Françoise Labouverie

SOE AGENT FRANÇOIS Reeve, who had led the GFP in Lille to the home of his network leader, Michael Trotobas, was condemned to death in what his captors described as a 'court martial'. Facing his interrogators, he argued that by organising specialised sabotage attacks, he had helped prevent the deaths which would happen if the 'RAF come and bomb'. He also used the fact that he led the GFP to Trotobas in his defence. In a courtroom in Arras he was told he would be able to appeal his death sentence, but once moved to Saint-Gilles, he heard no more about that. Another officer had told him he could 'expect to be shot at any time'. But the interrogation stopped.

Perhaps the Germans decided Reeve had told them everything he could. If so, they felt differently about two other SOE operatives. Robert Beckers had spent three years in a state of anger at the occupation without having any idea what he could do to oppose it. Then, in September 1943, a friend asked him if he would help carry radio equipment around Brussels for a British radio operator. The

23-year-old agreed and found himself not only part of the sabotage resistance group, *Groupe G*, but also assistant to SOE agent, Jacques Doneux, a courageous man who spoke French with a heavy English accent and was prone to the kind of gaffe which agents working in a second language could easily make, once bumping into a fellow traveller on a tram and exclaiming loudly, 'Sorry.'

Carrying a radio was dreadfully dangerous: it was not only heavy, but there was also no obvious excuse for a civilian to be caught with one. So Beckers came up with the idea of fitting it into a gramophone he had received as a wedding gift. A record would not play if it was put on the turntable, but the unit would pass a cursory inspection. He later installed another radio inside a vacuum cleaner.

For six months Doneux and Beckers criss-crossed the city and the countryside organising huge drops of arms which *Groupe G* used in attacks on fuel depots and airfields. They also worked on an audacious operation in which the printing works of the main Belgian evening newspaper, *Le Soir*, was sabotaged and dozens of trucks rushed across the city distributing 50,000 copies of an anti-Nazi version of the newspaper.

Doneux was eventually recalled to London for a break and replaced by Belgian Frans Flour, who was about Beckers' age. Flour was a dashing figure who Beckers felt bore a close resemblance to the Hollywood star Stewart Granger. Before the war, he had been a foreign student at Johns Hopkins University in Baltimore. Beckers now found himself busier than ever, as Flour had to organise supplies not only for *Groupe G*, but also the MNB and the *Front de l'Indépendance*. *Groupe G* sent out 20 sabotage teams one Sunday night to destroy electricity pylons, plunging much of the country into darkness and costing the Nazis an estimated 10 million lost man-hours in Belgium's factories.

But, using radio detector vans, the GFP and the Abwehr were on the trail of the two men and the small group they brought together as lookouts while Flour was on the radio, so the Resistance team were constantly looking for new locations, begging people to allow them to use a back room or outhouse.

On May 22, 1944, Beckers checked out one address suggested by the underground but saw too many men hanging around smoking cigarettes, seemingly doing nothing. The house was obviously under surveillance, so abandoning it, he took the risk of going back to an old address – the home of an elderly widow and her daughter.

It was mid-afternoon when Flour began to transmit. The street was busy, but everyone seemed to be going someplace, rather than stopping to watch. Beckers had four people on watch: two men and two women. If any felt any suspicion, they were to give the others a signal by taking out a handkerchief and blowing their nose.

Fifteen minutes passed – the maximum safe time Flour usually spent on a single transmission. Then 30, then 45. Beckers went upstairs. Flour said he was nearly finished.

Back down on the street, Beckers had a scout around the block and saw a van pull up. Seeing the aerial on the roof he knew immediately it was a radio-detecting vehicle. Walking quickly back to where he could be seen by a lookout inside the building, he blew his nose.

At that moment a man stepped out of a doorway, pushed a revolver into his stomach and said in accented French:

'*Haut les mains! Police Allemande!*'

As instructed he put his hands up and was shoved into the basement of the house and made to kneel. He was viciously beaten and his interrogators filled a bath, plunging his head under the water.

The whole team was rounded up, including the elderly owner of the house. Like Reeve, they were taken to Saint-Gilles, but *their* torture did not stop. They were regularly taken from the prison to GFP headquarters in Rue Traversière, where the brutality continued. Flour was twice tied to a stake in front of a firing squad and told he would be shot if he did not betray all those who had helped him. He and Beckers were beaten on the soles of their feet and told their families had been executed.

They also suffered the special treatment dished out in a torture chamber nicknamed '*die Kapelle*' – 'the chapel' – as there had apparently once been a religious building on the site. There, they were hog-tied, beaten with a leather strap, and had their faces smashed against a wooden table. Although an atheist, Beckers prayed to God. His interrogator told him God was not interested in people like him.

Eventually, Beckers was told he had been sentenced to death by hanging. He told the GFP officer in charge of his interrogation that he had one final wish: to see a photograph of his six-month-old baby, Christine, which he had been told his wife had brought to the GFP headquarters. The officer said he would consider the request, but Beckers was never given the picture.

Françoise Labouverie

FOR FRANÇOISE LABOUVERIE, THE YOUNG Resistance courier whose messages to London had included reports on V1 flying bomb sites, the Germans had reserved one of the 'dark cells'.

The GFP officer in charge of breaking the *Tégal* Resistance group, Captain Hugo Böhme, had decided the network must be completely closed down. As he knew several of its most senior figures, including Françoise's friend Franz Manderfeld, was still at large, he ordered that agents who might have information should continue to be interrogated and not yet sent to concentration camps. Consequently, the network founder, Pierre Hauman, was still in Saint-

Gilles when Françoise arrived there and would stay there throughout the summer of 1944.

To begin with, Böhme's approach to her was avuncular and protective. On snatching her from the Rexist group which had arrested her, he said: 'Your mother is very worried about you.'

It sounded gentle, but for Françoise it was a reminder he had been to her mother's house and he could go back and arrest her if he wished.

He had made a big fuss of her arrest, designed to make her feel important and to pretend it was all just a game which she had lost.

'Look what I've got! Françoise has come!' he told a group of men who saluted him as they arrived.

Böhme did not appear to be the aggressive figure she had imagined to be on her trail; he seemed more like a cunning detective, and she sensed he might be a dangerous adversary, capable of charm and an act to put her at ease.

He had the photograph of her that he had taken from her mother in a frame on his desk.

'You shouldn't have taken it away from her,' Françoise said boldly.

Böhme smiled.

'You shouldn't have played this dangerous game.'

Letters lay on the desk, the top one was in Hauman's writing and was addressed to his parents. Her blood ran cold. Was this meant to be his final letter home? Was Hauman to be executed?

'They were going away tomorrow,' Böhme told her.

There was a pause; Françoise tried to work out if he meant they were going to be executed or sent to a camp.

'But now that you have come, they'll have to wait.'

Böhme took the letters, tore them up and dropped them into a wastepaper basket. Farewell letters destroyed. The offhand way he carried out the act made her shiver.

Böhme questioned her about the rest of the group, not realising that with Hauman, Françoise and two others now in custody he had essentially broken the leadership of the network. Being taken to a cell, she passed faces she recognised as other members of *Tégal*.

After a couple of hours there was more movement in the corridor and the Germans brought in Roger Hanquinet's teenage son Jacques – the MNR boy who had been coming to hide with her – and put him in the next cubicle.

When the guard left, she asked him when and where he had been arrested.

'This morning,' he whispered. 'Your flat.'

Shortly after, Françoise was manacled to the wrists of other prisoners and put in a van. She could see through a small window in the back door and knew exactly where they were going before they slowed right down, turned sharply and drove through the heavy doors of Saint-Gilles prison.

Her arrival inside Saint-Gilles' walls was designed to be humiliating and degrading.

The prison officer who processed her made sniggering, sexual comments and, forced to hand over the pearl necklace which had been her grandmother's and the small diamond ring given to her by her godmother, she could see by the look on his face she would never see them again.

A female jail warder on the women's wing took her into a small glass lodge where she was given a spoon, a tinplate, a glass, and a very rough black blanket and small sheet. She then followed the warder through a wide corridor with cells on both sides and galleries above.

Inside her cell, she stood for a moment taking stock of her surroundings. An iron bed with a straw mattress, a hard wooden chair, and a small cupboard hanging on the wall. Beneath it was an enamel basin with a single tap and a tin bucket to be used as a toilet. Françoise looked up to the high window and a sliver of clear blue sky. She was a prisoner, but she still felt a strange relief at knowing her long hiding game was over.

As darkness fell, she held her tinplate to the little window in her door and took a watery gruel with green gooseberries from the warden outside. It tasted sour and thin, but she forced it down. As she made the bed and got under the blanket in her underwear – to keep the only dress she had from becoming dirty and creased – she began to hope that if she could make Böhme believe she was just an easily-led young woman on the periphery of the Resistance then he might just leave her alone.

However, the next time she was taken to Böhme's office, she found him in an angry mood.

'You have been lying to me,' he shouted, telling her a search of her flat had uncovered a stash of papers related to armed resistance.

Françoise shook her head, genuinely shocked: she had lost contact with most of her *Tégal* colleagues, as like her, they were in hiding. She knew the flat was clean. For a moment she was speechless; then she remembered Jacques Hanquinet had broken in and had no doubt brought papers belonging to the MNR.

The realisation was clear on her face.

'That is the MNR,' she said. 'The MNR resistance group.'

She explained that the group's plan had been to form an interim police force which would protect Brussels when the Allies arrived. They were concerned that the communist resistance would take over the city.

'We shall need a police force to keep order,' she stated, sensing that Böhme was persuaded by the idea of a conservative, royalist group being concerned about the power of the communists.

Böhme smiled and told her that her MNR friends were now in the hands of the Gestapo.

'I wouldn't like to have to pass you over to them,' he said.

He leafed through the papers, read them out loud and questioned her on different points. Over the next few interrogations, she learnt he knew 'Etienne' – Hauman – was the leader, he knew about Manderfeld – although Franz was still at large – and about the flat in the university quarter where she had lived and which the group had used as a meeting place. He asked who else came there but she said no one. There must have been other friends and contacts, he insisted. What about 'Little Victor'? She replied – and kept replying – that she knew no more than she had already said about Victor.

Eventually, the interrogations seemed to be over, and back in Saint-Gilles, she was moved to cell 469 on the second floor, which she shared with Jeanne, a large woman with thick jet-black hair and two Flemish sisters, Lena and Marieke.

Bedtime was complicated. There was only one bed, and it was Lena's turn to use it, so the others slept on straw mattresses on the floor. Each washed and changed at a rusty sink behind a dirty curtain hanging in one corner of the cell. By the time it was Françoise's turn to get ready for bed the iron bucket was full, and Jeanne had had to urinate in the sink.

As they settled down to bed Françoise learned the sisters had been arrested for selling stolen German cigarettes in a bar while Jeanne claimed she had been jailed unjustly. She said she had been sitting on a tram when the young woman sitting next to her had felt sick and jumped off, leaving a parcel for Jeanne to look after and take to the next station where her friend would collect it. But when Jeanne arrived at the station two German officers approached and arrested her. At the police station at Rue Traversière a German officer had opened the parcel and found a radio transmitter. Jeanne said she had been interrogated and beaten every day for the past week.

Françoise could not sleep, listening as a chorus of messages passed from one cell window to another. People shouted good night to their mothers or shouted a curse against *les Boches*.

'They asked me again, but I didn't tell them!' someone said.

And a reply came: 'Thank you, Simone. Have courage!'

The next morning there was a rush to get ready for inspection. The four women piled the mattresses, folded the bed clothes, and placed the mugs from a little corner cupboard onto the table. The near-overflowing bucket was placed by the door. The cell passed inspection, and the prisoners got their breakfast of water and stodgy black bread.

Afterwards the prison routine began with the chief warder – a cruel male army sergeant hated by the women – shouting out cell numbers for the other warders to unlock doors and bring the inmates downstairs for a shower. As the women washed themselves in the cold water, the guards sprayed chemicals on their clothes, leaving them stinking of disinfectant.

Every day Jeanne was taken for interrogation, normally coming back wincing in pain from bruises to her face and body, but she kept repeating it was all a mistake and there was no more she could tell the Germans.

Then, one night, Françoise was roused from sleep. It was Jeanne, pressing her face close to her ear. She had to talk to her.

'I can't keep it all to myself any longer,' she whispered. 'Françoise! All I have told you is a lie! I knew there was a transmitter in the parcel. There wasn't a young woman. But I can't tell them.'

Françoise put her hand on Jeanne's shoulder, telling her not to worry. But the next day Jeanne did not return from her interrogation and Françoise feared either she had broken or her night-time confession had been overheard.

After dark there was a hissed whisper from one of the cells.

'Françoise! Françoise!'

'Yes?' she responded, putting her ear to the spyhole in the door.

'It's Jeanne.'

They had put Jeanne in a neighbouring solitary cell. For the next few nights, they spoke after dark, until Françoise no longer heard Jeanne's voice. She prayed she had been released but never heard from her again.

Françoise's interrogations in Böhme's office resumed and one day there was a large parcel on the captain's desk. As he slowly unpacked the fruit, biscuits, cosmetics and clothes, he explained it had been left at the police station by her aunt Madeline who had spent days tracking her down. He said he could not allow her to have the food, but she could take the clothes and some of the cosmetics. That night she had pyjamas to sleep in. The next day Böhme gave her a letter from her mother.

But the friendliness of these visits began to contrast with the way she was treated in prison. Sometimes she was sent to a '*Dunkle Zelle*', where she crouched on a tiny seat, her feet on the cold stone floor.

Once she had controlled her panicked breathing, Françoise taught herself almost to enjoy the solitude.

In the darkness she wondered whether the order to send her to the cell came directly from Böhme himself, a ploy to make her even more grateful for the apparent kindness he showed her in his office.

Renée De Jonghe

ANOTHER YOUNG WOMAN WHO HAD risked her life to oppose the Nazi occupation was Renée de Jonghe.

In 1940, she was a happy-go-lucky teenager, enjoying a contented home life in Brussels with her father Robert, an engineer, her mother, Marthe, and younger brother Theo. Soon after the invasion, she had become determined to act against the Nazis. But, like Robert Beckers, she did not know how – until a strange invitation came her way.

She had just turned 17 and started university, where she came to the attention of a professor, a staunch Flemish nationalist who believed the Germans were there 'to liberate' the Flemish from the Walloon-dominated Belgian ruling class. He told his spirited new student that, as the blonde daughter of an old Flemish family, she had everything to gain by collaborating with the Germans.

Canny beyond her years, Renée did not commit immediately to the professor's cause, but went to see a friend who had been an activist in the Belgian Socialist Party before the invasion. She had a hunch he would be involved in anti-Nazi activities.

She was right. He told her to stay quiet for now and he would consult with friends. Renée wondered if they would decide to expose the professor as a traitor or even have him assassinated.

But the plan was much more subtle – and, for Renée, far more dangerous. When her friend returned, he said the Resistance wanted her to go along with the professor's suggestion and she would be contacted again later.

Over the next few years, she reported back to the Resistance on contact between the professor and other collaborators with the Nazis. The Resistance then used her as a courier, first carrying messages and then leading downed airmen through back roads from safehouse to safehouse. Men like Byron Buck, from New Jersey, and handsome Bill Edwards, from England, on whom she formed a schoolgirl crush. Like Françoise Labouverie, Renée created false identities for herself, firstly using her mother's maiden name, Van Meule, and later creating a young student named Marthe Massart.

The teenager kept her parents totally in the dark about her activities. In fact, seeing her in the company of so many collaborators, they began to question her loyalties. This suspicion grew when the Resistance encouraged her to allow the professor to use her as a liaison with the local Gestapo. One day, a German officer who had taken a liking to her, called at the house and asked if he could take her out to dinner. It caused a huge family row, and her parents asked her to leave the house. She felt terrible about deceiving them but it was the only way she could attempt to protect them from the potential consequences of her actions.

Renée's first job with the Germans ended abruptly when she argued with a German soldier and swore at him. Briefly jailed, she was sharing a cell with two nuns and two prostitutes, the latter sleeping with the guards to get extra food. Renée would go to sleep lying between the two nuns. After being released the Germans believed she had learnt her lesson. She was allowed into the Flemish SS and given a job as a switchboard operator at its Brussels headquarters. Renée realised she was one of two Resistance agents working in the building. The other worked as a motor transport driver and information Renée gained from her job would be passed to the driver for him to take to a Resistance radio operator. From there it would be relayed to London.

But during the summer of 1944, Renée's group was betrayed and 48 of them were executed. So, for now, she sat in a jail cell in Saint-Gilles, without trial or any information about what her captors had in store for her.

Gaston Masereel

THAT SENSE OF UNCERTAINTY WAS a feeling all the prisoners in Saint-Gilles shared. Some, like François Reeve, had been condemned to death and feared that any day they could be led out of their cell to the gallows or a firing squad. Others, like Françoise Labouverie, appeared to be still of use to the Germans and remained subject to interrogation or the torture of the dark cells.

Most, like Renée de Jonghe, received very little attention at all. They had no idea of their fate, other than a sense that they would remain here in Saint-Gilles or would, more likely, find themselves in a German concentration camp.

But, for Belgian SOE agent Gaston Masereel, who had killed four German soldiers after plunging out of a burning plane, incarceration in Saint-Gilles had come as something of a relief.

After his interrogators had found the secret plans in his suitcase and realised he was not a British airman, he was subjected to weeks of prolonged torture and mistreatment by the SS at Vught concentration camp in the Netherlands.

For a time, he had persuaded one of the Germans that he had been sent by the Belgian government-in-exile to liaise with a leading politician about Belgium's future under occupation. But the story did not protect him for long.

However, the terrible wounds he had received to his head and neck frequently allowed him to feign illness or, indeed, caused him to collapse for real. Eventually his interrogators gave up on him, and he was dragged onto a truck, wearing the rags of his clothes and two undersized wooden clogs.

In his cell in Saint-Gilles he was left to lie on his straw mattress, and he began to make a slow recovery.

It looked as if the Germans had forgotten him and, like the others, he would be freed by the approaching Allies.

PART THREE
THE ESCAPE

23

NACHT UND NEBEL

IN JULY 1944, Belgium's military commander Alexander von Falkenhausen was summoned to Berlin and arrested by the SS. Considered weak by the Nazi leadership, he was also suspected of having supported the July 20 plot to kill the Führer. He had, in fact, been one of the conspirators' candidates to become the new Chancellor of Germany.

His replacement was SS *Gruppenführer* Richard Jungclaus, a man who had spent some months in Brussels, on the order of Heinrich Himmler, collecting evidence of Falkenhausen's ineffectiveness. As a reward, he became commander-in-chief of all German forces – including the Gestapo – in Belgium and northern France.

Jungclaus, a 39-year-old from Freiburg, had joined the SS in 1931 and risen to a rank equivalent to lieutenant-general in the British or US army. Although the dream of European domination, which he believed was Germany's right, appeared to be collapsing into a nightmare for the Third Reich, he was determined that all its enemies should suffer.

It fell to him to ensure the successful completion of a new plan, drawn up by Himmler's security department, to transfer all Jews, political prisoners and *résistants* in the prisons of Breendonk, Saint-Gilles and Antwerp to concentration camps.

Such was the Reich's hatred of its enemies; even as it should

NACHT UND NEBEL

have been putting all of its military effort into halting the Allied advance, the transportations continued. During August, 1,703 prisoners were sent to Neuengamme, 420 to Ravensbrück, 827 to Buchenwald, and 131 to Vught in the Netherlands, where Gaston Masereel was interrogated.

The deportations were made under the *Nacht und Nebel* (Night and Fog) decree, which allowed for people who were suspected of opposing Nazi rule to be arrested and taken into custody without any contact with their families and banished into the prison and concentration camp system.

All at Saint-Gilles – apart from about 200 'juveniles' – were now listed for deportation under the decree. They would be sent to Neuengamme – and its satellite camps – where they would be worked to death or executed. Unusually, Jungclaus included the Allied airmen on his deportation list with the political prisoners – the status of airmen shot down and on the run no longer protected them from Nazi retribution. The men could fall foul of Hitler's Commando Order or the Führer's so-called Bullet Decree (*Kugel-Erlass*) which stripped escaping airmen of their rights as prisoners of war and was the basis of the 'Sagan Order' to execute 50 men of the 'Great Escape' from Stalag Luft 3.

Under the decree some Allied airmen from Saint-Gilles had already been sent to Mauthausen where French resistance fighter Maurice Lampe witnessed 47 British, American, and Dutch airmen beaten and forced to carry heavy stones on their backs to the top of a quarry. Twenty-one of them died within a few hours, some stoned to death as they lay on the ground. All of the rest were dead the following day. The camp administration office recorded they had been 'killed while attempting to escape'. Two airmen would also die at Buchenwald.

Jungclaus had a personal reason for hating airmen and any members of the underground who had helped them. The previous year Jungclaus had lost a friend in a bizarre RAF attack on Brussels.

On January 20, 1943, two Hawker Typhoons had taken off from RAF Manston on a strafing mission, to target any trains moving in the area around Ghent. Their mission accomplished, one waved the other 'adieu'. He took his aircraft down below German radar height and headed for Brussels.

The pilot was former Belgian cavalry officer Jean de Sélys-Longchamps, who had fled the country in 1940 and volunteered for a Belgian squadron attached to the RAF. In the intervening years he had received the occasional message from his family. One said his father had died while being tortured by the Gestapo; another told him the address of the Gestapo headquarters on Avenue Louise. De Sélys made a number of requests to his superiors for the building to be listed as one of his targets, but received no reply.

In the streets of Brussels people craned their heads to see what was happening as de Sélys' aircraft passed low overhead. Finding the Gestapo headquarters was not too difficult: it consisted of two tall apartment buildings which had been brought together to create a huge town house, and which towered over its neighbours. De Sélys unleashed a deadly burst of 20mm cannon fire. Concrete and glass shattered. As de Sélys flew away he threw small Belgian and British flags from the aircraft before heading safely home.

De Sélys left at least four dead, including SD chief *Sturmbannführer* Alfred Thomas, struck while sitting at his desk, and a dozen were wounded. Among the wounded was Brussels Gestapo boss *Obersturmbannführer* Müller. By coincidence, a meeting of high-ranking officers had been taking place at the time of the attack.

The daring raid was a huge morale boost for many Belgians and, the following day, hundreds of local people went to look at the shattered windows and bullet marks on the façade of this citadel of Nazi power. Angry soldiers pushed them back. The RAF demoted

31-year-old de Sélys for acting without orders – but also awarded him the Distinguished Flying Cross for his great courage and initiative.

The attack left Jungclaus with a burning hatred of the RAF. On taking over Belgium, he swore all airmen or *résistants* would be lost in a 'night and fog' from which they would not be heard of again[9].

That hatred included Jozef Craeninckx and his fellow villagers. Since being brought to Saint-Gilles on August 14, the people of Meensel-Kiezegem had been transported to the basement of the Gestapo headquarters on several occasions. Some were so distressed that they agreed to sign confessions stating they had been in the Resistance.

Teddy Blenkinsop, who was arrested with them, had become friendly with his cellmate and fellow Canadian, Pilot Officer Roy Brown, who turned 21 in Saint-Gilles. Blenkinsop told Brown he was being treated as a member of the Resistance rather than a prisoner of war. Shortly after, Blenkinsop was removed from the airmen's block and taken to one of the 'dark cells'.

The dark cell next door was occupied by JH Singleton, and the two men began tapping out messages to each other on heating pipes. Blenkinsop told Singleton he had been carrying out sabotage work with the Resistance but refused to talk after his arrest. The Germans had told him they were going to shoot him. After the last message Singleton tried several times to contact him again, but nothing came back.

Another airman, Flight Sgt Joseph Murphy – a 20-year-old New Zealander who had been trapped by the Dezitter organisation – met Blenkinsop in the queue for the shower. Blenkinsop told him he had been helping the Resistance when they had been overpowered by hundreds of German soldiers. He had fled but

---

9   Jungclaus's personal connection to de Sélys attack is based on an author interview with Jozef Craeninckx.

been captured. He had been threatened with torture but had not said anything. Three people from the Belgian Resistance had been tortured, though, and revealed their sabotage plans and implicated him. He had been told he would be shot. Blenkinsop asked Murphy to tell the story to the British authorities if he got back to England.

When Murphy saw Stuart Leslie in the prison, he told him about his fellow Canadian and whispered that he should remember and take home the name 'Blenkinsop'[10].

The last person to hear from Squadron Leader Teddy Blenkinsop was Dale Loucks when, on August 28, Blenkinsop tapped out a final message on the cell pipes

'I have been condemned to death. Goodbye.'

***

In the women's block, all the talk was about the liberation of Paris.

'The Allies are coming,' a fellow prisoner whispered to Françoise Labouverie.

The news created a sense of anticipation and joy. Seeing a parade of German soldiers right outside the women's block, Françoise lifted herself up to the window and shouted.

'Paris is free! They're coming! They're coming!'

The sergeant leading the parade turned and took his pistol out of its holster. As he lifted it towards Françoise's window, she jumped back down into the cell and realised the Germans had no intention of letting them go.

In Jungclaus's office at the Hotel Plaza, the final arrangements for the deportation of the 1,800 prisoners of Saint-Gilles had been completed. The clearance of the prison would be achieved in two phases.

---

10   Months later, it would be Leslie who would find Blenkinsop's parents and tell them about their son's days in Saint-Gilles.

NACHT UND NEBEL

In the early hours of August 31, 400 prisoners – including Blenkinsop and 70 of the villagers captured at Meensel-Kiezegem – were roused from their beds as the guards banged on the steel doors.

Told to get dressed and prepare to leave, they waited for three hours until the cell doors were opened and the guards screamed for them to hurry up. In the corridor SS troops swung machine guns and rifles towards the prisoners. The wings of the prison filled with the sounds of shouts, hurrying feet and whispers of confusion. As the prisoners lined up, they were given back some of their possessions and two Red Cross parcels containing food, cigarettes, and toiletries.

In the courtyard they were loaded into the backs of trucks, engines running, filling the early morning air with carbon monoxide. Some took a last look around the walls of the prison, wondering if their next destination would be even more severe. Then the trucks drove through empty streets to the rail station at Schaerbeek and the prisoners were loaded into cattle cars – 60 or 70 to each waggon.

The train left at 10am, but such was the confusion on the Belgian railways that it only covered a few hundred metres before it had to return to the station. None of the prisoners were allowed out of the waggons and they slumped in the trucks in the stifling heat until 7pm when the train moved again.

Sobs filled the air. There was no doubt where they were going. They were heading to Germany and the fact that the Allies were so close made it even more heartbreaking.

One man, Ferdinand Duerinckx, a father-of-six from Meensel-Kiezegem, wrote a note on the back of the label from a tin and threw it from the train[11].

'En route to Germany,' he wrote. 'Unknown destination, everyone healthy. We hope to return soon. Pray for a good quick homecoming.'

---

11   Remarkably, someone found it and it was delivered to his wife, Maria.

As night fell the train arrived in Antwerp and was soon across the Dutch border; then through Arnhem and Deventer, and late on Friday, September 1, it crossed the frontier into Germany. At the border post near Bad Bentheim, the German railway official counted the waggons and noted the train's destination: the concentration camp known as Neuengamme, just outside Hamburg. On reaching the city, the prisoners sat trapped in the rail trucks as the air-raid sirens blared. They arrived in Neuengamme – where half of the camp's 100,000 prisoners eventually died – on the morning of September 3.

Few from that train from Saint-Gilles would ever see their homes and loved ones again. Ferdinand Duerinckx was among those who would not return, as was farmer Vital Craeninckx, whose teenage sons remained in the prison.

Well before that train had reached the dark gates of the camp, the second and final clearance of Saint-Gilles had begun.

In his cell John Bradley raised himself up to look through the bars in the door, spotting German soldiers moving crates on a lower floor of the wing. He immediately realised they were getting ready to complete the evacuation of the prison.

One of the prisoners who acted as a servant to the guards whispered to Françoise Labouverie that the Germans were leaving.

'We'll be free in the morning,' the woman said.

Françoise felt a sickness in her stomach. She did not think that it was freedom that the Nazis had in store for them.

But, having seen the first train leave with so many of their compatriots, the Resistance and civilian population of Brussels now understood what the Germans had planned for the hundreds of people left in Saint-Gilles.

The question was, knowing so many had almost certainly gone to their deaths, could they save the rest?

24

THE TRAIN

THE LAST-MINUTE DEPORTATIONS ordered by Jungclaus outraged the diplomatic community in Brussels. For the past week a war of words – albeit in the moderate language of the diplomatic service – had raged between representatives of neutral nations and German leaders.

On August 23, humanitarian worker Max Séquin wrote to the head of the Red Cross delegation in Belgium, William Schmid-Köchlin, suggesting he demand the release of all political prisoners held by the Germans. Swiss-born Schmid-Köchlin took up Séquin's challenge, although he knew his own powers were limited: he had been denied the status of an IRC delegate by the Nazis and granted permission to help only his compatriots. He enlisted the help of the Swedish ambassador, Baron Kruuse of Verchou, the Belgian diplomat and Red Cross representative, Viscount Joseph Berryer, and a lawyer named Frédéric Eickhoff, who had represented hundreds of people accused of being members of the Resistance in German courts throughout the occupation.

On the morning of August 25, Baron Kruuse invited German ambassador Ludwig Mayr-Falkenberg to the Swedish Consulate. Forty-nine-year-old Mayr-Falkenberg was a Bavarian lawyer who spoke several languages, including English and French, and who had represented the German foreign office in many countries around the world. Eickhoff told Berryer that Mayr-Falkenberg was a decent and humane man who had previously supported his efforts to commute death sentences for Belgian prisoners.

At that point the diplomats calculated there were still 5,000 political prisoners in Belgium, including those in Saint-Gilles, and they requested they remain where they were. They also asked that the planned deportation of the remaining 500 Jews at the Dossin Barracks in Mechelen be halted. The international diplomats agreed on the text of a request to Jungclaus. But Mayr-Falkenberg would not sign it, almost certainly out of fear of Jungclaus.

On August 31, Schmid-Köchlin's committee of diplomats from Switzerland, Spain, Finland and Sweden stressed to Mayr-Falkenberg in writing that their request was motivated by humanitarian rather than political reasons.

By the time Mayr-Falkenberg received the letter on Friday, September 1, the clearance of Saint-Gilles had begun, and 400 prisoners were onboard the first train. Kruuse and Berryer urged Mayr-Falkenberg to do more.

'I have done everything in my power to help you,' the German ambassador said. 'But another attempt may mean my own arrest.'

But even as they argued, 130 Belgian women were being sent to Ravensbrück and a complete round-up of prisoners was being made north and west of the capital to take more than 800 men to Sachsenhausen. Even with the might of the Allied armies right at their heels, there remained a determination in the SS and Gestapo to hold on to and punish its *häftlingen*.

Then, late on Friday, September 1, and into the early hours of Saturday, SS guard detachments brought 32 boxcars into Brussels-South (Bruxelles Midi/Brussel Zuid) train station. Not wishing to alert Belgian railway workers that they were clearing out Saint-Gilles, the Germans had assembled the train in secret and without the use of Belgian personnel. It was due to leave at 8.30am on Saturday, September 2.

First, the trip north to Mechelen, then on through the Netherlands and into Germany. The guards on the train were to be drawn from the SS.

Paperwork for the final train showed around 1,400 Saint-Gilles prisoners. Belgians, French, Russians, Americans, Canadians and British. Resistance and evasion line men and women – and often their families. SOE agents, Resistance couriers or helpers. Plus, the airmen.

In the prison, ever since the 400 prisoners had been taken on August 31, everyone had speculated about their own future. Where were the Allies? They could hear their guns. Would they get here in time? Or would the Germans still have time to evacuate them?

Or, if the city were under siege, would they just be shot?

Throughout the evening of September 1, the women's wing was alive with rumour and chat. Although the guards tried to shut them up, the women shouted about liberation and loudly discussed who had already been taken away in trucks. Messages were passed from husbands in the male wing to say they were still there or to say that their impending execution had been cancelled.

Rumours that Saint-Gilles was going to be evacuated spread through the city and family and friends of prisoners came to stand outside the prison walls, hoping the Germans would simply let their loved ones go. National anthems were sung. Belgian, Dutch, French.

Throughout this display of love and patriotism, the German guards did nothing, adding to the sense that they were no longer interested in the prisoners. In fact, they were busy getting ready for the move.

At 1.30am, the guards began banging the doors with their fists and hammering the rails along the prison wings with wooden batons and metal sticks. They planned to move through the first three wings, A, B, and C, and then the D wing, where the women prisoners were kept. At 3am, they reached B Wing, where police officer Jean-Marie Moortgat, who had worked for the MNB under the codename 'Brochet', was crammed into a cell with about a dozen others. The door opened and a guard shouted:

'*Fertig machen* – transport!'

'Get ready – transport!'

'Now we know,' Moortgat thought, 'our "protectors" are taking us with them.'

In Cell 333 on C Wing Jozef Craeninckx listened as the guards approached. His brother was elsewhere in the prison; his father, although Jozef did not know it, had already been deported. Jozef was under no illusions about his own fate: a wireless operator who had been in the cell when Jozef had arrived had been taken out a few days earlier.

'Your friend was executed at ten o'clock,' the guard came back later to tell him.

Craeninckx sat watching the door as it swung open and a German soldier entered.

'Come along, get ready, take everything with you.'

In the punishment cells Stuart Leslie and John Bradley sweated as if in a fever. Not only was it a warm September night, but the heating pipes were burning hot, fuelled by the raging furnace fire: the Germans were burning piles of documents as they prepared to flee.

The airmen were almost delirious as the doors swung open, light flooded the tiny rooms, and hands pulled at them roughly.

'*Raus! Raus!*'

'Out! Out!'

Most prisoners had no time to get things together; they pulled on their shoes and stumbled out onto the landings.

THE TRAIN

Stuart Leslie was half-marched, half-shoved back toward his regular cell, surprised to find the corridors lined with prisoners. He saw fear and confusion on many faces, as the guards shouted and their boots echoed as they ran back and forth. All the Allied airmen had been gathered together.

'They're emptying the nick,' an English prisoner whispered to Leslie. 'They're taking us to bleeding Germany.'

And with horror, Leslie realised he must be right. They were marched outside and into a courtyard. The fitter prisoners helped those who were weak with their bags and belongings as they were corralled through the two rows of machine guns to where a line of trucks waited, their engines lumbering in the dark.

But inside the prison there was a problem and some of the SS soldiers rushed inside. A riot had started in A block, prisoners were smashing up furniture and shouting insults. The Germans used rifle butts and clubs to subdue the troublemakers and Leslie watched as men from A block were dragged, pushed and kicked into the courtyard. The uprising seemed to have achieved little, but it had delayed the departure from the prison, and every delay would be critical.

As Françoise Labouverie came into the yard, she was met by women from the Red Cross who were handing out emergency ration packs.

'Eat it carefully,' one said. 'You'll get nothing else to eat.'

Each box contained hard tack – a long-lasting biscuit – and a can of meat.

Planks had been laid out as ramps up to the back of the lorries and the women were pushed inside until the last space was filled.

For two and a half hours the prisoners were loaded into the vehicles. Waiting in the trucks with the canvas flaps pulled down, the airmen got curious. Stuart Leslie lifted the flap, and a German soldier struck him with the butt of his rifle. Some guards shouted for silence, but the prisoners carried on talking under the noise of the engines and the shouts of the soldiers. They couldn't be quiet: there had been weeks of discussion about the approaching Allies and, now, right at the moment of liberation, they were being swept away.

Finally, the convoy moved off and swung out into the streets. John Bradley could see that soldiers had been stationed along the route. Police officer Jean-Marie Moortgat thought about making a jump for it but realised that to try to escape would have been suicidal.

The prisoners were uncomfortable, confused and terrified, but, near the railway station, some in Françoise Labouverie's truck started to sing *La Brabançonne* – the Belgian national anthem – and others quickly joined in. It was an act of defiance which left many with tears rolling uncontrollably down their cheeks.

An SS man fired a shot into the air to silence them.

People in the street hurled insults at the German guards. Others ran alongside the trucks and began to collect bits of paper being thrown down. The prisoners were hurriedly writing notes on scraps of paper and on the backs of labels from food tins.

The onlookers rushed to collect them.

'Help us!' some said.

And: 'Please take a message to my parents. They are…'

Many contained simply three words: 'Stop the train!'

25

THE STATION

THE SCENE AT the station was chaotic. Angry soldiers drove the prisoners from the trucks, waving rifle butts and bayonets in their faces. Françoise Labouverie watched the brutal scene, noting how old women – their limbs stiff from the journey in the trucks – and those who were ill or injured were pushed just as roughly as the rest. Some fell or stumbled, and dropped personal items, mirrors or toothbrushes, which the soldiers kicked under the train.

Again, Red Cross workers tried to get close to hand out small packets of food, but the Germans pushed them away this time. One packet, however, was grabbed by Stuart Leslie, who found chocolate, figs and tinned meat inside.

Jozef Craeninckx searched for his father and brother but could not see them. In fact, he could see no one who had been detained after the raids on Meensel-Kiezegem.

The railroad trucks waited with their doors flung open. Most were made of timber with no gaps for air. Robert Beckers saw the words '40 men, 8 horses' on the side of the truck as he was pushed in. He reckoned between 80 and 100 men were in with him. Arms, legs and heads were about to crush into each other. Resistance worker Renée de Jonghe, the young woman who had pretended to be a Nazi to infiltrate the Flemish SS, counted 83 women in hers. All were standing.

Timber sides on some of the waggons had cracks in wooden slats through which the prisoners searched for their friends, relatives, and wives as they passed on to the next boxcar. Françoise Labouverie saw her network leader, Pierre Hauman. She lifted her mouth to the gap in the wall and shouted his name. Realising who it was he asked whether she had seen his wife. Françoise said she had not and found herself overcome with emotion. Two friends from the jail tried to comfort her.

After each car was filled up its heavy door was slid shut and, until the prisoners' eyes were accustomed to the gloom, it seemed terribly dark. Some shouted and cursed the Germans; others cried or quarrelled. Françoise turned angrily on some, forcing them to come to terms with what was happening and urging them to keep control of themselves. Slowly, some of the stronger ones managed to arrange the car so each had some space to either sit or crouch.

When fully loaded the train contained 1,370 political prisoners – 800 were Belgian. Many were Comet Line and EVA, the people who helped airmen such as John Brown and Bill Grosvenor. Elisabeth Wassenhove who had helped Canadian Stuart Leslie was there, as was Elvire Willemsen who had hidden Ryckman and Cozzens. And 13 men and women from Meensel-Kiezegem, including Maria Boesman; Pauline Bollen – whose husband had been executed during the first raid on the village; the village doctor Hendrik Goyens; and Constant and Germaine Wittemans, Resistance leaders from the community. Many of Françoise Labouverie's colleagues from *Tégal* were there and a large number of members of the Luc-Mac intelligence agency (later known as Marc), including Captain Robert Sauveur, aka Robert Prévot, who had gathered intelligence in Liège.

There were several who had worked directly for SOE, such as Gaston Masereel and Frans Flour, and many who had helped them. François Reeve, from Michael Trotobas' Resistance network, was

THE STATION

in the car with the airmen, who included the dozens betrayed by Dezitter. Unlike the others, the airmen were not in a cattle truck: they had been corralled into a baggage section which took up half the length of a railroad car. William Ryckman did a head count and found 42 airmen in all, plus Reeve.

Old friends and crew members were reunited. Kleinman reconnected with his pilot, 'Bud' Brown. Some, such as Staff Sergeant Cecil Spence – in civilian life a grinder at the Vickers factory in Detroit – and Technical Sergeant Kenneth C Holcomb, from Freeport, Illinois, had experienced the whole war together. Still aged just 20, they had trained together, flown 18 bombing missions together in their B-24 – which they dubbed 'You Can't Take It With You' – and baled from their burning aircraft together. Finally, of course, they had shared the experience of having been betrayed by Dezitter.

Joe Murphy searched in vain for Blenkinsop, the airman who told him he was going to be shot. Bill Grosvenor was in a terrible state, still hearing voices from his torture in the dark cell and was convinced the Germans were going to take everyone to a concentration camp and kill them. John Brown tried to comfort him.

Each man flinched as the door slammed shut. To save energy they slid to the ground and listened as the German soldiers hurried to get the train ready. There was a desperation, even an anxiety, in the way the Germans moved: after all, a Guards Armoured Division was now closing in on Brussels.

The crowds who had stood outside the prison had reached the station, peering over fences and climbing up streetlamps to get a view of the train. They watched for the most part in silence, but some shouted insults at the soldiers who walked by.

One SS man turned angrily on a prisoner in Françoise Labouverie's railcar and laughed.

'Tomorrow you will be in Berlin!'

But soon after a Belgian railway worker came close to where Françoise was looking out of the truck and whispered.

'Don't worry, you won't cross the frontier.'

The station's assistant manager, Michel Petit, had watched the hundreds of prisoners arrive with a sense of revulsion and anger. He had been on duty all night and received a message at 6am to tell him Saint-Gilles was being cleared out.

Unbeknown to the German soldiers who greeted him curtly that morning, Petit was an active member of the MNB Resistance group. He had already discussed the deportation with others from the group as many of their comrades were on the train, including the policeman, Moortgat.

The sun was now rising on a sunny September morning and a suffocating heat started to build up inside the railroad cars. Seeing the prisoners' discomfort, Petit's colleague, Duverger, ignored German threats and started to open the ventilation slots on the closed cars, so fresh air could get into the wagons.

At 7.30am Petit walked along the platform, the train to one side, a line of SS soldiers on the other. He reckoned there were between 150 and 175 of them. Back in his office, he met with other members of the MNB and told them the locomotive requested to pull the train must be sabotaged. He had a message sent to the Laeken resistance group: it must make sure that every group between Brussels and Antwerp is aware the train is coming and that it was not to cross the border.

'*This train must not reach its destination.*'

The Germans were already impatient. An officer came looking for Petit and told him to prepare to receive a *Wehrmacht* hospital train which was being diverted to Brussels-South. Petit nodded. When alone, he considered using the explosive charges he had hidden in a box to damage various sections of track. But there was no way he could carry the heavy box, secure the charges, set them off, and get away undetected with so many Germans at the station. Instead, he found a colleague and they managed to slip away, fixing an explosive charge to one rail switch.

In the meantime, another of Petit's messengers went to meet the station chief – Léon Petit. He was no relation to Michel and was not an active member of the Resistance, but he shared his assistant's hatred of the Nazis. Michel's messenger told Léon he must do everything he could to stop the train leaving.

'We are trying to persuade Jungclaus to stop the train,' he said, 'so it must be kept here until the decision is made.'

Agreeing to let his office become the headquarters for the clandestine operation to stop the train, Léon Petit said the first plan had to be to delay the delivery of the locomotive. He sent the Resistance man to his colleague, Piette, who immediately told the driver, Roelants, the plan. All the locomotives were in different locations around the marshalling yard so Roelants and his two fellow foremen, Deshorme and Masquelier, had them moved to the railway depot, further away, to cause a delay when the Germans requested a locomotive.

First World War veteran Masquelier had, in fact, been leading a small Resistance cell for two years, preparing ways to sabotage engines once the Allies reached Belgium. He had also been falsifying data in the logbooks of locomotives, drivers and firemen, losing the Germans thousands of hours of railway time each month, as well as distributing underground anti-Nazi newspapers.

The railway Resistance group – including Léon Petit's assistants, Parmentier, De Coster and Gevaerts – gathered in the station manager's office for a discussion. *Should they take up arms against the German guards?* No, that plan was quickly dismissed: who knew how many might die in a gun battle against such a force of SS and the prisoners would be trapped and dangerously vulnerable onboard the train. Even a successful violent intervention would likely kill as many prisoners as it would save.

'We will not feel the shame of having helped deport our compatriots,' Parmentier told them.

Everyone agreed the Germans were to be constantly misinformed on the number of locomotives available. More messages were sent out. Some drivers were told to disappear or report to the office that they were ill. The signalmen were told additional 'stops' must be put into the network's schedule to slow up all rail traffic in the Brussels area. Piette sent word to the drivers already in work or out on the track to converge their trains on Brussels-South, the line north or the marshalling yard to help clog up the local network. Everyone was told that whenever they damaged a part, they must also ensure that its spares were also broken or lost. In the confusion of war, they reckoned they could get away with it.

A German officer arrived at 9.15am with documentation for the train – including its convoy number: 1.682.508. The Germans wanted a powerful locomotive of 'Type 33'. Only a small number existed on the Belgian railways and the engineers now knew exactly which locomotive they needed to sabotage.

Around the same time the railwaymen became aware of a difference of opinion among the senior German officers at the station. The army train director had no stomach for the deportation, seeing the need to move ambulance trains of wounded soldiers as a much greater priority. The SS officer in charge of the guard turned on him angrily, but the train director, in his subsequent conversations with Léon Petit and Parmentier, did little to force the issue of finding a locomotive.

The driver assigned to the engine was named Georges. Roelants sent a man to meet him on his way to work and tell him to report sick. The station doctor, Dr Genot, signed him off. Another driver, Van der Veken, was brought in.

An answer came back from the depot regarding the requested locomotive. The Type 33 engine had broken down, the message stated. In fact, Roelants had gone to locomotive number 3302 and damaged an oil pipe used in the lubrication of the engine.

A new locomotive, number 1202, was assigned but when the engineers 'checked' it they discovered a broken pump. Roelants had torn out the lubrication pumps with his own hands. They all knew that had the Germans time to investigate these acts of sabotage Roelants and others would have been shot on the spot.

The Germans were told the pump on 1202 could be fixed but it would take some time. Masquelier went to the maintenance department and told the two men charged with fixing the pump to work slowly. Indeed, both men did nothing at all.

But the Germans were getting suspicious and an officer announced they were bringing in their own army mechanics. Every repair job would be taken over by them. The Belgian engineers wandered off as the Germans fixed the pump.

It was midmorning by time the locomotive finally left the depot, but now the Belgians were back in control. The driver and signalman arranged for it to head in the wrong direction, becoming trapped in a corner of the marshalling yard. At noon an impatient SS officer set out to track it down, finding it jammed into a dead end by other trains. Seeing a German freight train coming into the station, he demanded its locomotive be reassigned to the prisoner train. The locomotive was uncoupled from the freight train and word of the Resistance operation was quietly passed to its driver by Parmentier. In the continuing confusion of the busy station the locomotive was sent to a carousel to be turned but was 'misdirected' and headed to the Schaerbeek marshalling yard to the north of the city centre.

In the railroad trucks rumours and speculation continued to spread. The shouts from those that feared they were being taken to Germany to be gassed were hard to ignore. Others said the Germans just wanted to get the prisoners out of the city so they could be shot without any witnesses. No, said some, the Allies were too close; their murderers would be arrested.

In the distance came the crump of explosions and the rattle of small arms fire. But the train still did not move.

A message came to Petit that the Resistance was going to make a threat to Jungclaus: they would machine-gun a nearby hospital train if the deportation went ahead.

***

By 2pm, the heat in the packed wagons had become almost unbearable; the prisoners were tired, frightened, hungry and thirsty. In Jean-Marie Moortgat's car the air was becoming unbreathable and several people had fainted. The prisoners forced open two air shafts in the roof which the Germans had tied down with barbed wire.

Renée de Jonghe watched as an elderly woman licked the sweat off the back of another's neck to get some moisture to slake her thirst. Another appeared to be already dead, jammed into the corner by a group of people so her inert body had nowhere to fall. Was it possible that, in the heat of the railcar, they would all die through a lack of water? Renée tried to pry open the boards of the cattle car. But she had little room to move and very little strength. Her fingers bled.

At 20, Renée was one of the youngest political prisoners on the train – although a few were still in their teens. One of the very youngest, Jules Buedts, was just 16. For a year he had worked as a courier for the NKB, carrying information about troop movements between his hometown of Keerbergen and Louvain and Mechelen. He had once crawled along a dry stream and spent the day noting the movements at an airfield close to the town. But before dawn on June 19, 1944, the street outside the family's café and home had

THE STATION

suddenly been filled with German soldiers. Pulling on his trousers and throwing his socks into his shoes, Buedts climbed out of a back window but was spotted and arrested. He had been betrayed by a member of the Resistance. Tortured for three days in the jail at Antwerp, he told his GFP captors he was only 16 and 'the older men would not tell me the secrets, so I don't know anything.' Buedts had been moved to Saint-Gilles only a few days before the final deportations had begun.

In his cattle truck was a big Dutchman.

'As we pass through the Netherlands we must escape,' he told Buedts, 'because if we get to Germany we will die.'

Robert Beckers, meanwhile, was 'thrown toward the back of his car and it was practically impossible to move to any other position'. He watched people near him use a spoon or fork stolen from the prison to make an extra hole in the wooden wall.

From her vantage point at a crack in the wall of the railcar, Françoise Labouverie realised the German retreat had become chaotic. Trucks drove wildly, ignoring other traffic, while some soldiers packed onto horse-drawn carts or rode from the city on bicycles.

Stuart Leslie looked around at the faces in the baggage car. Most seemed sadly resigned to their fate. They had come so far, having spent months on the run, but now they were locked up and on their way to Germany. A prisoner of war camp had never been mentioned to them and their fate seemed very uncertain. Someone slammed his fist against the wall in anger and frustration.

There was anger on the platform, too – or at least there appeared to be, as the SS guards watched a fight break out between two Belgians.

Roelants shouted at his boss, Piette.

'I have been in work for hours,' he yelled. 'My shift should be over.'

It was a drama faked for the Germans' benefit. With a shrug, Piette agreed to let the engineer go home and called for another driver, Deshorme, who arrived grumbling, 'It is Saturday; I have to go and collect my wages otherwise I won't get paid.'

Deshorme then disappeared for the next two hours.

The other driver, Van der Veken, had been wandering around the railway station since before lunch, staying one step ahead of anyone who might be looking for him. When the Germans finally found him, he said he was waiting for the correct locomotive. But, realising the Germans were losing patience with his excuses, Van der Veken took drastic action.

Standing on the footplate of an engine he deliberately threw himself off it, pretending to fall, badly hurting his leg. The SS looking on turned on him angrily but there was nothing they could do as comrades carried him off to see a doctor.

By 3.15pm an armed unit of SS arrived at the locomotive depot, demanding to see Deshorme, but, as he was still off getting his pay, two of the SS dragged out another driver, Louis Verheggen, and stoker, Léon Pochet, telling them to drop whatever they were doing and drive the locomotive for the prisoner train. Verheggen had just arrived on his shift and did not know what was happening. Pochet whispered they were going to be driving a train load of prisoners.

Engine 1202 had by now been freed from its corner of the yard and brought to the engine house. The foreman, Masquelier, and the other mechanics in the depot had done all they could.

The stakes were getting higher. The German army train director had already shown little stomach for the deportation, and a morning and half an afternoon of sabotage and deception had tried the patience of an SS unit already furious and apprehensive about their inevitable upcoming retreat.

As Verheggen and Pochet climbed onto the footplate, three SS guards took up places behind them. For the next 18 hours these two railwaymen would stand with loaded guns at their back.

Even so, Verheggen and Pochet had decided to continue to delay and sabotage the train. Both knew they would be aided by the fact that 1202 was not of the powerful type required to pull such a large train.

Exchanging glances, they saw the determination in each other's eyes.

At about 3.30pm Verheggen and Pochet manoeuvred Locomotive 1202 out of the depot and headed towards Brussels-South. But Verheggen immediately took a great risk. With a signal open for slow local trains going south to Ruisbroek, he went ahead and, with a colleague quickly switching the points, entered the busy marshalling yard on the wrong track and headed into a cul-de-sac. The driver and a railroad official faked a row for the benefit of the Germans as the locomotive was directed towards Forest South train station.

At Forest, the assistant station manager, Vanderstricht, was a member of the Resistance and had been briefed about the prisoner train. He had therefore already permitted a 72-wagon German freight train priority for entry into Brussels-South, blocking the line. Verheggen was forced to move slowly into another dead-end track.

Vanderstricht told the SS men holding their guns on Verheggen that German orders gave the freight train priority as it contained army supplies and their locomotive must wait. Verheggen and the others now had a little help from the exasperated German driver of the freight train who got into an argument with his superiors, which became so heated he was eventually arrested.

To clear the track the locomotive on the freight train was uncoupled and the long row of waggons separated.

While Verheggen waited he let the 'blower' run so his locomotive wasted steam and water. Every tiny bit of time he could waste would count towards saving the passengers.

Eventually arriving in Brussels-South, Verheggen and Pochet set about the time-consuming job of coupling the locomotive to two lengths of train consisting of 32 boxcars, including one at the head of the train which contained a detachment of German soldiers and officials, all eager to get away. It took the two men 45 minutes to bring the train together. As they worked, they looked down the track, along the long train of misery and the lines of SS soldiers. Two machine-guns had been set up next to the track, giving the operators a field of fire which took in the length of both sides of the train. The SS officer in charge was determined there would be no escape.

Verheggen went to speak to one of the German railway officers.

'Because of the size of the train and the length of the journey, we should carry out a brake test,' he insisted.

'The workshop foreman has already done one,' the German replied, waving him away.

'But the workshop foreman does not have to drive the train,' Verheggen told him.

As Verheggen wandered around, a *Reichbahn* foreman who would be riding in the car at the head of the train came to make an unofficial request.

'I will pay you a lot of money if you can take me to Frankfurt,' he said

Verheggen turned his back, disgusted at the cowardly way some of those who had lorded it over him and his nation for four years were now acting.

Climbing back into the engine he was even more determined to prevent the Germans from getting out of Belgium. He did not know all that his colleagues at the railway station had done in secret to delay the train, but he knew there was little more they could do.

THE STATION

It was down to him and Pochet now. It was time to leave.

In the baggage car, the airmen were arguing over how close the Allies were.

'Ten to one our boys get here before Jerry gets steam up,' one said.

'You're on,' someone replied miserably.

At that moment the train lurched into motion and the whistle blasted, sending shivers down the spines of each on the train and of those watching.

'You owe me,' said the pessimist, unhappy to have won his bet.

26

A JOURNEY TO NOWHERE

LOUIS VERHEGGEN WAS an ordinary working man in his early 40s. He had not been part of the organised Resistance, but everything now depended on what he alone could improvise. Trains had been carrying Belgians to Germany throughout the occupation, sometimes with *Reichbahn* crews but always with the help of Belgian workers. Now it was his turn to be in the cab, and he was determined to make a difference. As someone later noted: 'One man in the right place can be worth a regiment'.

The last person Verheggen spoke to before the train moved off from Brussels-South was Deweiger, one of the station's assistant managers, as he leaned down from the footplate:

'Paris is liberated, the Allies will soon be in Brussels. This train will not cross the border.'

He and Pochet released the brake and opened the throttle. It was 4.50pm and the train was more than eight hours behind schedule. Then, on being asked by the Germans to return to Forest to collect a flatbed wagon holding an anti-aircraft gun and attach it to the rear of the train, Verheggen took the opportunity to take on water and waste more time at Forest. It was 5.55pm before they started moving again.

Throughout the journey, each time Verheggen moved off, he did so abruptly, hoping to cause a break in the coupling.

Moving at a painfully slow speed – about three miles an hour – the train trundled towards Schaerbeek marshalling yard. The signal into the yard was set to 'safe' but, guessing the SS guards on the footplate did not understand the signals, he set the brake and started to get off. One of the guards swung the machine-gun around into his face as Verheggen said he needed a yard 'pilot' for negotiating the network of tracks through the yard.

The bluff failed. Verheggen was dragged back on board by his collar. The guard pushed the gun into his side: '*Maschine kaput, du kaput!*'

***

In the baggage car occupied by the Allied airmen everyone was discussing the stop-start of the journey.

'The Resistance has blown up the tracks,' one said.

Some of the airmen tried to pull out the bars on the windows. Reeve told them to stop as the Germans would check if they had been damaged.

'Besides,' he said, 'I can open the door.'

Taking out a concealed knife he unlocked the door and a frisson of excitement went through the huddle of men.

'We should not try to escape until night falls and when the train is running along a sloping bank,' he told them.

In Françoise Labouverie's railcar, suspicion rose that all the to-ing and fro-ing was part of a German plan to cover the military evacuation. On one long curve they saw there were huge red crosses on the roofs of their trucks and they suspected the Germans were running the train up and down the line to stop the Allies bombing retreating troop trains.

One cynic said the reasoning made no sense because the Allies would judge that an attack on a retreating army was far more of a priority than a 'handful of prisoners'.

'If there is bombing to be done,' she said glumly, 'then we won't be spared.'

Still, the train moved north, leaving Brussels and reaching Vilvoorde on the way to Mechelen. The signal here was set to 'stop', the signalman having received a message from Brussels-South.

Although the guards were angry, there was nothing they could do: they could not risk ploughing into an oncoming train. But as the wait went on and no other train came through, one of the guards lost patience and stepped down to walk a little way up the track.

Climbing back onto the footplate, he ordered Verheggen to ignore the signal and to drive on. The driver protested they would all be killed in a collision but was threatened with the gun: it was becoming too dangerous to push the guards too far.

At Eppegem, the Resistance had again set the signal to 'stop', but the Germans ordered Verheggen to ignore it, and they crawled on towards the busy railway hub at Mechelen, which they reached at 11pm. Verheggen knew he would need to stop here: the signals had been put out of operation by Allied bombing and he explained to the guards he would have to make a phone call to get the 'all-clear' to continue down the track. They were suspicious, but less willing to risk a head-on collision now darkness had fallen.

Two of them climbed down from the footplate with Verheggen, escorting him to a track telephone while Pochet and the third guard waited in the train. Pochet cautiously allowed steam to be steadily released, with the guard unaware what was happening. When Verheggen got back on with permission to drive ahead the two Belgians continued to allow the engine to lose boiler pressure. They watched the needle on the gauge fall slowly, again hoping the SS guards would not notice.

Still only half-an-hour from where they had started, Verheggen came up with another plan. Knowing the water tanks at Mechelen had been damaged by the same bombing that smashed the signals, he risked claiming the locomotive needed water – even though he had enough to get to Antwerp. A German railway official and the assistant manager at Mechelen stood by the side of the train and joined the discussion. Verheggen believed that they might agree to uncoupling the locomotive and sending it south-east to Muizen, the source of the nearest available water supply, but when the German official suggested taking the whole train, he smiled inside. That would take even more time.

The Mechelen assistant manager also explained the line to Mechelen was snarled up with German trains. Verheggen argued it would be best if the train were diverted, back via Brussels, to Liège and on to Germany from there. Reluctantly, on hearing elements of the British army were bypassing Brussels to head towards Antwerp, the German railway officer agreed.

All the while, Françoise Labouverie could hear the German guards shouting and threatening Verheggen, while other soldiers patrolled the track outside.

Inside her car, the discomfort was even worse. The heat of the day had gone, and the sweat grew cold on the prisoners' bodies. They shivered in the dark. The bucket of water they had been given to drink was empty. No one had been able to use a toilet. Moments of singing, designed to keep their spirits up, had ended. No one wanted to speak.

In one corner a nurse looked after a young woman who was eight months' pregnant. Everyone felt pity but most had become lost in concern only for themselves. All the same, despite their exhaustion, some stood in the dark, allowing space on the floor for the expectant mother to lie down. She cried in pain for most of the night.

It was 20 minutes to midnight when the train pulled into Muizen for the water it did not need. By now so far off schedule and planned route, it had become *le train fantôme*, the 'Ghost Train', no longer 'visible' to officials beyond the train itself.

Verheggen and Pochet worked slowly but tried to seem busy, looking for a chance to escape even as the SS kept their guns trained on them. A German messenger came to say the train was not allowed to leave during the darkness.

Françoise Labouverie's fitful sleep was disturbed by a splintering of wood from the next truck. A woman near her whispered in horror: 'Oh God, they are trying to escape!'

'Please don't let them be caught!' said another.

Everyone listened. There was more splintering, then the crunch of footsteps on the ballast at the side of the track. Everyone held their breath. A few moments later came a burst of machine-gun fire and then silence. Someone cried out, like a howl in the night, but it was not anyone outside; it was someone in Françoise's railcar going into panic. A nun began to pray.

'Oh God, have mercy upon us!'

One of the other prisoners whispered to Françoise.

'Perhaps it wasn't a prisoner escaping. Perhaps the *Boches* are opening the truck and shooting prisoners.'

Françoise took a deep breath and gripped the other woman's hand. But outside everything had gone quiet.

Jean-Marie Moortgat told the others in his car that the shooting and two explosions they could hear must be his colleagues in the Resistance carrying out acts of sabotage. Shortly afterwards, an SS guard came to stand outside.

'If anyone tries to escape two or three prisoners will be picked out, stood against the side of the waggon and shot.'

Despite the warning some planned to escape. Dick Pagenstecher, the son of a Dutch mother and German father, had deserted from the German army and gone into hiding with his family in Brussels. He had been arrested when he went to the home of his friend, Petronelle 'Nel' Van Gellicum, and found the German police waiting: Nel had just been picked up for aiding Dutch people who were hoping to escape to Britain. Both she and Pagenstecher ended up on the train and Dick's sister, Charlotte Ambach – herself a member of the EVA network – watched as her brother and others tore up the planking in the floor of their cattle car until they made a hole large enough to escape.

Verheggen and Pochet were finishing taking on water for the engine when the shooting broke out. Both men pulled themselves back onto the footplate and everybody took cover. Verheggen had been planning to escape into the streets here, but the thought that the Germans were getting easy on the trigger persuaded him to forget that idea.

In the trucks the night was long and cold and cramped. Airmen picked at the Red Cross parcels. Some tried to eke out what they had. Items were exchanged. Guards had been placed all around the train making escape through the door opened by Reeve seem impossible. Besides, the prisoners were so tired and confused, and the journey so strange, they did not know where they were. It had been a day of agony for the prisoners. But they had covered barely 15 of the 400 miles to Neuengamme.

Their fates remained in the balance; they felt vulnerable and alone. But they weren't: the fight continued to save their lives.

***

Early on September 2, Schmid-Köchlin, the head of the IRC in Belgium, had resumed his plea for the estimated 5,000 political prisoners who were being detained under the threat of deportation.

As yet unaware that Saint-Gilles had been emptied and a final trainload of prisoners was waiting to leave Brussels-South, the Swiss wrote to Jungclaus in the Hotel Plaza via the ambassador Mayr-Falkenberg.

'It is my duty, as representative of the only body currently dealing with the prisoners, to draw Your Excellency's attention to the fact that the IRC would find the planned deportation of the prisoners difficult to understand.'

On hearing nothing, a delegation of the diplomats went to the Plaza and tried to find Jungclaus or Eggert Reeder, the military administrator who had been in charge of deportations under Falkenhausen. They were not there.

It was then that word had reached the diplomats about the train which was at that time waiting to leave Brussels-South, and they sent an urgent message to Mayr-Falkenberg at the German Embassy:

'The *Wehrmacht* prison in Saint-Gilles now appears to have been cleared. We have noticed that this measure has caused great concern among the population, and we are firmly convinced that if Your Excellency wanted to rescind it, the unconditional gratitude of not only thousands of Belgian families, but also of the whole world, would be expressed to you.'

Mayr-Falkenberg spent two hours in negotiation with Jungclaus. But was unable to get him to agree to stop the transport.

The ambassador knew that the German military was withdrawing as quickly as possible from the city and was debating whether to leave hundreds of its own wounded behind. A huge hospital train was being organised, but it might easily face Resistance attacks – especially if the Germans were seen to deport thousands right at the moment of their retreat.

This gave Mayr-Falkenberg an idea: he decided to reach out to an ally in uniform with the courage and intelligence to face down Jungclaus and persuade him to help save thousands of lives.

27

A BATTLE OF WILLS

DURING THE OCCUPATION, the German military had taken over the Bordet Institute, a hospital in the Boulevard de Waterloo. It was run by General Werner Wachsmuth, a 44-year-old veteran of the First World War and one of Germany's most respected surgeons.

Despite becoming such a high-profile figure, in 1935 he had taken the dangerous stance of refusing to join the Nazi Party. Therefore, to be 'sheltered from Hitler' he rejoined the army. On September 1, 1944, with the British getting closer to Brussels, Wachsmuth had 'received a direct order from Hitler's staff' to prepare to leave the Bordet with all his staff, evacuating only the walking wounded.

'I was ordered to abandon the others, all the others,' he said later. 'To leave behind 1,000 sick, crippled and dying people.'

Wachsmuth instantly decided to disobey the order and, gathering his medical staff together, he told them: 'The medical oath forbids me to abandon my patients, under any circumstances.'

On Saturday, September 2, 1944, at around 9pm, when the train was negotiating the 'stop' signals on the way to Mechelen, Wachsmuth was checking the bandage of a wounded man when he was called to the telephone: it was Mayr-Falkenberg ringing personally to say he wished to see him urgently at the German Embassy

Mayr-Falkenberg said he, the International Red Cross, and the consuls of Spain, Sweden, and Switzerland had all appealed 'in vain' to Jungclaus to stop the train now leaving Brussels.

The ambassador looked grave and added: 'There is only you left.' He told Wachsmuth he must stop the deportations 'in the name of humanity and to save the honour of our fatherland.'

Wachsmuth immediately understood that the last-minute deportations put any of the wounded he wished to evacuate at risk, both from Resistance action and also because transport was scarce and he would need trains to evacuate his patients.

He drove to the Hotel Plaza and was led into Jungclaus' rooms. It was an intimidating atmosphere. Jungclaus was flanked by his SS chief of staff; Reeder, representing the views of Gauleiter Josef Grohé, who Wachsmuth knew to be 'a convinced Nazi'; and another officer who the surgeon did not know.

'We do not have the right to send 5,000 hostages across the Rhine in the current circumstances,' Wachsmuth stated. 'This crime will cost Germany dearly and those responsible will risk the most just punishments after the war.'

Jungclaus cut him off. 'It is by deporting the hostages that we hold the Belgians in our hands! Do you forget, Doctor Wachsmuth, that no one will harm your dear wounded, if the hostages are in a safe place?'

Wachsmuth then distilled his argument to two points: firstly, that stopping the deportations would 'make amends for some of the injustices that were done to the people during the difficult years of occupation' and 'such a generous act would have an echo throughout the civilised world'.

Secondly – and this was the point which swayed the debate – he argued for the protection of the German wounded. 'It is my duty to care for the hundreds of wounded, who, as they are not fit for transport, we have to leave to the generosity of the Belgians. I am willing to stay with my wounded men in Brussels with all my medical personnel once all the German troops have left – and will require that the Belgian people show generosity in protecting the wounded who remain behind.'

There was then a silence. Wachsmuth wondered whether he had overstepped the mark. But the safety of the German wounded in military hospitals in Belgium – most significantly the central one run by Wachsmuth – was a crucial factor. One estimate made later that week suggested there were 10,000 wounded German soldiers who went into Allied hands when their comrades retreated from Brussels.

Jungclaus looked at Reeder. The latter, who was not a fanatic like Grohé, declared: 'I agree, these prisoners must be released. We should do it for Professor Wachsmuth, who is asking for this for himself and his wounded.'

Jungclaus' chief of staff nodded in agreement.

The question seemed to be settled. But the meeting was interrupted when an orderly brought Jungclaus a written message.

He opened it and read it to the others: 'A train of 1,600 deportees has arrived in Diest. You agree, gentlemen, this train must continue its journey to Germany?'

After a short argument, Jungclaus again backed down and agreed to send a message to Diest to tell the 'Ghost Train' to stop and return all the prisoners to Saint-Gilles.

But overnight, on September 2-3, the Germans had become confused about the location of the 'Ghost Train'. It was not at Diest to the east of Brussels, where it would have gone if it had travelled via Leuven. It was in a siding 25 miles to the west in Muizen. Jungclaus' messenger went to Diest.

***

At 5.30am on Sunday, September 3, Verheggen and Pochet – with the armed SS guards at their backs – began the return towards Mechelen, planning now to go back to Brussels and then onto Liège, as had been discussed the night before.

The train had been reconfigured: at first light Verheggen took the locomotive to a turntable so it would be at the other end of the train to take it back towards Brussels. This meant that the flatbed with the anti-aircraft gun – previously at the rear of the train – was now next to the engine.

As the train approached the station at Mechelen, the wheels began to slip and spin. The train slowed and stopped. Verheggen explained to his guard that something was wrong with the distributors which dropped sand onto the track in front of the wheel to increase the traction of the drive wheels. These were essential for a locomotive to pull a train of this size, he explained. The Germans agreed to let him ring for help. Under guard, Verheggen walked the full length of the train to the nearest track telephone and requested a new locomotive which could tow him and the train.

'The new driver will be Gérardy,' the voice said on the other end of the line.

'Good,' Verheggen replied. 'And Gérardy understands the contents of the train?'

'He does,' came the voice on the other end.

Returning to the locomotive Verheggen walked into an argument among the SS. Those manning the anti-aircraft gun felt too exposed next to the engine – the main target for Allied aircraft – and wanted to be moved to what was now the back of the train. Verheggen shrugged: anything that would waste time suited him.

He and Pochet began the manoeuvre once they reached Mechelen, unhooking the flak waggon with the anti-aircraft gun and pulling it into a siding before relinking the engine to the train.

The three SS guards remained on the engine footplate and had no idea what was happening more than 30 wagons back. They were now bored and tired.

The Belgians exchanged glances. When they moved off they didn't pause. The men on the gun waggon waited for it to return to the siding but the train kept going. They had been abandoned.

Further down the track the train met up with Gérardy, who hooked up to tow the train back towards Brussels.

The prisoners sensed the change in direction the train was travelling. This time the attitude among the passengers was at first confusion and then a restrained sense of joy. They strained to look through the slats.

The air was filled with smoke and the sound of gunfire. Trains passed slowly in the opposite direction, loaded down with equipment and soldiers – many nursing injuries. From their confined and uncomfortable vantage point the airmen were witnessing the retreat of the German army from Belgium. They couldn't help wondering how their guards must feel, knowing they were on a train heading back into a city they were losing control of.

Most passengers on the train were Belgian and looked out in silence at the black smoke which hung over their city: the large copper dome of the Palais de Justice thick with flame, a fire set by the Germans to destroy documents of the occupation. There was a gasp as the dome collapsed in upon itself. It was a heartbreaking sight for people struggling to maintain both their morale and their physical strength. Some, weak and tired, began to cry: some muttered again that the Germans would machine-gun them rather than set them free.

Between 9.30am and 10am the train arrived at Petite-Île freight station in the suburb of Anderlecht. Having taken so long to reach Mechelen, it returned to the south of the capital in just 30 minutes. Even at its starting point at Brussels-South, the train had never been further from its destination.

As soon as it arrived a group of German and Belgian Nazis demanded that Gérardy's locomotive be detached. Holding him at gunpoint, they made him attach the engine to another train on which they planned to escape to the Netherlands. Gérardy's own safety was now in doubt – but he and his fireman were able to escape from the train when it reached Mechelen.

All along the route to Petite-Île, Verheggen had noted the stations were empty, personnel having agreed to leave their jobs and head home, both for their own safety and to cause the Germans more confusion. However, having followed reports of the prison train, a small number of staff with links to the Resistance had returned to Petite-Île to try to ensure it did not leave again.

They were led by the station manager, Van Beveren, the son of a veteran of the First World War, who had been on duty for almost 14 hours but had no intention of leaving. He was supported by two Great War veterans, Gansberg, whose son – a *résistant* in the Ardennes – was missing presumed dead, and Neyt, who kept open the signals to ensure that any potential replacement locomotives rushed through and were not available for the train.

All were heartened by the news the Allies were in Tournai. They were further encouraged by the promises of Fernand Adam, a French *Deuxième Bureau* agent working with the Resistance networks *Groupe G* and *Zéro*, who said the hour of liberation was close.

The prison train pulled up next to an army hospital train – one of which Wachsmuth was evacuating the wounded who were well enough to be moved quickly. The prisoners watched a steady flow of German army ambulances bring lines of walking wounded and stretchers to be taken on board. Every carriage on the ambulance train became crowded with soldiers.

The SS guards on the prisoner train were also furious at having been sent back towards the advancing Allies. When they realised

A BATTLE OF WILLS

Gérardy's locomotive had gone, they grew even more angry. On the road they could see their comrades escaping in army vehicles.

Some of the SS found cognac on an abandoned delivery truck at the station and began to drink it. As they did, *Witte Brigade* snipers started to shoot at the train.

Verheggen's locomotive had already been detached from the prisoner train and moved onto a side track and two of the guards wandered off, leaving only one. Verheggen carefully took his identity papers from his jacket which was hanging in the cab and got down, pretending to inspect the wheels and the sandboxes. His stoker remained on the footplate and managed to let the flames go out in the firebox.

As soon as Verheggen was out of sight of the guard, he walked swiftly, but as naturally as possible, across the tracks, passing the signal box in full view of a group of Germans. Expecting a bullet at any moment, he was shocked to find no one took any notice of him.

Walking down the embankment to the river Senne, planning to hide in the ruins of a nearby gasometer, he began to worry about being tracked by police dogs. Wading through the water in a storm drain to throw any dogs off his scent, he eventually found his way into the streets.

Reaching his home, he checked with a neighbour if the Germans had been there looking for him, but they had not. Reunited with his wife, he told her they were heading quickly to her sister in Ixelles, just to be sure he faced no last-minute retribution from the Gestapo.

Amazingly, he would simply return to work as normal the following day.

Fortunately, the SS did not take out their frustration at Verheggen's escape on Pochet. But there was a frightening moment as one of them – feeling tricked by the Belgian – angrily fired his machine gun into the work clothes Verheggen had left in the cab.

Even as Verheggen made his escape, the German officer in charge of the prison train had still not received word from his superiors.

Angrily, the German officer confronted Pochet who said his engine could not run. The officer went off to demand another locomotive, but the only other one in Petite-Île was reserved for the Red Cross hospital train.

A small number of railway personnel had returned to Brussels-South when they had heard the prison train was at Petite-Île. They called all available locomotives to block the tracks at Schaerbeek and left every signal open, so the SS on the stranded prison train had to watch as several lone locomotives passed. Some ran out along the track and yelled at them. But it was hopeless.

Ryckman noticed the drunken soldiers were becoming riotous.

***

At 10.30am, a delegation of diplomats was summoned to a meeting with the German Ambassador, Mayr-Falkenberg. He told them Jungclaus had ordered the immediate release of the prisoners and that the train had appeared at Petite-Île. The delegation headed out to the station.

A Mr Roberte of the Red Cross, was already at the station, having received a call earlier that morning to say the Germans were transferring the prisoners back to Saint-Gilles. He had rushed to the prison with German-speaking Belgian, Dr Van Dooren, whose wife was one of the prisoners on the train, and discovered the train had actually arrived at Petite-Île.

Standing on the platform, Mr Roberte started negotiations with the German railway commander, while the doctor was allowed to tend to the sick. First aid boxes were brought out of the station and passed into some of the wagons.

Van Dooren spoke with Gansberg and Adam as he worked.

'What are your plans?' he asked them.

'The train will not leave the station,' Gansberg said.

'Are you sure?'

'Absolutely.'

Gansberg told him he would shoot the German in charge of the train if necessary.

Further acts of sabotage were also being carried out to ensure the train did not leave Petite-Île. Various pieces of equipment, such as valves on the water tower, were removed and buried. Telephone lines were cut and the Belgians told the Germans their headquarters must have abandoned Brussels.

Fernand Adam climbed unseen into the guard's wagon and carried out a trunk; he had rescued a box of jewellery and personal possessions belonging to many of the prisoners.

Françoise Labouverie watched trains passing, jammed full of soldiers and saw several guards from the prisoner train leave their posts and run to jump on slow-moving passenger trains.

Looking south-east towards Halle, the German officer in charge of the train could see the smoke of explosions. The sound of the guns was getting closer. A Belgian railway staff member suggested he should get on the hospital train and get away as soon as he could.

Then he received Mayr-Falkenberg's instructions. Still unsure, the train commander sent a dispatch rider into the city to obtain clarification. He came back, having found no-one – the military headquarters had been abandoned.

Confused and with little time to spare, the train commander agreed to let the political prisoners go.

At about 12.30pm, Gansberg and Adam ran along the length of the train, pulling open the doors of the cattle trucks.

The SS guards watched and took no action.

Close to the boxcar in which Françoise Labouverie waited, there was a corporal who had not left his post. Françoise sensed from the look on his face that he was a veteran who had seen enough of the war and was perhaps now waiting to be taken prisoner.

'What's happening?' she called.

He looked up and down the track to check nobody was watching and then took a step towards her.

'It's all right,' he said, and she realised there were tears in his eyes. 'You're going home. We are all going home. The war is over.'

But even as the doors of the cattle cars were finally thrown open and the occupants told to come out, there was some hesitation. Many passengers argued with each other about where they were: they were not familiar with the goods station.

In Renée de Jonghe's car there was fear that the Germans were outside with machine guns and flame throwers, ready to mow them down, and the most vocal shouted to the others that they were better off inside. Robert Beckers couldn't help thinking 'we're goners.'

But then a new sound reached their ears. Family members of the prisoners had found the train and called out to loved ones. Belgian voices shouted it was safe. A few stepped down, then more, then everyone.

People searched eagerly for their loved ones. The lucky few found them very quickly and fell into each other's arms. Some wandered off alone. Others hesitated, afraid that there might be German soldiers in the streets, or they might be shot as soon as they left the station.

Friends urged them to hurry away in case the Germans changed their minds.

Jozef Craeninckx stood aside from the crowd and looked down the track, seeing his brother, Frans, and together, they found the others from Meensel-Kiezegem. There had been 13 people on the train, including Pauline Bollen, whose husband Oscar Beddegenoodts had been executed by the Nazis; the town doctor, Hendrik

A BATTLE OF WILLS

Goyens; and Constant and Germaine Wittemans, who had endured abuse and torture rather than give up their sons to the Nazis. They had no idea what happened to their friends from the village. Once united, the weary little group began the long walk home.

In Françoise Labouverie's railcar the nurse and some other prisoners improvised a bed on the platform and the heavily pregnant woman was able to lie down. Stretchers were brought for her and for other prisoners who could not walk. As Françoise walked along the platform she found her Resistance network boss, Pierre Hauman, and together they sought out other members of *Tégal*, such as the Liberal Party politician Ernest Demuyter, who had been in the same railcar as Robert Beckers.

Beckers himself was delighted to find his friend Frans Flour, the SOE wireless operator, safe among the crowds on the platform. Together they boarded a tram and headed for Beckers' home. When the ticket inspector asked for money, Beckers explained he didn't have any and why. An argument broke out until the other passengers told the inspector in no uncertain terms to leave Beckers alone.

As 16-year-old Jules Buedts was walking through Schaerbeek he saw a friend from his hometown and asked to borrow money for a drink. Walking into a cafe to buy a beer he encountered strange looks – people thought he was German because of his strange, prisoner's clothing.

'I have just escaped from the train,' he said to the woman in the cafe.

Suddenly he was surrounded, strangers buying him drink after drink until he had 10 or 15 glasses in front of him.

As he headed through the northern suburbs of the city, he witnessed celebration and retribution. People were already starting to set fire to the houses of Belgian collaborators. But some Germans were still shooting and he feared for his life.

Françoise Labouverie found herself walking through neighbourhoods where in one street people were cautiously celebrating and in others there were German convoys, tanks and sometimes ragged bunches of soldiers on foot. At first, she feared she would be re-arrested or shot out of hand by a panicked soldier but none of them even looked in her direction: they were all intent only on escaping.

At every corner excited crowds shouted about the Allied advance.

'They are at Porte d'Anvers!'

'The English are at Porte de Halle!'

When a British tank swept into the street it was surrounded by local people, some of whom threw flowers onto it. Françoise Labouverie found herself lifted onto it by her friends.

As night fell, this time there was no curfew. The sky was lit by the orange flames of the blaze at the Palais de Justice, but the city buzzed with the singing and dancing of a liberation party.

At the Bordet Institute, General Wachsmuth and his staff were fulfilling their promise to continue to care for the patients who were too ill to be moved when Allied troops stormed the hospital and took them all prisoners of war.

28

THE LAST PRISONERS

THE ORDER JUNGCLAUS had sent to the German guards at Petite-Île specified the release of all the 'political prisoners', but there was confusion about the airmen. The train commander said the message he received said the Resistance would not shoot trains carrying German wounded if the 'political prisoners' were released. Neither he nor the diplomats had been told anything about the prisoners of war, and the Red Cross decided it could not claim responsibility for them. In the confusion, everyone agreed the airmen must remain on the train.

It was soon reconfigured to become a Red Cross train, featuring carriages filled with German troops and the baggage car packed with the airmen. The guards had kept aside a German-born engineer found among the prisoners and forced him to drive the train. German soldiers brought the airmen a five-gallon can of water and told Liberator gunner Hugh Bomar, who was standing near the door, the Resistance had agreed to let their train leave Brussels. Before the Belgian conductor locked the baggage car, he secretly handed SOE man François Reeve a spare key. But John Brown noticed another soldier had been added to the guard on the car.

At 2pm on Sunday afternoon, after all the political prisoners had left and were finding their way home, the new train started moving towards Schaerbeek in the north-east of the city. There were signs of fighting in the streets beyond, explosions and tank fire. In the confusion of battle, the train was fired upon but kept going.

Then, as it slowed down on its approach to Schaerbeek, the silence was shattered by a crack of wood. Some of the airmen had managed to lever open one of the doors, splintering part of the frame. There were hushed exclamations of excitement as several men jumped down: James Levey, William Muse, from 'Cawn't Miss'; and turret gunner Ralph Lynch from Kansas. Spitfire pilot Brian Harris followed them. The men ran across the rail tracks and took shelter, hoping they had not been seen. If they had, no one seemed to be pursuing them. Harris shook hands with the others and headed off alone, while the crewmen Levey, Muse and Lynch stuck together. They eventually banged on the door of a brewery on Avenue Van Volxem where the owner, Fernand Dewerpe, gave them food and he let them eat and sleep in an office behind a large room containing the fermentation vats.

The sporadic battles the men could hear from the train now intensified around the city. The Resistance were blowing up garages filled with German lorries and attacking road convoys as they looked to escape. Rexists were executed. Other former collaborators gathered at the station in the hope of getting a train to Germany. Nazi soldiers in the Avenue Louise were shooting at passers-by. Rail lines leading in every direction out of the city were now in the control of the Resistance and tracks had been blown up in skirmishes fought with the last remnants of the German army.

The airmen's train came to a halt in a siding alongside the main highway leading north, which was jammed with German trucks, tanks, and staff cars. Stuart Leslie watched as a half-track stuttered and stalled. The officer wasted no time, ordering his men out and waving down a truck. A soldier tossed a stick grenade into the half-track, and it exploded. It would burn for hours.

THE LAST PRISONERS

Across the city Allied demolition crews set about disarming booby-traps and explosives left behind by the Germans. Soldiers of the Welsh Guards fought battles with the city's defenders. The airmen could hear tanks in the distance. At first, they thought they must be German but one of them said the flares from the Verey pistols being used belonged to the Allies.

The prisoners dived for cover as the *Witte Brigade* fired on the train, which stopped and started, such was the chaos on the track ahead. The airmen kept their heads down, occasionally looking out to try to work out what was going on. They could see marshalling yards, lines of tracks, and hear confused shouts and the pounding of feet. Maurice Muir reckoned the train reached Mechelen again, at about 8pm, before stopping for some time and then running backwards towards Schaerbeek.

Then suddenly, as darkness fell, there was a lurch as two of the cars jumped the track. Everyone fell to the floor. The *Witte Brigade* had blown up a section of track. There was now a huge amount of activity as the Germans tried to reorganise the train. The airmen heard guards jumping down and noticed one SS officer had changed into a *Wehrmacht* uniform. Everyone listened, identifying each noise. A Red Cross train moved slowly by, packed with German wounded.

The airmen's baggage car was shunted back and forth, and then jumped off the damaged track. A paralysing fear set in; the Germans might shoot them and abandon the train. Soldiers rushed alongside the train. It was hard to work out what was happening in the darkness but the airmen realised the Germans were getting into the cars ahead of those which had been derailed. They were going wild and scattering.

Then even more hope: the unmistakable sound of the engine being driven off.

And suddenly it seemed very quiet.

For some time the airmen stayed down, afraid to move. Unsure what might happen next.

Eventually, Al Sanders – pilot of B-24 Liberator, dubbed 'Mike, the Spirit of LSU' – slipped from the baggage car and got up into the next carriage. It had been used by German soldiers, but was now empty. Many had left bags and packs in their rush to flee. He rifled through a few hoping to find food but there was only spare clothes and equipment. Other airmen followed, dropping cautiously out of the baggage waggon and looking both ways along the track. Further up the line they could see the locomotive and two passenger cars containing German soldiers. It appeared the track ahead of the locomotive was blocked, as a working party was busy in the distance.

The Germans were still dangerously close.

With the streets in darkness and the situation in the city so uncertain there was confusion about what to do next. As he spoke German, Canadian Flight Lieutenant Thurmeier was elected the group's leader. He suggested it would be too dangerous to wander through a strange and chaotic city at night, where there might be booby traps or snipers. It would be better to lay on the floor of the car until morning and then venture out in search of forward units of the Allied forces. Ted Kleinman went out to scout the area around the station and, when he returned, also said it was best to wait until dawn. There was a real fear that the Germans had laid a trap for them.

But by 3am disagreement was growing. Air gunners Ray Smith, from Denver, and Hugh Bomar, from El Paso, who had been captured together by Dezitter's team, talked with an Australian, most likely Lancelot Bodey, and decided that waiting around in the baggage car was just as risky as leaving.

'The Germans could come back and recapture the whole group,' they reasoned.

Others voiced warnings.

'You're risking being court-martialled for disobeying orders.'

But they decided to make a break for it anyway.

The three men headed into the darkness, got well away from the train and then knocked on the door of a house. The people there promised to contact the Resistance and the civilian police to find out what was happening in the Battle for Brussels. The airmen attempted to return to the train to tell the others, but got lost in the strange, dark streets, and ended up hiding back near to the house they had called at. Eventually they set off again and walked into a Canadian armoured unit who turned them over to a British captain.

There were other sporadic escapes before dawn. James Wagner and Cecil Spence snuck out together soon after Smith's group. On hearing gunfire, they hid until daylight. Halifax flight engineer Maurice Muir and his aircraft's co-pilot, Canadian William Elliott, who had evaded and been betrayed together, left the car at about 4am and wandered into Brussels. They met a local family and were invited into a house where they stayed for several days.

François Reeve had befriended a young Australian airman named Kevin McSweeney in Saint-Gilles. McSweeney had been shot down over the Netherlands but made it to Belgium alone and had found help. He had been arrested while waiting in a café for a contact. Having seen the marks of torture on Reeve's back and chest, McSweeney had gained huge respect for the SOE agent. They escaped from the train together.

As day broke British artillery was firing on the area and the remaining airmen agreed that anybody who wanted to leave could. It was felt that by continuing to move out in small groups they stood a better chance of breaking through the German line and getting to the advancing Allied soldiers.

Flying Fortress pilot JH Singleton and his tail-gunner, Harry

Blair, left together; B-24 radio operator James Dykes left with bombardier Wallis Cozzens, from the 'Carpetbagger' crew. Bob Piarote partnered with Canadian Bill Cunningham. As they ran from the train there was more shooting, bullets ricocheting off the tracks. It was impossible to know if the Germans were shooting directly at them, or whether it was just the chaos of battle. Either way, they were striking dangerously close. Lieutenant Ford Babcock, a B-17 bombardier, was one of those who went alone. Sneaking through the streets of Schaerbeek, he managed to find a Red Cross station later that day. Roy Brown, Murphy, and Mason met up with Cunningham and stayed in a man's shed all through the next night, until the morning of September 4 when they found a Catholic priest who took them to a British major.

'Carpetbagger' bombardier Bill Ryckman and B-17 navigator John Bradley left the baggage car together. They crossed the marshalling yards and disappeared into a gas works which had been knocked out by Allied bombing. Coming out the other side, they found a narrow back road and followed it until they reached a small canal. They could see a bridge, but it seemed too exposed to gunfire to cross. There was movement and Al Sanders appeared, alone. He had got separated from 'Carpetbagger' pilot Henry Wolcott, the man with whom he had spent much of evasion.

Then Royce McGillvary and Stuart Leslie – captured together when the German checkpoint found Mac's dog tags – appeared. They had recced the canal and found nowhere to cross but that bridge. They were going to try it. If they got arrested, they said, they would shout and scream.

Ryckman, Bradley and Sanders watched them go, waited 15 minutes, and then made the crossing themselves. The three entered a factory yard, beyond which was a main road and a larger canal and were joined by Wolcott.

They edged out onto the canal bank and saw a church spire – a place to find refuge. They headed towards a rowboat tied up next to a barge but suddenly heard the heavy tramp of the boots of German soldiers behind them. A torch swung in the morning gloom and a guard dog barked.

It looked as if they were trapped. But Bradley jumped down onto the barge, and the others followed. They remained hidden as the soldiers passed.

The captain of the barge opened a window and Ryckman tried to speak a few words of Flemish. Bradley said in English: 'American aviator.'

'Queen Wilhelmina,' said the barge owner.

Sanders smiled. 'President Roosevelt,' he replied.

'Comrades,' said the man, opening the door and hurrying them in.

The barge owner was a Dutchman named Wijs who said he had heard them speaking English when they approached. They must hide, he said, as there were running battles in the streets of the city. He offered them coffee and what little food he had.

Later, they held their breath as a German patrol passed along the bank, but it made no attempt to come inside.

* * *

After running on ahead Stuart Leslie and Royce McGillvary had tried to get into a number of warehouses, but the doors were all locked. They had no option but to continue walking through the dark streets, where vehicles and sometimes buildings were burning. Somewhere in the distance they could hear the heavy rumble of tanks, but they saw none. They walked in silence, almost afraid to speak; when they did, they only whispered words of encouragement to each other.

As dawn was breaking the pair asked a man which was the way to the city centre. They headed on, passing queues of women waiting for the daily ration of bread at a bakery. One of them whispered in broken English: 'The Germans have gone!'

'Can you help us?' Leslie asked the woman, who agreed to take them to her home. The tired and weary men were able to bath and shave, and feel the pleasure of putting on clean clothing which the woman kindly gave them.

Having tucked into some of the freshly baked bread, Leslie shook McGillvary by the arm.

'Let's go downtown and welcome our liberators.'

***

The barge owner woke Sanders, Ryckman, Bradley and Wolcott with a breakfast of coffee, hot cakes and jelly, bringing out a radio which he had hidden in the bottom of his boat since the fall of Holland in 1940.

They listened to the news together. Tanks were encircling Brussels, some were heading directly for Antwerp.

The airmen went outside and saw all the barges along the canal raise Belgian and Dutch flags. The barge owner's son came back from along the canal shouting 'Tommy, Tommy!' There were army trucks with a big white star crossing a bridge a quarter of a mile away, he said.

The airmen rushed along and, as one truck slowed, Bradley waved his arms and shouted: 'Americans!'

The driver stopped. They were Canadians attached to a British unit. A soldier gave them cigarettes and they all hopped onboard.

In the main square in front of the Gare du Nord, locals had been gathering for a few days to watch the retreat from their city.

'Dust-covered, exhausted Germans, passing on tireless bicycles, in lorries showing traces of the recent fighting, in carts drawn by lank horses, could see the people of Brussels seated outside cafes sipping beer and lemonade,' observed one journalist.

When the British arrived, cheering mobs of people climbed onto their tanks as they rumbled through the city. A crowd gathered outside the Bourse de Commerce to see a portrait of Hitler set aflame.

The airmen were sometimes hailed as liberators themselves. Leon Panzer – who four months earlier had only just survived a jump with a badly-damaged parachute – was carried on the shoulders of a crowd. Unshaven and unwashed, he was presented to a group of local dignitaries. All around him people were singing, and many were in tears. He described it as the 'maddest mob I've ever seen.'

'Carpetbagger' radio operator Dale Loucks walked straight through town and stood in front of a British tank. Its crew were stunned to hear the dishevelled young man in civilian clothing talk excitedly to them in an American accent.

At a Canadian army camp Sanders, Ryckman, Bradley and Wolcott were turned over to an RAF liaison officer who took them to a signal truck where their details were transmitted back to England.

They were then taken to the mess tent for beef stew. 'Boy, did I lose it!' said Sanders when he recalled later how much food he wolfed down. The meat made Bradley feel dizzy; it had been so long since he'd had any. The men were given clean clothes and taken to the Hotel Metropole, which had been taken over by the British Army. There was a party, but Bradley and others declined as they were so tired. That night they showered and slept between clean sheets and on a soft pillow.

In the morning there was coffee before they joined an army unit heading back towards Amiens and another lift to Paris. The driver gave them a few francs for beers. The next day they got a lift out to an airfield and had a ride back to England on a Canadian-crewed

C-47. Bradley had been out of England for 10 months. He had lost two and a half stone in that time, 10 pounds while on the run and a further 25 as a prisoner in Saint-Gilles. He was 6ft 3in and weighed under nine stone.

***

Among the last to leave the train were John Brown, Ted Kleinman, Bill Grosvenor, Ken Holcomb, Nigel Beamish and Charlie Hillis. Donald Swanson and Jack Terzian were also probably in this group.

Events almost came to a tragic end when they walked into a nervous teenager with a rifle who thought they were Germans. Believing they were going to be shot, they finally managed to persuade him to take them to a police station where an officer realised who they were.

They headed to the Metropole and found many of the airmen from the train – all had made it to freedom safely. Terzian sat in the bar with a bottle of beer and a corned beef sandwich on white bread.

'You never tasted anything so good!' he said.

Outside the hotel the Belgian flag was flying and people were crying with joy. To protect them from collaborators or Germans who might have stayed behind to fight on, the airmen were given police protection for the next couple of days.

Brown was pleased to be able to meet up with Marguerite Quintard-Legrain and Madame Claes-Frix and find that all the helpers who had been on the train were also safe. They had a big party. Bill Grosvenor's friends Jeanne Drieghe and her daughter Suzanne were there too.

Brown and Grosvenor decided to stay together and befriended Bill White, a newsman for the *Associated Press* who had been covering the British advance to Brussels for *Time* magazine. White agreed to take them to Paris in his Jeep.

JH Singleton went back to Templeuve to tell the people who had helped him how they had all been betrayed by Dezitter and Giralt. For Father Dropsy and Gilberte Watteau-Picard the betrayal was a huge shock. Watteau-Picard and Micheline Cyprès drove to Wodowosoff's hat shop which had been a 'mail drop' for Dezitter. Wodowosoff told them very little; and the next day she disappeared to Spain. The two women then reported Dezitter to the British Military Police.

Ted Kleinman travelled around the city looking for people who had helped him. It was then he learned that the man he knew as Captain Barbaix had been captured after ambushing a German convoy and shot by a firing squad in Lessines. His wife had also been arrested; refusing to talk to the Gestapo, she was tortured and later died.

Determined to capture the people who had betrayed the airmen, Kleinman persuaded a Belgian army officer to drive him to the Rue de Forestière to show him where so many had finally lost their liberty.

But the 'Dog House' was empty. The traitors had fled.

29

AFTER THE TRAIN

ON SEPTEMBER 2, the day the 'Ghost Train' rolled out of Brussels-South station at the start of its journey to nowhere, a small convoy of cars – including a Graham-Paige and Chevrolet – screeched away from 16 Rue Forestière and followed the line of retreating Germans.

Prosper Dezitter and Flore Giralt were in one car; their driver, Nicolas Fetissoff, and fake courier, Suzanne Bertherand, were in another; and Jean-Marcel Nootens and Giralt's former lover, Vania Gristchenko, who had rented the 'Dog House', were in a third and fourth. Fetissoff and Bertherand fled to Würzburg in northern Bavaria, 300 miles away from Brussels. Soon after they were joined by Gristchenko but were later sighted without him in Berlin and Lübeck. They were never apprehended.

The young Comet Line courier, Michou Dumon, who had exposed the traitor Jean Desoubrie and his links to Dezitter, returned to Belgium with MI9's Airey Neave to join the search. One day an American officer asked to speak to her and showed her a photograph of a suspect. She immediately identified him as Desoubrie: he had offered to work for the Allies. He was tried in July 1949 and executed that December.

In November 1944 a unit of eight men from the Luc-Marc and *Zéro* formed a search and snatch squad roaming the Liège area to find Dezitter. An officer of the US Counterintelligence Corps in Liège and two local police officers were providing them with information. Agents of a sabotage section of the *Armée Secrète*, the Hotton group, bribed one of Dezitter's Brussels accomplices and set up a trap for him. But the man who turned up was not Dezitter and, despite being fired on by three American soldiers, he got away.

Early in 1945 Major John Delaforce, of SOE, arrived in Brussels to interrogate enemy agents under arrest in the city. He combed Resistance reports, and Belgian *Sûreté* and police records to build up a picture of Dezitter's activities and to try to work out where he was now. But the myth of Dezitter had not ended with the liberation. Delaforce gathered a huge amount of material – including the claim that Dezitter had met Hitler in Munich after fleeing Brussels – but acknowledged that 'many reports about him cannot be taken too literally'. One eyewitness claimed to have seen Dezitter on a Belgian train, another on a bicycle near Mechelen. Delaforce even investigated reports that Dezitter had been parachuted back behind Allied lines as a spy and had been seen in US Army uniform and driving in a Jeep.

'If he is posing as an Allied officer and keeps on the move all the time,' noted Delaforce, 'he may not be so easily caught.'

Giralt's estranged husband, Paul Dings, told SOE he believed Dezitter and his wife had gone to Switzerland. Delaforce agreed he was most likely there, or in the Netherlands or Germany.

Then, a breakthrough. In February 1946, after receiving medical attention for his bad back, Gristchenko was traced to his lair in Würzburg. He denied being a traitor and said he believed Giralt had worked for the Allies.

Dezitter and Giralt were, in fact, hiding nearby, with a pro-Nazi doctor. They were eventually arrested four months after Gristchenko.

But what then? A former member of the Resistance saw Dezitter at Eisenhower's counterintelligence headquarters in Frankfurt, not under arrest, but apparently helping the Americans track down Nazis. Did the US Army Counterintelligence Corps (CIC) also believe he might help in the search for possible Soviet spies in Belgium? After all, like Klaus Barbie – the SS 'Butcher of Lyons', who would become a CIC informer – Dezitter was an expert at hunting communists, having betrayed so many in the Resistance. Nootens was also apparently helping them.

If Dezitter had any value to the CIC it did not last for long. They either realised it was time he faced justice, or he simply outlived his usefulness; either way, he was put in front of a court. Dezitter secured a postponement to his death sentence 'by promising sensational revelations', but it was just one final lie from the dangerous trickster, and at 5.45am on September 17, 1948, a police officer came to Dezitter's cell in the Avenue de la Couronne and led him out in front of a firing squad to be shot. His lover, Florentina Giralt, was executed in June 1949.

* * *

SS General Richard Jungclaus' decision not to carry out the deportation of Belgium's political prisons did not go down well in Berlin. He was reprimanded and demoted by Heinrich Himmler and sent to fight in Albania and what was then Yugoslavia. He was killed in action in April 1945.

Ambassador Mayr-Falkenberg was unable to continue in the diplomatic service after the war. He returned to law and also worked with the Red Cross in Bavaria. He died in 1962.

After being taken prisoner with hundreds of his patients on September 3, 1944, Professor Dr Werner Wachsmuth spent almost two years as a prisoner of war, holding the position of commandant at POW hospitals in Watford and Swindon. Returning to

Germany in 1946, he continued his career in medicine, becoming director of surgery at the University of Würzburg. He died in 1990, aged 90.

After the liberation of Brussels, Viscount Berryer told *Le Soir* that of the 5,000 political prisoners they knew about 'no one was killed and everyone was freed'. This included the 'Ghost Train', a further 1,500 prisoners at the Beverloo prison at Leopoldsburg, and the remaining 500 Jewish prisoners at Mechelen.

Sadly, hundreds of prisoners at Breendonk had already been transported to Germany by the time of the agreement with Jungclaus. A recent estimate for those of the Resistance who were executed in Belgium put the figure at 350, with a further 1,570 having died in concentration camps in Germany.

***

After being taxied back to England in a series of rides on C-47 Dakotas from Paris, the airmen were debriefed, giving the intelligence officers the details of their evasions, who had helped them and how they came to be captured.

Some needed treatment for undernutrition and exhaustion. When a sergeant dragged Sanders aboard an aircraft to England he looked him up and down, taking in the greyness in his face and his tatty, torn civilian clothes, and told him he could relax now. In hospital in London an American army doctor visited Sanders and laid something on the bed sheet.

'This is yours,' he said.

It was a Purple Heart.

Far more important to Sanders was the fact he had been able to get a message to his wife to say that he was safe. Millie had believed him to be dead. In fact, when Western Union rang her and said they were ringing on behalf of Alfred Sanders she had shouted,

'That isn't funny!' and hung up. Fortunately, they rang back, and she listened to the message.

'Dearest, I am safe and well. Will be home soon. Letter following. Alfred Sanders.'

Millie replied to Al to say his son, Mike, had been born two days after his plane had gone down. Al went home, but stayed in the air force to fly jets. He later returned to Europe with his second daughter, Winki, to find the people who had helped him.

He was one of many evaders who returned to Belgium over the years to thank their helpers. 'Carpetbagger' Henry Wolcott learned there were 56 members in the Resistance group which helped him in May 1944, but only five remained alive by the end of the war. During his visit in March 2001, he was also determined to find out what had happened to his tail-gunner, Dick Hawkins.

Former members of the Resistance gave him a small plastic box of mementos: a piece of Hawkins' parachute silk and some twisted metal and plastic from the wreck of their plane. They also gave him a small American flag and a photograph of Hawkins from his wallet which had been kept for 57 years by local man Georges De Cooman. Hawkins' parachute had not opened. De Cooman and his brother had carried his body away as the Germans opened fire and he had been given a hero's funeral at a local convent.

Wolcott's co-pilot, Lieutenant Robert Auda, from Tiffin, Ohio, veteran of 16 missions and the 'Ghost Train', sadly had little time to enjoy the peace. He was killed when his car swerved to avoid a motorcycle and overturned on a road near Rantoul, Illinois, in June 1945. He was days away from his discharge from the service. At age 25, he was survived by his wife, Rita, whom he had married shortly before going on active service, and their baby daughter.

Wallis Cozzens returned to his hometown of Eldorado in Texas and worked as a geologist in the oil industry. He died in 1990.

AFTER THE TRAIN

Navigator William G Ryckman returned to Fresno, California, and started a family. He died in 1971, aged 50.

Although a quiet man, radio operator Dale Loucks had a very social manner and became a successful car salesman. While proud of his military service, he rarely talked about the war or the night his plane went down and the young tail-gunner that died. He never flew again and, if he travelled, he went only by car. He died in 2018, aged 93 in Yakima, Washington State.

Although he had received much help in Belgium, JH Singleton was deeply affected by Dezitter's betrayal. When interviewed by Military Intelligence about his experiences and asked his advice for others, he stated: 'Trust no person and give no person a chance to give you to [the] Gestapo!'

He stayed in the air force after the war and retired in 1961 with the rank of colonel. A father of five, he died in Orlando, Florida, in 2013, aged 93. His former navigator, James Levey, had continued to serve in the air force with him. Their top turret gunner Bill Muse went home to Laurinburg, North Carolina. He died in 1973, aged 52. The crew's tail-gunner, Harry Blair, who was just 19 when he was shot down, returned to Pittsburgh, graduated from university, married and had nine children, and enjoyed a successful career as the owner of a manufacturing company. He died in 2008, aged 83.

Ted Kleinman's wife of two months had received a 'missing, presumed dead' telegram, but had never given up hope that he was still alive. They went on to have four children, seven grandchildren and eight great grandchildren. He served in Korea as a navigator instructor, where his friend and pilot John Brown was recalled to serve as a pilot. Brown was killed when his plane crashed in heavy weather into Mount Fujiyama in Japan.

Bill Grosvenor settled in Abilene. He worked as a civil airline pilot for many years. In 2001, he returned to Belgium for the documentary, *The Last Best Hope*, where was reunited with P-47 pilot

Jack Terzian and with the guide who had helped keep him free, Marcel Harnie. Terzian also made his home in Abilene. He stayed in the service after the war, eventually retiring in 1963 to become a life insurance representative.

Stuart Leslie returned to civilian life, working for Air Canada as a flight dispatcher until his retirement in 1989. He loved to travel and returned to Belgium with his family to attend the wedding of the granddaughter of one of his helpers. Stuart's son fell in love with one of the guests and they got married – and a new union between an airman's family and the Resistance began. Stuart died in Vancouver on February 21, 2018 – the morning of his 94th birthday.

Royce McGillvary, whose dog tags had caused the problem at the checkpoint on the way to the Ardennes, became a steelworker in California. He died in Los Angeles in 2011, aged 88.

John Bradley recovered from his time at Saint-Gilles and returned to Matawan, New Jersey. Graduating university with a Bachelor's then Master's degree in finance, he went on to work in the finance department at American Airlines for 25 years. Always community-minded, in his spare time, he volunteered to help older people prepare their taxes. Like many veterans, he maintained an aura to those he met. His daughter, Kat, said: 'To me, my Dad was like John Wayne. A hero. Tall, honest, handsome. Loyal to those he called friends. Kind. Inspiring. Super smart.'

He died in 2005, two weeks short of his 88th birthday.

***

Airmen who had been helped by the Resistance did not generally go back into operations over Europe, for fear that if they were shot down, they might give away the identities of people who had previously helped them.

AFTER THE TRAIN

Likewise, for many of the resisters, the end of occupation meant their war was over.

Françoise Labouverie married one of Belgium's liberators, Hugh Rigby, and moved to London, where she founded Lifeline, an organisation devoted to rebuilding the lives of former prisoners and slave labourers in what was then West Germany. Over 15 years, Lifeline sponsored 8,500 families. She achieved the rare distinction of receiving not only the Belgian *Croix de Guerre* and the *Cross of Chevalier de l'Ordre de Leopold II* for her wartime gallantry, but also, in 1960, the German *Verdienstkreutz* for her work with displaced persons. She spent the last years of her life in Henley-on-Thames with her second husband. She died in 1999, aged 77. The family home where she grew up in Céroux-Mousty was bought by *Tintin* author Hergé in 1949.

'Michou' Dumon, the 23-year-old Comet line courier who looked 15 and whose feet 'barely touched the floor' when she sat on a tram, worked with MI9 at the end of the war to find Resistance members who had been deported to Germany. She later married Pierre Ugeux, a major in the French section of SOE who knew all about her courageous work during the occupation. Her father, Eugène, died in Gross-Rosen concentration camp. Her younger sister, Andrée – known to friends by her wartime codename 'Nadine' – survived Ravensbrück and Mauthausen. For many years she was an honoured guest at the meetings of the Evasion Lines Memorial Society. She was respected for her courage, and loved for her mischievous smile and wit.

Radio operator Frans Flour was one of the few who had been rescued on the 'Ghost Train' to go back into action. In March 1945, he was part of a two-man team trained by the OSS which managed to infiltrate a garage used by the SS in Munich. They gathered information which would help the Americans round up 60 top Bavarian Nazis after the war.

THE NAZI GHOST TRAIN

Gaston Masereel slipped back into the shadows after the war. But in 1958 gossip columnists reported the 'biggest collection of secret agents and cloak-and-dagger men to assemble in the free world since the war' had met at London's Hyde Park Hotel as guests of the Special Forces Club. Masereel was listed among them.

***

The sacrifices made by those who resisted and helped Allied airmen can be seen in the story of the Biernaux family and the people who worked with them around the town of Hasselt.

Florent and Olympe Biernaux – and their two children – helped up to 60 airmen, including John Bradley and Royce McGillvary. Arrested on August 5, 1944, Florent was tortured but rescued from the 'Ghost Train'. But his wife, Olympe, a fearless Resistance leader, had by then already reached Ravensbrück.

She came home late in May 1945, having lost more than three stone in weight, and spent the following months awaiting the return of her son, Raymond. As the family waited and suffered, Florent wrote to one airman he had helped and signed off: 'I hope that God will give us back my son, Raymond, and then we can begin again a new life.'

But eventually the family discovered that Raymond had died in Neuengamme on March 1945. He was 20.

The family never recovered and, Olympe – whose courage had never failed and who had been showered with honours, including the US Medal of Freedom – succumbed to a nervous breakdown and took her own life.

Father and son Jules and René Jaspers, who had been arrested on the same day as the Biernaux family, suffered different fates because of the people who stopped the 'Ghost Train'.

René had been sent to Breendonk before being transported to

Neuengamme. He was forced to spend Christmas 1944 keeping the runway of a Luftwaffe airfield free of snow. He was finally liberated from Wöbbelin by American soldiers.

When he returned to their home in Zonhoven, he found his father Jules, who had been rescued from the 'Ghost Train', waiting.

But this brave Belgian family, which had done so much for the liberation of their homeland – sheltering Allied airmen and Russian and Polish prisoners of war, undergoing pain and torture – had paid a heavy price.

The youngest son, Roger, had just come from church in his Sunday best on November 2 when his friend urged him to come and watch the excitement of a huge British convoy passing through their village. Roger's mum said he was allowed to go, provided he changed his best shoes for a pair of clogs.

The two boys ran to the road and Roger's friend nipped between two trucks and across the road to get a better view.

Roger went to follow, but his wooden shoes were heavy in the mud. He was struck and killed by a British army motorcyclist.

He was seven.

***

The Merckx family of Meensel-Kiezegem were put on trial in 1946. Clementine Merckx-Swinnen was sentenced to life imprisonment while her three surviving sons were handed down the death sentence in absentia – they had fled Belgium. Six other jail sentences were given to collaborators who had supported the family and their actions. All had been released by 1951.

Robert Verbelen, the Flemish SS officer who led the two raids, and had also been responsible for a number of killings and attempted killings as the head of a unit called the *Veiligheidskorps* (Security Corps), fled to Germany and, after the war, was recruited by the

American army's CIC in Austria. Codenamed 'Herbert' his role was to spy on Communists in Vienna, although he turned out to be 'of little or no value'. He was convicted in absentia and sentenced to death in Belgium in 1947, but he was never extradited. He died in 1990.

His accomplice in the killings and torture at Meensel-Kiezegem, Tony van Dijck, was caught and tried. His death sentence was later commuted to a 17-year jail term which he served. He later wrote a book on the war on the Eastern Front.

***

In the pretty red-brick houses of Meensel-Kiezegem those who had survived the 'Ghost Train' kept waiting for their loved-ones to return.

'We just hoped that the others, like us, would all come back safe and sound,' said Jozef Craeninckx. 'But the rumours arose about the concentration camps and when the first villager returned, he was a skeleton. He had to be carried.'

Those villagers who had been among the group of 400 prisoners which left Saint-Gilles on August 31 had arrived at Neuengamme concentration camp in the early hours of Sunday, September 3, while the 'Ghost Train' was stuck in the siding at Muizen.

At Neuengamme about 50,000 prisoners worked and lived in terrible conditions, and faced not only typhus but were subjected to medical experiments. Many, like Jozef's father, Vital Craeninckx, slaved in the brickworks.

On November 16, 1944, Vital was digging clay in a pit. The clay was heavy underfoot and, when Vital was ordered by a German guard to climb out, he was too tired to do so quickly enough. The guard shot him dead. Talking about his father's fate was still overwhelming for Jozef more than 70 years later.

AFTER THE TRAIN

The Canadian airman, Teddy Blenkinsop, who joined the Resistance of the town, died on January 23, 1945 – most likely in Neuengamme, although his family was informed his death occurred in Belsen. A Neuengamme official recorded the cause of his death to be *Hernschwäche*, a weak heart. Over the past months he had been tortured and starved; he was exhausted and probably suffering from tuberculosis. He had turned 24 during his incarceration. After the war he was posthumously awarded the *Croix de Guerre* by the Belgian government.

Of the 71 people from Meensel-Kiezegem who went on that first transport – mostly the men of the community – only eight came home, and they were broken by their time in Neuengamme and its satellite camps.

By contrast, all the prisoners from the second transport – the 'Ghost Train' – returned safely. The fortunes of those on two trains 48 hours apart could not have been more starkly different.

A few weeks after the events of the 'Ghost Train' Louis Verheggen and many of the railwaymen who had saved its passengers were invited to a special event at the town hall hosted by politician Ernest Demuyter, who had been on the train. Afterwards, the men wrote a joint letter to thank him for the welcome.

'The political detainees locked in the waggons of the September 2 convoy represented the elite of the country, the soul of the Resistance,' they stated, 'and if we were able to contribute to the liberation of these valiant patriots, we did it solely out of duty to serve our country, justice and the law.'

However, they insisted they wanted no further publicity for their exploits and they 'formally reject any idea of reward'.

'Consider us as soldiers of the resistance,' they concluded. 'That will be our fondest memory.'

For Jozef Craeninckx, Verheggen was one of the truly great unsung heroes of the Second World War. 'We were all destined to die in the concentration camp, there's no doubt about it,' he said years later. 'But we were saved by the engine driver. And there isn't even a monument to him. A hero!'

Teenage *résistant* Jules Buedts, who lived to be 87 thanks to the acts of Verheggen, met the driver once but did not know what to say. In the end, he just said: 'Thank you for saving my life.'

Verheggen told him: 'It was my duty as a good Belgian.'

The rescue of the people on the 'Ghost Train' was down to delay. Delay by the men at the station when crucial hours were lost in the train's departure and by Verheggen and Pochet. Their combined actions to keep the train in Belgium were even more important than they could possibly know; had the train crossed into the Netherlands and out of Jungclaus' jurisdiction, it is extremely unlikely that his decision to rescind Hitler's deportation order would have been obeyed.

As it was, the prisoners went home, lived their lives and started families. The men and women who stopped the train saved not only 1,400 lives but also guaranteed the futures of thousands more in Britain, Belgium, France, Canada, Australia, and the United States.

ACKNOWLEDGEMENTS

SPECIAL THANKS TO my agent Andrew Lownie; and to Claiborne Hancock and all at Pegasus Books, and Clare Fitzsimons and her team at Reach, for their enthusiasm, skill and support.

My family – Moira, Evan and Caoimhe – have lived with the 'Ghost Train' for some time now. They've read drafts, joined me on research trips, and listened to my stories (and grumbles) as I have worked to bring the book together. My thanks and love go, as always, to them.

SOURCES

INTERVIEWS AND CORRESPONDENCE

SPECIAL THANKS TO the following people who have helped with my research over the years, as correspondents, interviewees and supporters: Tinca Bodson, widow of former *résistant* and author, Herman (correspondence 2016); Jules Buedts, 'Ghost Train' veteran (interview June 2013); Marie Cappart, historian; Claudette Claereboudt, daughter of Renée Marie Germaine de Jonghe (correspondence 2015); Jozef Craeninckx, 'Ghost Train' veteran (interview June 2013); Régis Decobeck, evasion historian (correspondence 2008); Karin De Greeve, historian (correspondence 2020); Tom Devos, of Museum44 Meensel-Kiezegem (correspondence 2024); Susan Willis Dunlap, daughter of evader Alan R Willis (correspondence 2020); Michou Dumon, Comet Line veteran (correspondence 2012); Andrée Dumon, Comet Line veteran (correspondence and interviews 2012-2015); John Evans, evader (correspondence and interviews 2006-2010); Ellen Geeraerts, Buedts family (correspondence 2013); Georg-Hermann Greiner, Luftwaffe veteran (correspondence 2009); Guy Jaspers, son of *résistant* René (correspondence 2013-2025); Michael LeBlanc, evasion historian (correspondence 2008-2020); André and Ingrid Le Jeune, family of Remi Diependaele (correspondence 2019); Elizabeth McDade, of the Air Force Escape and Evasion Society (correspondence 2015) ; Jo Ann Michel, Biernaux researcher (correspondence 2008-2009);

SOURCES

Darryl Rehr (correspondence 2016); Rudi Schellinck, friend of Jozef Craeninckx (2013); Henry 'Dutch' Schultz, B-17 waist gunner (correspondence 2016); Victor Schutters, grandson of *résistant* (correspondence 2008-2013); Neil Singleton, JH Singleton's nephew (correspondence 2015-2016); Kildine Van Staey, Craeninckx family (2013); Kat Taylor, John Bradley's daughter (correspondence 2023-2025); Walter Verstraeten, 'Ghost Train' researcher (correspondence 2009-2020); Dirk Vijverman, historian (correspondence 2009-2016); Nathan Ware, Dale Loucks' grandson (correspondence 2016-2024); John Wells, James Dykes' nephew (correspondence 2020); Henry W. Wolcott IV, son of Henry Wolcott (correspondence 2016); Jan Zoons (correspondence 2010-2015).

I'm also indebted to the following people for their various research posted online and in an email research group: Bruce Bolinger, John Clinch, Oliver Clutton-Block, Philippe Connart, Michel Dricot, Fred Greyer, Fred Heathfield, John Howes, Keith Janes, Brigitte d'Oultremont, Edouard Renière.

NATIONAL ARCHIVES – UK:

WO 208/3322/22 STEPHEN BRIAN HARRIS; WO 208/3322/31 Roy C Brown; WO 208/3323/2418 Leon Panzer; WO 208/3324/2 Joseph Murphy; WO 208/3324/3 William Cunningham; WO 208/3324/20 Kevin McSweeney; WO 208/3324/197 William Mason; WO 208/3325/88 Maurice Muir; WO 208/3350/1499 Stuart Leslie

KV2/961/3 Englandspiel; KV/2/962 Herman Giskes; KV/2/1732 Prosper Dezitter; KV/2/1733 Prosper Dezitter; KV/2/233 Christian Lindemans; HS 14/1 Andre – De Zitter; HS 6/28 Andromache/Masereel; HS 6/101 Hillcat/Jacques Doneux; HS 6/105 HORATIO mission/Frans Jacques Flour; HS 9/665/8 Harniesfeger; HS 9/997/9 Gaston Masereel; HS 9/1241/4 François Reeve.

NARA – US:
Escape and evasion (E&E) reports from the files of MIS-X London. These reports are available for download from the US National Archives and Records Administration (NARA) at Maryland.

EE-1287 Clarence Barsuk; EE-1590 John J Bradley; EE-1591 William Ryckman; EE-1592 James Dykes; EE-1593 Hugh C Bomar; EE-1594 Ray Smith; EE-1595 Alfred Sanders; EE1695 Gerald Miller; EE-1781 Thomas Smith; EE-1789 Jack Terzian; EE-1841 John Brown; EE-1846 William Muse; EE-1847 JH Singleton; EE-1848 James Levey; EE-1849 Harry Blair; EE-1856 Cecil Spence; EE-1858 Kenneth P Holcomb; EE-1861 Donald Swanson; EE-1862 Charles Hillis; EE-1868 Ralph J Lynch; EE-1870 James Wagner; EE-1877 Henry W Wolcott; EE-1881 William Grosvenor; EE-1891 Ford Babcock; EE1902 Percival Goewey; EE-1915 Robert Auda; EE-1916 Wallis Cozzens; EE-1918 Dale S Loucks; EE-1952 Robert Piarote; EE-2082 Henry Young; EE-2101 Theodore H Kleinman; EE-2143 Royce F McGillvary.

John Brown crew's Missing Air Crew Report (MACR), number 2564.

CEGESOMA – BELGIUM:

CEGES AB 179 (AVIATION DEPOT (Strongroom); CEGES AB 348 (Aviation depot (Strongroom); the letters and documents of Oscar Catherine.

NATIONAL ARCHIVES OF AUSTRALIA

434/2/3 BODEY L.R.

SOURCES

NEWSPAPERS:

ABILENE REPORTER NEWS; *AGE, THE*; *Alexandria Times Tribune*; *Austin American Statesman*; *Daily News, Lebanon*; *Daily Telegraph*; *Del Rio News Herald*; *Durham Morning Herald*, North Carolina; *El Paso Times*; *Evening Courier*; *Galion Inquirer, Ohio*; *Leader-Post*; *Lebanon Daily News*; *Le Patriote Illustre*; *Le rail*; *Le Soir*; *Manchester Evening News*; *Minnesota Legionnaire*; *Notre Metier*; *Oakland Tribune Sun*; *San Angelo Standard-Times*; *Sidney Daily News,* Ohio; *Sunday Telegraph* (Australia); *Times-Colonist*; *Urbana Daily Citizen*; *Vancouver Daily Province*; *Vancouver Sun*; *Waverley Gardens Newsletter*; *Windsor Daily Star Ontario.*

SELECTED BOOKS:

BODSON, HERMAN, *AGENT FOR THE Resistance*, Texas A&M University Press, 1994

Bodson, Herman, *Downed Allied Airmen and Evasion of Capture: The Role of Local Resistance Networks in World War II*, McFarland & Company, 2005

Bowman, Martin W., *The Bedford Triangle*, Sutton Publishing, 2003

Caine, Philip D., *Aircraft Down!* Potomac Books, 2005

Celis, Peter, *One Who Almost Made It Back*, Grub Street, 2008

Charles, Jean-Léon & Dasnoy, Philippe, *Les dossiers secrets de la police allemande en Belgique*, Editions Arts et Voyages, 1972

Clutton-Brock, Oliver, *RAF Evaders*, Grub Street, 2009

Cosgrove, Ed, *The Evaders*, Simon & Schuster, 1976

Debruyne, Emmanuel, *La guerre secrete des espions belges*, Éditions Racine, 2008

Deem, James M., *The Prisoners of Breendonk*, Houghton Mifflin Harcourt, 2015

De Jong, Ivo, *Mission 376*, Stackpole Books, 2012

Doneux, Captain Jacques, *They Arrived By Moonlight*, St Ermin's Press, 2000

Dumon, Andrée, *I haven't forgotten you*, privately published, 2022

Etherington, William, *A Quiet Woman's War*, Mousehold Press, 2002

Foot, M.R.D., *SOE in France*, HMSO, 1966

Foot, M.R.D., *SOE in the Low Countries*, St Ermin's Press, 2001

Foot, M.R.D. & Langley, J.M., *MI9: Escape and Evasion 1939-1945*, The Bodley Head, 1979

Jackson, Robert, *The Secret Squadrons,* Robson Books, 1983

Jones, RV, *Most Secret War*, Wordsworth Editions, 1998

Kent, Stewart & Nicholas, Nick, *Agent Michael Trotobas and SOE in Northern France*, Pen & Sword Military, 2015

Lokker, Claude, *Des bâtons dans les roues* : Les cheminots belges durant la deuxième guerre mondiale, MIM Fonds Ortelius, 1985

Miller, Donald, *Eighth Air Force*, Aurum Press, 2006

Moszkiewiez, Hélène, *My War in the Gestapo*, BCA, 1985

Neave, Airey, *Saturday at MI9,* Hodder and Stoughton, 1969

O'Connor, Bernard, *Tempsford Academy*, Fonthill Media, 2012

Parnell, Ben, *Carpetbaggers*, Eakin Press, 1987

Persico, Joseph. *Piercing the Reich*. Sphere Books Ltd, 1980

Rigby, Françoise, *In Defiance*, Elek Books, 1960

St George Saunders, Hilary, *Royal Air Force 1939-1945 Volume 3 The Fight is Won*, HMSO, 1974

Sarkar, Dilip, *Spitfire Voices*, Amberley, 2012

Trigg, Jonathan, *Hitler's Flemish Lions*, Spellmount, 2007

Ugeux, William, *Histoires de Résistants*, Duculot, 1979

Van Laere, Stefaan, Frans & Jozef Craeninckx, *Een Klein Dorp, Een Zware Tol*, Manteau, 2004

SOURCES

Veranneman, Jean-Michel, *Belgium in the Second World War*, Pen & Sword Military, 2014

ARTICLES AND DOCUMENTS

'A YOUNG BOY AND THE Good War' by Edouard Renière (airforceescape.org)

Office de la Résistance documents of the Belgian Ministry of Defence

'Le train fantôme', *Notre Metier* magazine, May 1947

Various editions of the Air Forces Escape & Evasion Society newsletter

Robert Jan Verbelen and the United States Government, A Report to the Assistant Attorney General, June 16, 1988, accessed at http://www.justice.gov/sites/default/files/criminal-hrsp/legacy/2011/02/04/06-16-1988verbelen-rpt.pdf

'The Great Escape' by Al Zdon, *Minnesota Legionnaire*, January 2016.

'Al Sanders' by Myrna Camp and Winkie Ruiz, *Waverley Gardens Newsletter* (date unknown) (AFEES)

'Rapport sur le Groupe Drion' by the Belgian government (April 29, 1949)

WEBSITES

AMERICANAIRMUSUM.COM; AROLSEN-ARCHIVES.ORG; BELGIUMWW2.INFO; COMETELINE.ORG; CONSCRIPT-HEROES.COM; evasioncomete.be; freebelgians.be; freidok.uni-freiburg.de; http://www.lwha.be; 100thbg.com; theescapeline.blogspot.co.uk; wingsofmemory.be; ww11-netherlands-escape-lines.com; ww2escapelines.co.uk

DOCUMENTARIES:

LAST BEST HOPE (2006), PRODUCED by Beth Hames and Mat Hames; Nazi Ghost Train (2000), produced by Darryl Rehr and Damian Weyand.

UNPUBLISHED MANUSCRIPTS:

'DIARY OF LIEUTENANT JOHN BRADLEY'
'Evading Capture' by William (Robbie) Robertson RCAF, written for the RAF Escaping Society (courtesy of evader Robbie Robertson)
Letters to John Evans and Robbie Robertson from Florent Biernaux, June 20, 1945 (courtesy of evader John Evans)
Oscar Catherine's report of his written exchange with Louis Verheggen (1981) (CegeSoma)
'Train fantôme', a summation of the events by Oscar Catherine (1981) (CegeSoma)
'Ceci est la relation exacte et précise de l'odyssée du train fantôme', by Louis Verheggen (CegeSoma)

For further source notes and references please see the author's website at: https://greglewisinfo.com/